Setting the Records Straight

How to Craft
Homeschool Transcripts and
Course Descriptions for
College Admission and Scholarships

*"Your transcripts and records were the best organized
and documented I have seen."*

*~ Bryan Jones, Associate Director of Admissions,
Seattle Pacific University*

Setting the Records Straight

How to Craft
Homeschool Transcripts and
Course Descriptions for
College Admission and Scholarships

Lee Binz
The HomeScholar

Dedication

This book is dedicated to all the hard-working moms and dads who are doing the wonderfully challenging job of homeschooling high school. One day you'll look back on these years fondly, the way I do now.

Special thanks to my husband and best friend, Matt. Without his vision and business sense, The HomeScholar would consist of a business card and phone number.

Thank you to my ever-patient editor, Jill Bell, for her perseverance and wonderful eye for detail. You have a real gift.

Finally, thank you to my sons, Kevin and Alex, who have provided the raw material for this book and The HomeScholar business. I love you guys!

Train up a child in the way he should go
And when he is old he will not depart from it.
~ Proverbs 22:6

Foreword

Six years ago when our family made the decision to home school, high school was tucked in the back of my mind. It seems that one day I woke up to find that I had a high schooler! Home school through high school? Then at just the right moment Lee Binz came into our life! Among the first words of her book, Setting the Records Straight, she reminded us, "You will be successful. Do not be afraid. Take it one step at a time."

Lee's practical approach and her own success in homeschooling high school students into the colleges of their choice (with scholarships!) are encouraging and reassuring. In Setting the Records Straight she outlines the fundamentals for successful transcripts and home school course classes and descriptions to help guide the college bound student to the college of their choice. The chapters include answers to many of the questions that home school families ask, the very questions I myself was asking.

- Why make a home school transcript?
- What should it look like?
- How can we determine and calculate high school credit?
- How should grades be assigned?

For each question, Lee has a thorough and detailed answer. She speaks from experience and from speaking to college admission offices all over the country. In Setting the Records Straight, Lee offers samples of academic records by year, subject and in the case of Dual Enrollment. These transcript samples are invaluable!

In the final section of the book, Lee tackles the subject of course descriptions. As homeschoolers, the world of course descriptions can be an overwhelming one. She clearly outlines the three steps in compiling course descriptions into language that makes sense. Tackling the core subjects as well as electives and even outlining courses without records are helpful in making this section of the book worth its weight in gold.

This is not just a book for home school families educating through high school, this is truly a resource. There are extensive appendixes that detail course descriptions so that a home school parent has a reliable guide with which to work from.

This book was the most VALUABLE tool I've seen on the nuts and bolts of transcripts and course descriptions! EVERY question that came to mind was answered in such thorough detail. It's given me the confidence to move into the high school years unafraid. This is certainly a book that I will refer to often. This book is a practical resource for the home school community and one that will alleviate fear in many a home school parent.

Lori MacMath,
Heart of Matter Magazine

Prologue
Step-by-Step

Is homeschooling high school an overwhelming task? Instead of looking at the big picture, sometimes it helps to focus on smaller, simpler tasks to achieve your goals. If you just look at the end result, "High School Transcript" or "College Admission," you may become overwhelmed.

Consider the story in the Bible about Jesus changing water into wine. He didn't tell the servants to "change water into wine." Instead, he gave them three easy steps. Each step was possible, and manageable. Read his instructions in John 2:1-11. He gave his servants very small, manageable tasks.

A Step-by-Step Guide to Changing Water Into Wine:

Step 1: fill jars with water

Step 2: draw some out

Step 3: take it to the master

Jesus did not even MENTION the end result. He just gave the steps. In fact it was Jesus who was in charge of the scary end result and final consequences. The servants (that's us!) only had to handle the small, individual steps. If the servants had focused on changing water into wine, they would have become overwhelmed. Instead, they were simply asked to fill jars. God was in control of the quality of the wine. They just had to do one simple thing at a time. Jesus brought the joy to the event, and he brought the highest quality of wine. He can bring joy and quality to your homeschool as well when you focus on one step at a time.

In this book, you will learn about the large task of creating homeschool records. I encourage you to think about two smaller tasks: making a transcript and writing course descriptions. In the first section you will learn the step-by-step directions to make a Homeschool Transcript. In the second section you will learn about course descriptions, and how to compile a comprehensive academic record of your homeschool.

Please consider each section as an encouragement. You only need to complete small, manageable tasks. I will help you identify easy ways to complete each task, and will encourage you to take it one step at a time. Your job is to focus on raising your child today. Keep your eyes on the prize – producing a well-educated and happy grown adult.

You will succeed at homeschooling high school, because your child has been given to you – because God knew in advance this day would come. He knew what you needed for this day.

I can do all things through Him who strengthens me.
~ Philippians 4:13

Do not panic! You are completely capable of doing this! Your child has been given to you – it's been planned this way forever! You have what it takes to do the work – God promises to strengthen you! This is a completely doable task.

The secret of your success will be the love you have for your child. The love for your child will teach you what they need to know, how they learn, what they are missing, and how to prepare them for the future. Love won't teach you calculus, but you don't need to know calculus in order to homeschool high school. Instead, the love for your child will motivate you to find a way for it to happen. Love will urge you to seek resources and curriculum choices that will fit your child.

Above all, love each other deeply, because love covers over a multitude of sins.
~ 1 Peter 4:8

The love you have will cover the difficulties you face. You will fail at some small tasks, because we all fail at small tasks every day. Even high-powered professional executives will fail at small tasks regularly. But we will succeed at the big task: raising and educating our children.

Your child has been given to you, so you know you can homeschool high school. You know you are capable, because you have the strength of the Lord behind you. And when small missteps occur, the love of your child will cover you.

You will be successful. Do not be afraid. Take it one step at a time.

. . . .

Prologue Step-by-Step

Table of Contents

Dedication v

Foreword vii

Prologue Step-by-Step ix

Chapter 1 The "Love Language" of Colleges 1

Chapter 2 Why Make a Homeschool Transcript? 7

Chapter 3 The Nuts and Bolts of a Homeschool Transcript 13

Chapter 4 Making a Homeschool Transcript 19

Chapter 5 Determining High School Credit 25

Chapter 6 Calculating Credit Value 31

Chapter 7 How to Assign Grades 37

Chapter 8 Calculating Grade Point Average 49

Chapter 9 Academic Clearing House 53

Chapter 10 Delight Directed Learning 59

Chapter 11 Transcripts: A Work in Progress 69

Chapter 12 Course Descriptions Demystified 81

Chapter 13 How to Write a Course Description 87

Chapter 14 Course Descriptions in Real Life 95

Chapter 15 How to Avoid Writing Course Descriptions 109

Chapter 16 Knowledge, Wisdom and Character 117

Appendix 1 Making a Transcript Guide 119

Appendix 2 Transcript Templates 121

Appendix 3 The HomeScholar Comprehensive Record 127

Appendix 4 Ann's Example 199

Appendix 5 Christina's Example 209

Appendix 6 Expanded Transcript 221

I hope this book will encourage you as you homeschool your child through high school.

Blessings,
Lee

The HomeScholar

Chapter 1

The "Love Language" of Colleges

Homeschool transcripts are better than chocolate! OK, maybe not better than DARK chocolate, but certainly better than milk chocolate. That's because transcripts are legalized bragging! That's right – your job is to write down the wonderful things about your child onto a piece of paper – and you get to call it their "permanent record." What fun! This is the good stuff! Even though it's just a piece of paper, there is nothing mundane about it!

Some parents fear making a transcript because the process sounds intimidating. This is absolutely not the case. **Creating an impressive homeschool transcript that colleges will love is easy and eminently possible.** In fact, this book will show you exactly how easy and rewarding making a high school transcript can be!

The best thing about transcripts is that **there is really no right or wrong way to do them**. The process is more of an art than a science. There are so many ways you can make a transcript, and each way is OK! There is nothing to fear, and in fact there is a lot of freedom in making your homeschool transcript! In this book you will see the homeschool transcripts I created for both of my sons. I'll show you our transcripts by subject and by year, so that you will get a general idea of what is possible. But truthfully, my transcripts are nothing particularly fancy. I created them in a Word document on my home computer and printed them on regular printer paper. **I gave it to the colleges – and they LOVED IT!**

Parent-made homeschool transcripts work! My students were admitted to all four colleges they applied to, and they were given fabulous scholarships from each one. In fact, both of my sons were given **four-year full-tuition scholarships to their first choice university**. They applied using my homeschool transcript with my own "mommy grades." You don't need to worry about accreditation or fancy paper or getting the right computer program to do it the right way. You can make your transcript the right way just by doing it yourself.

RETAIN YOUR STATUS AS AN INDEPENDENT HOMESCHOOLER!

Why would you make your own homeschool transcript? By making your own, you retain your status as an independent homeschooler. **That gives you complete control over your student's academic record, and you can make sure that it truly represents who they are and what they know**. A homeschool transcript can include all your academic experiences. Your transcript can also save you money, if your children go to college. Properly documented transcripts can earn big scholarships. Creating your own transcript is a very important piece of documentation that colleges need from all applicants. Your transcript is as official as your homeschool. Don't be shy about it!

Document your homeschool "as-is." Remember that a transcript is your homeschool experience translated into words and numbers that

colleges understand. It is really just communicating in the "love language" of colleges. When homeschoolers are talking amongst themselves, they may say, "*Today we had so much fun! We had a great lesson, and combined it with a wonderful hands-on experience, and then read a book in the park together. It was wonderful!*" A transcript is just translating these conversations into words like "course titles" and numbers like "grades and credits."

You don't have to change the way that you homeschool to make it fit your transcript! It goes the other way. You take what you are already doing in your homeschool – what is already working – and create the words and numbers that colleges understand. What you are doing is taking your wonderful educational experiences and translating them into "college-ese." Believe, me, it's much easier than learning Latin, and I will tell you how! These days, almost every college will accept a homeschool transcript made by a parent. **Homeschooling is a very popular educational option, and colleges want our students!**

The military academies accept homeschoolers with a homeschool transcript. I have talked with them at length at college fairs. Every single military academy now accepts homeschoolers. Two of the three major academies actually have a homeschool adviser. One even has a homeschool adviser who is a homeschooling parent. Military academies can be harder to get into than Ivy League schools, so the difficulty getting in  may have nothing to do with being homeschooled and *everything* to do with the competition. At a recent college fair, I spent a long time talking to several military academies, most particularly the Naval Academy in Annapolis. They confirmed that **all of the military academies accept homeschoolers, even when Mom makes the transcript.** The big-time military academies are as concerned about leadership and physical fitness as they are about grades. Most even have a "homeschool admission" webpage, which is always very helpful.

WHAT DOES A HOMESCHOOL TRANSCRIPT LOOK LIKE?

Below you will see one of my son's homeschool transcripts. It's the same transcript I submitted to colleges, but without the personal information. When you look at it, remember that I created it in a Word document on our home computer. It was

> A transcript is your homeschool experience translated into words and numbers that colleges understand.

printed on regular computer paper. We submitted it to colleges with our application. My children were admitted to every college. They even got full-tuition scholarships! Go ahead and peek at the next page to see a transcript. Don't worry, though! There is no reason to feel overwhelmed. By the end of the book, you'll know what it all means – and you'll know how to make one yourself.

Homeschool Senior High
Home Address * Our Town, WA Zip Code

Student: Binz, First Name   **Gender:** Male   **Birth Date:** 09/09/99
Parents: M/M Matthew Binz   **Address:** Street Address, Our Town,   WA 98ZIP

Academic Record by Year

Year	Class Title	Completion Date	Credits	Grade
Early High School Credits	Algebra 1	06/01	1.0	4.0
	Latin 1	06/01	1.0	4.0
	Geometry	06/02	1.0	4.0
	Latin 2	06/02	1.0	4.0
	French 1	11/02	1.0	4.0
2002-2003	English 1: American Literature & Composition	06/03	1.0	4.0
	Algebra 2	06/03	1.0	4.0
	Biology with Lab	06/03	1.0	4.0
	**American History	06/03	1.0	4.0
	Latin 3	06/03	1.0	4.0
	French 2	05/03	1.0	4.0
	Music: Piano 2 with Performance	06/03	1.0	4.0
	Fine Arts 1: American Art	06/03	0.5	4.0
	Bible: Christian Manhood	06/03	0.5	4.0
	Critical Thinking in Chess	06/03	1.0	4.0
	Public Speaking	06/03	1.0	4.0
	PE 1	06/03	1.0	4.0
2003-2004	English 2: World Literature & Composition	06/04	1.0	4.0
	Novel Writing	06/04	1.0	4.0
	Pre-Calculus	06/04	1.0	4.0
	Chemistry with Lab	06/04	1.0	4.0
	**Ancient World History	06/04	1.0	4.0
	Washington State History	06/04	0.5	4.0
	French 3	06/04	1.0	4.0
	Music: Piano 3 with Performance	06/04	1.0	4.0
	Fine Arts 2: History of Art	06/04	0.5	4.0
	Bible: Apologetics	06/04	0.5	4.0
	Occupational Education	06/04	0.5	4.0
	Russian History	06/04	0.5	4.0
	Formal Logic	06/04	0.5	4.0
	PE 2	06/04	1.0	4.0
	Driver's Education	07/04	0.5	4.0
2004-2005	**English 3: Honors Literature & Composition	06/05	1.0	4.0
	Calculus	06/05	1.0	4.0
	Physics with Lab	06/05	1.0	4.0
	**Modern World History	06/05	1.0	4.0
	**American Government	06/05	1.0	4.0
	Music: Piano 4 with Performance	06/05	1.0	4.0
	Fine Arts 3: Art and Music Appreciation	06/05	0.5	4.0
	Bible: World View	06/05	0.5	4.0
	PE 3	06/05	1.0	4.0
Activities:	Soccer Team 9, 10,11: Swim Team 9,10, 11 Coaches Award 10: Competitive Chess 9, 10, 11 Student Teacher 9,10, 11: Youth Mission Team 10: Youth Group 9, 10, 11: Worship 9, 11			

SAT Results	Grade Point Equivalents	Summary	
March 2005: Reading 740, Math 710, Writing 760, Total 2210	A =90-100% =4.0		
June 2005: Reading 790, Math 770, Writing 690, Total 2250	B=80-89% = 3.0	**Credits**	**GPA**
**Denotes Honors course, documented by passing CLEP exam	C=70-79% = 2.0	35.5	4.0
	D = 60-69% = 1.0		

Chapter 2

Why Make a Homeschool Transcript?

There are many advantages to making your own homeschool transcript. One great advantage is that you can let the personality of your child shine through. I knew a young girl in public school, who was extremely gifted in art and languages, but who did poorly in science and in math. Consequently, her public school transcript didn't look very attractive and really did not reflect her giftedness. When you

are homeschooling, however, you can **highlight the strengths of your children** with additional coursework in their gifted areas. Certainly you record the areas they don't necessarily excel in, but you also have the freedom to include all of their extracurricular projects, to make their transcript really shine with individuality.

A transcript can demonstrate your family values. You'll notice that I boldly put "Bible" on my transcript. I wanted colleges to see that Christian instruction was taken very seriously in our home. I knew that this would appeal to Christian colleges, but I also reasoned that the public universities might see us as bringing a bit of diversity to their schools – a win-win!

Consider the purpose of a transcript. Homeschool parents will often save some of their students' school records with other mementos. Trophies, tutus and tiaras line our shelves. While these are wonderful keepsakes that have deep meaning, they are not, however, a transcript! There's a BIG difference between record keeping and scrap booking!

A transcript is only for high school. It isn't for every homeschool activity you have ever done at any age. A transcript is only an academic record; it isn't a character record. Character-building experiences will be described on a college application, but generally not within the transcript.

> There is a BIG difference between record keeping and scrapbooking!

Some experiences, such as a church youth group, are better placed on an "Activities" list than a transcript. **You may want to keep some great high school experiences off the transcript itself.** Save them for a work list or community service list, or use them in a college admission essay. Not everything is a formal high school "course." You don't have to put everything down as a class! Some wonderful things are best saved just for your scrapbook.

Your transcript will be a great planning tool. Work on it regularly, so you don't forget things. Update it regularly, so **you know where you have been and where you are going.** If you keep it updated, you can see if you didn't quite complete something you need for graduation. You'll see what you need to work on next year. In general, a high school transcript will help you keep track of your homeschool graduation plans.

A transcript can also be used to give your student feedback. Maybe it's just my children, but it seemed that when I wrote down a grade on paper, it somehow carried a lot more weight than when I simply said, "Honey, I need you to do this again." Some kids even like to have feedback on an actual piece of paper when they get older. If it motivates your child, use what works!

Of course, the primary use of a transcript is for college applications, but that doesn't happen until your student's senior year of high school. **Students will sometimes need a transcript before their senior year** because they are applying for a college scholarship, or filling out a form for an essay contest. There are good reasons to keep a running transcript throughout your student's high school career.

HOMESCHOOL TRANSCRIPTS AND PUBLIC HIGH SCHOOL

A homeschool transcript is a wonderful thing indeed! Although your homeschool transcript will almost certainly be accepted by colleges, the credits on your transcript may not be accepted by a public high school. Sometimes I hear questions about high school students returning to public school. There is no guarantee that a public high school will accept the credits from a homeschool transcript. It's very easy to pull a child out of public school to homeschool. However, **it can be difficult to put children BACK into public school and retain their homeschool credits and grade level.**

Let's be clear about one thing, though. It may be true that public high schools are difficult to reason with. But colleges don't give us nearly the trouble about our homeschool transcript! Colleges are used to seeing transcripts from

> Your transcript may not be accepted by a public high school.

unaccredited schools, even unaccredited public schools! They are also accustomed to seeing kids with accredited transcripts who are poorly educated. They know that "accredited" isn't all it's cracked up to be. So **colleges will usually accept a homeschool transcript with the same wary eye as any other transcript,** and we aren't at a disadvantage at all. Not so with public high schools. Perhaps they view homeschoolers as the competition – our business as homeschoolers threatens their business. For whatever reason, they are far more concerned with having control over a transcript.

Depending on the school district, you may have little chance of having any or all of your homeschool classes accepted at face value by the local public school. One parent taught her child physics and calculus at home. She wanted a "real" transcript, so she took all her homeschool records to the local public school, so they could be accredited. Her beautifully intense "Physics with Lab" course became "High School Science Requirement Met." Her calculus course was renamed to "High

School Math Requirement Met." Each of her wonderful classes was re-named according to the state graduation requirements. **Although it was accredited, it really didn't represent her homeschool very well.** Her

child's academic record was watered down and misrep-resented. When you submit your transcript to a public high school, it may not be accepted at face value.

If you want to home-school high school, it's a good idea to go into it know-ing you'll continue for the full four years. If you know you will only homeschool for a year or two, you may want to choose an accredited program, or an accrediting agency, which can give you greater security that your credits will transfer into a public high school.

If you are homeschooling, and you know you want to continue for all four years, do NOT worry about whether or not the public schools will accept your transcript. If you continue homeschooling through high school, **there IS NO REASON to give a public high school your transcript.** You don't have to give it to public schools at all - you give your transcript to the college. And colleges understand.

I hope you feel stronger, and know that your transcript has value to colleges! Don't worry about those persnickety public high schools. You don't have to interact with them if you don't want to.

If you purchase an "accredited transcript" from a homeschool or private school agency, you will lose control over your transcript. They may give a grade that you know does not reflect what the student has learned. There are no "take-backs" when you deal with an accrediting program. If your child receives a poor grade, once you have it on their official transcript, it's... well... official. Even a very poor grade will be part of their "permanent re-cord." When your children apply for college, they will ask you to submit all tran-scripts for all schools, and even a rotten transcript is a "real" transcript that has to be submitted.

> There are no "take-backs" when you deal with an accrediting program.

That's one reason why I prefer homeschool transcripts. We can re-take a class, or a test, or a semester without reporting how many tries it took. **In homeschooling, only the results matter, not how long it took to get there.** In general, homeschoolers teach for mastery, and mastery can be such messy work! Sometimes it will take a few tries before the student learns!

If you do have **some truly rotten grades** on an official transcript, consider having your child re-take the class. Teach it again at home, until your child has mastery. It may take a long time for them to learn, but they may catch on pretty quickly the second time. Once they have an understanding of the concepts, then you can provide grades again. If you do that, it would be  a wonderful thing to explain in an application essay. You could talk about "stick-to-it-iveness," perseverance, and the love of learning that homeschooling provides.

HOMESCHOOL GRADES ARE OFFICIAL

Are your homeschool grades official? Shouldn't homeschool grades and credits be left to real "professionals?" I believe that homeschool parents really are professional educators. **Your homeschool grades really are official** grades, because you have an official homeschool.

I know there are accredited high school credits that "educators" believe are official. However, I firmly believe that parents do know best - even in the area of high school grades and credits. There are times when the parent will know better than a "professional" what to put on a high school transcript.

I know a parent who unschooled, and never forced their child to do math in high school, and yet his son ended up knowing pre-algebra (which was verified by testing.) The class "Pre-algebra" was on his transcript even though he hadn't done math since 5th grade. There are times when things will

> Homeschool parents really are professional educators.

go on a transcript because you as the parent are 100% confident that it is accurate and true. On the surface, "trained professionals" may not understand.

I encourage people to go with their heart. **If you have thought through your reasoning, then trust yourself to do the right thing.** If you know it to be true, just be honest on your transcript. Don't leave something off just because you are afraid of what a "professional" might say.

Chapter 3

The Nuts and Bolts
of a Homeschool Transcript

Surprisingly little is actually required on a transcript. To begin with you need a title. I creatively chose the title **"Official Homeschool Transcript."** I prefer to be simple and to the point, so my title was not fancy at all. The student's name is required, obviously, but also other identifiers as well. Some people will include their social security number, but I did not feel comfortable with that, so I used my student's birth date instead. Parents' names can also be an identifier for the student and should be included, as well as the name and address of the school. In keeping with my creative transcript title, I imaginatively named my school **"Homeschool High School."** We also included the titles of courses, and a final graduation date. You need to indicate the expected graduation date on their transcript, so I just indicated the month they would finish.

Some of the optional parts of a transcript sound like they should be required. You can decide for yourself if you want to include these elements: credit value, grades and a grading system, course completion dates, and grade point average. Again, these things are not required. I included them on my transcript so it would look as much like an ordinary transcript as possible. Some homeschoolers will indicate a class rank, but aren't all homeschoolers first in a class of one? Some people use their "percentile ranking" from their standardized testing to be their class rank. Sometime parents like to include test scores, like the SAT or the ACT, but it's not mandatory since the colleges they apply to will get their official score reports. Other optional attachments for your transcript include reading lists or course descriptions. That's a topic for later, but I do think that a separate list of course descriptions is a great idea.

As I worked to make my transcript look ordinary and normal, I discovered something shocking! **There IS no normal!** In my business,

I have seen many, many transcripts; homeschool, public school, and community college. They all look different! The format of your transcript really is not that significant. The only thing that really matters on a transcript is that it is typed. A handwritten transcript does not carry the weight and importance of a typed transcript. **Typing it is absolutely essential.**

While acknowledging that there is a wide range of "normal" I do think it's important to have a "typical" looking transcript with grades. Some parents want to have a transcript without grades, or will choose to use a narrative transcript. That's completely acceptable if that's what you want to do. I felt that my grades carried the weight of any other school system, and that my grades had just as much value. I wanted to have my grades on the transcript.

Remember to think of yourself as a foreign language translator. Your job is to translate what you have done in your homeschool into words and numbers that colleges understand. **Your job is NOT to change your homeschool** – just do what works for you. You job is only to trans-

> I have seen many transcripts: homeschool, public school, and community college. They all look different!

late your experiences (whatever they are) into the "love language" of colleges.

I know that some colleges don't mind a narrative explanation of a homeschool. At a college fair I attended last year, there were some colleges where 15-20% of their student body had been homeschooled. The admissions staff spoke about narrative records in a very warm and open way. However, the majority of colleges may not understand anything as well as a typical transcript, as it will seem like a foreign language to them.

Some persnickety **colleges will ask for things that don't make a lot of sense** for homeschoolers. Some will want your student's transcript notarized. One of the colleges that we applied to wanted my students' transcripts in sealed envelopes with my signature on it, so we put them in sealed envelopes and signed the backs. Having two students graduating the same year, I experienced a moment of panic! Had

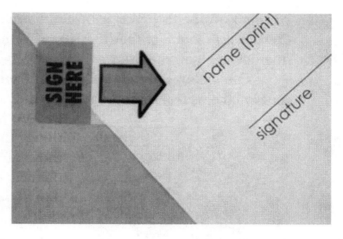

I put the right transcript in the right envelope or mixed them up? I quickly opened them up and made sure I had each student's transcript with their correct application (I did not.) So I switched the transcripts, put them in new envelopes, and sealed and signed the backs again! Which makes you wonder: **what did they think was going to happen** when they had a homeschool mom seal and sign the envelopes?!

Yes, each college will have their own preferences. Yes, they can be inconvenient. As long as requests are reasonable, I encourage you to submit your records the way the colleges want.

ACTIVITIES AND AWARDS

There are some things, however, that don't go on a transcript. As you submit your transcript with your college application, you will see that there are a variety of places to record different experiences. The transcript is the backbone of the application, but there are other parts as well. As mentioned before, not everything goes on the transcript itself. It may help you in the long run to **keep a list of your child's activities.** This list can be extremely helpful as you try to recall four years of high school activities. What kinds of things should you put on the "Activities and Awards" list when the college asks for that? I have GREAT news! The activity and awards list is only for successes, so failures don't go on the list!

Keep a list of their awards. Did your son work at a fabulous job? It goes on the list! But the twenty-eight job interviews with rejections do NOT go on the list. Was your daughter awarded $200 in scholarship money by a community organization? It goes on the list! If she applied to ten big-money scholarships and didn't win any of them, that does NOT go on the list. Was your child a member of the wrestling team? On the list! The fact that they never actually WON a wrestling match does NOT go on the list.

Our failures are always right in front of our eyes, and can sometimes make us feel discouraged. It's negative feedback, telling us what

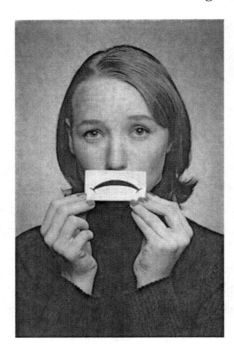

we do not do well. But there are things that our students do well, and those are the things that you put on the activity and award lists. You don't have to list the bad stuff, just the good stuff. All you have to do is remember to write down those wonderful activities and awards when they happen, so you won't forget anything. Keep your awards list just for the positive feedback, and forget about the negative experiences.

Keep a list of activities. What groups are your students involved with? What does your calendar look like each week? List these things on your transcript as "Activities." Some activities are just "fun," but others will demonstrate an elusive and much sought-after trait: leadership. Colleges LOVE to see leadership in students! If your child has a position of

> The activity and awards list is only for successes, so failures don't go on the list!

authority in an activity, you will want to make a note of that. Think of it this way: any groups, clubs or teams can be listed on the activity list.

Some transcripts will include activities as well as courses. I did that myself. I think this aspect of a transcript is more of the "art" than the "science", and is completely up to the parent to decide. There are no real "rules" about activities on a transcript. I consider the transcript activity list for clubs and groups – and positions held in the club or group.

If you list activities on your transcript, keep the description limited to just a few words, and indicate what year the activity was completed. So for example, you might list "Soccer team, 9, 10, 11, 12" to indicate that it was done all four years. You could say "Worship Team 11, 12" to indicate that it was done for just the last two years of high school.

You can also **list special honors for each activity**. For example, "Youth and Government 9, 10, 11, 12 – Governor 11." If you are putting a list of activities on a transcript, first put down activities that were done all four years with any honors, and then list those that were done for all four years, and then list them as the amount of participation decreased. You're trying to demonstrate your student's passion and consistency with each activity. Emphasize their specialization by listing those activities first in the list.

With some activities, it can be extremely difficult to determine if the experience should go on the transcript as a course, or be listed as an activity. Either way is fine, so if you have a preference, feel free to do it that way. When I consult with families, **I suggest that if the experience is enough for a high school credit, then I would put it on the transcript.**

Consider, for example, a teen working on the computer. What kinds of things might qualify for a technology or computer credit? One parent wondered if PowerPoint, keyboarding, website creation and audio-visual work at church could count toward a technology or computer credit. I'm not familiar with homeschool laws in every state, but ALL of those experiences sound just GREAT to me!

Often I see parents expecting too much from **delight-directed high school courses.** One parent scoffed at labeling his son's activities as "computer science." As he told me "I have a degree in computer science, and his programming is not as much as I learned in my computer science classes!" You know what? I'm a nurse, and when I taught my kids health, I didn't require them to know as much about the subject as I know before I gave them a high school credit. **They don't have to know it "all" before you give them a high school credit. They just have to know a "high school amount."**

Keep a record of everything technological that your child can do. Sometimes that will mean keyboarding, ten-key, Word and Internet basics. For other children it will mean HTML, C++ and website design. I'm constantly amazed at the variety of subjects that homeschoolers learn. If your child has a lot of sound and studio experience, you may even have 180 hours for "audio-visual communication" and another 180 hours for "computer and technology." **Your goal is to give them credit for the work they do.**

Chapter 4

Making a Homeschool Transcript

What are the steps toward making a transcript? All the information about "why" is just great, but parents also need to know how to actually MAKE the transcript. To begin with, you should review your homeschool records, making a note of the month and year each class was completed. After reviewing your records, you should name your classes, determine credits, and decide on a grade. This may sound a little scary, but as we go over these steps one at a time, you will gain the confidence you need to create a great transcript. This chapter is about the very first steps: reviewing records and naming course.

REVIEW YOUR HOMESCHOOL RECORDS

Look over the records you have kept. If you haven't been diligent with your record keeping, now is the time to review the planning guide that follows. The guide will prompt you to consider ALL subject areas, not just the most hated and most loved ones.

Subject	9th	10th	11th	12th	Comments
The HomeScholar Planning Guide ™					
English					4 years literature, writing, composition, speech
Math					3-4 years - algebra, geometry, algebra 2, trigonometry, pre-calculus or calculus
Social Studies					3 -4 years world history, US history, economics and government
Science					3 years - 1 with lab usually biology, chemistry and physics
Foreign Language					2-3 years of a single language
Physical Education					2 years ½ credit per year
Fine Arts					At least 1 year Music, theater, art, dance
Electives					Bible, driver's ed, keyboarding, logic, computer science *specialization*
Advising		Optional: October PSAT- for fun?	October: PSAT, Spring SAT or ACT, and visit colleges	**Fall: College essays,** college applications. January: FAFSA	AP or SAT 2 Subject Tests if needed after each course complete.

Usual graduation requirement: 19 credits. Usual college preparation requirements: 24 credits or more

Making a Homeschool Transcript

Look at every item you have saved, and **use it to remember courses** and accomplishments. As you look over each item, try to remember as much as you can about the course. This does assume that you are keeping homeschool records, and of course, I encourage you to do that!

NAMING HOMESCHOOL CLASSES

After reviewing your records, it's time to name your courses. Don't be worried, though. Naming courses is easy; there is so little pressure. Remember, naming homeschool classes is an art and not a science. There is simply no right or wrong answers. **You can be as specific or as general as you want**. For example, you could keep it simple and call their first high school language arts classes a very general name; English 9, English I, Freshman English, or English. Or instead, you could be specific and call it Novel Writing, American Literature or Literature and Composition.

You can be creative in your course names, but **I encourage you to stay within the bounds of normal educational terminology.** Each year that you teach a class, you can name it a different thing as it fills a different niche in your homeschool. Throughout his high school career, my son Kevin spent many hours every day studying chess! The first year studying chess, we named the class *Critical Thinking*, because that is what chess is all about – critical thinking and logic. The second year, he presented weekly chess lessons to our local homeschool group so we called it *Public Speaking*. The third year, Kevin worked for a major chess employer in our area teaching at many public and private schools, so that year we called chess *Occupational Education*.

Be thoughtful naming your classes; they don't have to be the same year after year. If you get writers block and simply can't think of a title, look at a course catalog from a local college. Sometimes just reading the catalog titles can give you ideas about what to call your courses.

When you are looking at your course title, perhaps you'll wonder if your class is an honors or AP class. The description "AP" is actually owned by The College Board, and they don't want anyone to put an "AP" designation by a course unless you use their approved curriculum. You can contact them for more information at www.collegeboard.com. You do NOT have to use their approved curriculum to take the AP exam, however! **Any high school student can take the AP exam.**

> "Honors" means that a course was more challenging than a regular high school course, and it usually means the course was approximately college level.

Putting AP on your transcript means you have used a curriculum approved by the College Board, but you can take an AP test and call it "Honors" to get the same thrill. To call a course AP on your transcript, you are supposed to use the AP curriculum.

The designation of "Honors" can be applied to homeschool courses. "Honors" means that a course was more challenging than a regular high school course, and it usually means the course was ap-

proximately college level. If your curriculum choices say they are "honors" then it's easy to conclude that you can put "honors" on their transcript. But if your student passed an AP or CLEP exam in the subject, then you can also say the course was an Honors course. Sometimes the parent will KNOW that a course was an honors course. Go with your gut – you know best, write it down. **As with the entire transcript, our job is to be honest. If you know it's an honors course, your job is to be honest and write it down that way.**

It may not matter whether you label your course "Honors" or not. Colleges will adjust your courses without you knowing. Some high schools call advanced courses "honors" and others call them "AP." Some high schools will say an honors class "A" is worth 4.0, and others will say an honors class "A" is worth a 5.0. That's one reason you hear about grade inflation and public school kids graduating with ABOVE a 4.0 grade point average. Colleges aren't fooled by elevated numbers. They have formulas that will try to make all high schools across the nation equal. So if your honors course receives a 4.0 or 5.0, it probably doesn't matter. **It's your transcript, and your preference will work** just fine. Just be consistent.

For myself, I chose to have honors courses for every class that received a passing grade on a CLEP exam. I chose to have each honors class carry the usual grade of 4.0 for an A. Knowing that it didn't really matter, I decided my children's transcripts were very strong already, and I didn't want to appear desperate by inflating numbers on an already extensive transcript. That was my decision, knowing the full story about my own students. You know YOUR student, and you are in the best position to make a decision for them.

Chapter 5

Determining High School Credit

Determining high school credit is the next step in making a transcript. High school credit sounds like such a scary and official thing, but it's really not difficult. A credit is simply a reflection of how long and how hard a student has worked. Usually classes are listed on a transcript as either one whole credit or one half credit. Numerically that looks like 1.0 or 0.5. In this chapter you will learn the four ways to determine high school credit.

METHOD 1: CREDIT FOR HIGH SCHOOL LEVEL WORK AT ANY AGE

High school credit can be awarded at any age. As homeschoolers, we know this better than anyone. Credit is based on a student's ability within a subject. If your child is younger than high school age, but is doing high school level work, you can include that work on their high school transcript. When you look carefully at my own transcript, you will see an example. On my **"Transcript by Year"** I labeled those courses **"Early High School Credits."** The top part of that transcript looked like this:

Homeschool Senior High
*Home Address * Our Town, WA, Zip Code*
HIGH SCHOOL DIPLOMA AWARDED JUNE 11, 2006

Student: Binz, Kevin   **Gender:** Male   **Birth Date**: 01/01/00
Parents: M/M Matthew Binz   **Address:**   Home Address, Our Town, WA Zip Code

Academic Record by Year				
Year	Class Title	Completion Date	Credits	Grade
Early High	Algebra 1	06/01	1.0	4.0
School	Latin 1	06/01	1.0	4.0
Credits	Geometry	06/02	1.0	4.0
	Latin 2	06/02	1.0	4.0
	French 1	11/02	1.0	4.0
2002-2003	English 1: American Literature	06/03	1.0	4.0
	Algebra 2	06/03	1.0	4.0

Give high school credit for high school level work completed at any age, even if your children aren't old enough for high school. Once they have completed something that is high school level, include that on their transcript. The big question, then, is how can you determine if a course is high school level?

The textbook company is a good place to start. You will know a course is high school level if a textbook company says so. When Saxon says Algebra 1 is a high school freshman course, then you record it as such. If Apologia labels their Biology book as high school level, then you can feel confident doing the same.

You can also determine high school-level curriculum according to its catalog listing. A Rainbow Resource or Sonlight catalog might say something is appropriate for a 9th through 12th grader, for example. Look at the homeschool catalogs that list your curriculum. When it is listed as a high school level course, you can too. By the way, any time "9th grade" is included in a description, it is high school-level.

Sometimes you can tell high school level work by the description from an accrediting program. Every once in a while I will hear that North Atlantic

---

Tips to Determine High School Level:

- Textbook Author

- Catalog Supplier

- Accredited Sources

- Parent Knows Best

Regional High School (NARHS – an accrediting program in Maine) has considered a course of study as high school-level. For example, Rainbow Science is often considered high school level general science if you complete it in one year. **If an accrediting agency identifies a course as high school level, then the course is high school level for your student as well.**

Sometimes the **parent will simply know best.** For example, one year we used Bob Jones World History over two years, even though it was supposed to be a one-year course. While using each half of that textbook, we piled on the reading and added Teaching Company college level lectures. My students dove deeply into the subject. I knew beyond a shadow of a doubt that everything we were doing to beef up that World History course would make each year one whole high school credit, even though the book was only supposed to be a one-year course.

METHOD 2: WORK COMPLETED AT HIGH SCHOOL AGE

Give high school credit for every class your student completes at high school age. If a high school student takes a class at home, in a co-op, or in a school setting, it goes on their transcript.

This may seem obvious enough if your child is working at grade level, and doing the ordinary classes seen in high school. But this strategy also is valid for other situations. If your child was enrolled in a public school, and was not quite up to grade level in English, all their classes would still be included on their transcript. Each class would be labeled accurately – something like "Remedial English" or "Basic English Composition," – but the class would still be on the transcript. **Whether your student is above or below grade level, when they are doing work at a high school age it should be included on their transcript.** Don't put your kids at a disadvantage just because they aren't at grade level in every subject. Clearly labeled remedial work can go on the high school transcript.

This does NOT mean, however, that you have to graduate every student when they reach a certain number of high school credits. You determine graduation requirements for your student. They can remain in your homeschool until you decide they are ready to graduate. You can decide they will graduate in five years instead of four. However, I do suggest that you include on their transcript all work they do at a high school age.

METHOD 3: COLLEGE LEVEL WORK AT ANY AGE

If your student does any college level work, include it on their transcript. When kids are homeschooled, and they love their particular area of specialization, they can get to a college level while still in high school. This works for public schooled children as well, so don't think for a minute that you are cheating! When a child is enrolled in a public school and is enrolled in a community college at the same time, it's called "Dual Enrollment" and it just means that a student can receive college credit and high school credit at the same time. Parents with younger children might be surprised that a high school student can work at a college level – but it can happen!

> Parents with younger children might be surprised that a high school student can work at a college level – but it can happen!

You will know it is college level material when your student can pass a college level test, like a CLEP or AP exam. Students attending community college while in high school are doing college-level work. Your transcript should include all college-level courses, including dual enrollment in community college, AP exams, CLEP tests, and any college credit earned with correspondence school or distance learning. All of them should be included as high school credit.

METHOD 4: CREDIT BASED ON DEMONSTRATED EXPERTISE

If a student is working with **adult-level expertise**, you can give them high school credit. High school credit can be awarded to a student based on demonstrated expertise. For example, if your child has work published in a magazine, they are functioning on an adult level in their area of specialization. I know a homeschooled student who was published by

National Geographic. He wrote an article on the migratory patterns of birds, and sketched all the artwork himself. This certainly demonstrates expertise! Christopher Paolini wrote Eragon when he was a 15-year-old

> Demonstrated Expertise Tips:
>
> - Published as an adult
>
> - College professor recommendation
>
> - High school teacher recommendation
>
> - Professional in the field recommendation

homeschool student. It became a New York Times Bestseller. Don't you think his mother included that on his transcript? I'm sure she could have! **Feel confident about putting expertise on your transcript.**

My son had his essay on the economist, Friedrich Hayek published in a national magazine when he was sixteen. This demonstrated his expertise in economics, and I was able to include that credit on his transcript. There are other ways to demonstrate adult level knowledge. You can also tell that your child has demonstrated expertise when a college professor, high school teacher, or professional in the field tells you your child is working at an adult or expert level.

INCLUDING DRIVER EDUCATION ON A TRANSCRIPT

I am often asked about including Driver Education on a transcript. As with most things, there are many "right" ways to do it, and you can choose to do it any way that you like! With my boys I simply put "pass" because I had read a book that suggested it. Since that time, I've read other books that suggest grading it, and other books that suggest you leave it off the transcript altogether. Based on all of that information,

I'd say that including Driver Education on your transcript is completely and totally 100% your preference. Keep in mind that if a college doesn't want to use that grade, they will just drop it. Colleges often take the classes they LIKE and figure the GPA of those grades only. With that in mind, anything you do for Driver Education class will be fine – you make the call.

Chapter 6

Calculating Credit Value

You have now figured out how to determine whether the work done by your student should be included on their high school transcript. This begs the question, however, of **how many credits should be awarded for each course.** Calculating credit value can be a difficult question to answer if, like me, you don't use a lot of textbooks. It's also complicated because different school districts may use different numbers for a high school credit. As a homeschooler, however, you can calculate credit value the way that fits your homeschool best.

Textbook manufacturers will often tell you the credit value of the course, and whether the class is high school level. Sometimes, however, there is no ready-made answer to the question of whether a course is worth a whole credit or a half a credit. What do you do? **One approach is to count hours**. In order to do this, you will need to know how many hours constitute one credit.

Unfortunately, even the experts disagree on how many hours constitute a high school credit. Some books say one credit is 120 hours of school, and other books say 180 hours of school. Some books go into more detail, and say that a credit is 120 hours, but each hour should really only be 20 minutes – because homeschooling is much more efficient than other educational settings. Other books say that a credit is 180 hours, but you cannot count homework. Now really – isn't ALL homeschool "homework"!? Other books would claim that 150 hours was the right number for determining credit. None of the books agreed, and I found that very frustrating when I was creating my transcripts! I read all the books, and I really wanted "THE ANSWER." Ultimately I found (again!) that there is no one, single, correct answer that everyone agrees with. **So I came up with a strategy of calculating credit value that is much less stressful!**

In my research, I found that one credit is somewhere between 120 to 180 hours of work. The books didn't agree on an exact number, but they do agree on that general range. The good news is **you can calculate hours of work without counting**. I found that out the hard way, after trying to count hours using the "one-to-one correspondence" that we learned in elementary school. We started off calculating hours for swim team, and I quickly learned that we had FAR more hours than we needed for one credit. All the effort of counting our swim team hours was a complete waste of time!

Estimating is SO much easier than counting! And since the range is 120-180 hours, most of the time you don't have to calculate the number of hours perfectly anyway. Let me share some easy formulas, so that you can quickly and easily calculate the credit value of your courses.

Working for one hour a day, five days a week, for most of the school year, will constitute one credit. Add it up for yourself, and you'll see that **using this formula will total 120-180 hours of work,** depending on how long your school year is. Even if you don't follow a "school year," you'll still know that by studying that much most of the year, you are still within the range.

```
One Credit

COUNT
120-180 hours of work

ESTIMATE
1 hour 5 days a week most of the school year
```

If you are working on a course for a short intense period of time, consider the hours of work per week. Multiply that by the number of weeks your student worked, and see how many hours you achieve. In our area, we have a very popular theater program that many home-schoolers enjoy. When they are preparing and performing a play, it's not unusual for the student to practice 30 hours per week. If the production of the play is five weeks, you don't have to literally count each hour. Multiply 30 hours times five weeks, and see that 150 hours is a whole credit.

Using that same technique, calculating the hours for a half-credit course is equally easy to do. **If you work half that much, it would be worth a half a credit.**

If your student works for 30 minutes every day, five days a week, most of the year, it's a half credit. If your student works two or three hours per week most of the year, then it's a half credit. It's that easy.

You do not have to count hours when using a measured textbook. **Calculating credit value is done either by counting hours OR by using a textbook with a defined credit value.** You don't have to do both. In fact, I recommend against attempting to do both, it will only frustrate and confuse you. Consider, for example, if your student gets through the entire Algebra II textbook in six months instead of eight – should he be punished, and granted fewer high school credits because he finished early? No! He has earned a full credit at the end of the book.

> Half Credit
>
> COUNT
> 60-90 hours of work
>
> ESTIMATE
> 1 hour 2-3 days a week
> OR
> 30 minutes a day 5 days a week

Count once, not twice, even if math takes "forever." One complete high school course like algebra is one whole credit. One math textbook is one credit, even if it takes forever. If you are counting hours, even if you go over 120 hours, it's still just one credit. When we did swim team, for example, it was HUNDREDS of hours, but still just one credit a year. **Math is just one of those things, like organized sports, that can take a LOT of hours to complete each year.**

Although you probably won't give more than one credit, remember the good news here! **You don't have to count hours AND count textbooks.** If you have a textbook, that becomes your measure for a credit. If you are counting hours, then 120-180 hours is a credit.

You may feel very strongly that your child deserves something more than just one credit on a transcript. If so, you might consider giv-

ing him an honors credit to account for all the additional work he did for this class. **Remember: the parent always knows best.** Although I don't usually recommend it, there may be times when excess hours could represent an extreme situation, and you MIGHT feel the need to award your student more than a credit. You are in control of your child's education, you know the details of your homeschool, and you know best.

You can combine experiences together to make a credit. If you have smaller amounts of credit from different experiences, you can add them up until you get a whole credit. When I help parents with their transcript, this comes up frequently.

One homeschool family has a "dancing daughter." They combined all of her different dance experiences into one PE course. She had 30 hours of ballet and 30 hours of hula and 30 hours of swing dance. When added together, that was 90 hours, so the mother gave the student one half credit of PE. If you have more than 180 hours, you can divide it into different subjects, and if you have less than 180 hours, then you can **combine hours together** until you have enough for a half credit or a whole credit. **Credits are usually assigned in half-credit increments** – either a whole or one-half credit. Only very rarely do you see one-quarter credit given. Only very rarely do schools give 2 credits for an honors course. I suggest that you simply use either a half or a whole high school credit per course.

College credits are different than high school credits. When you are putting college credits on a high school transcript, make sure you translate those credits into high school credits. Why? In a community college, they don't spend a whole year going through a calculus text-book; they do it in three months. In a community college, they don't go through one level of French in one year; they finish in three months.

In high school American History, it takes a whole year to get a credit. In college, you will finish the course in a quarter or semester. In college, students will usually just take three full courses at a time. Three months later they take another three classes, and then another three classes. In high school, almost everyone takes more classes than that. In high school, calculus covers... well, just calculus. In a year of college calculus, students cover calculus 1, calculus 2, and dif-

ferential equations. And so that is why... **what a high school calls one credit will be covered in one year, while a college will cover the same material in three months.** In other words, three months of college work can equal one whole year of high school work.

College Credit On a High School Transcript

5-6 College Credits = 1 High School Credit

Different high schools will have their own way of translating college credits into high school credits. Some colleges don't like credits for community college classes, and won't give you credit for those classes anyway. As always, my advice is to **be honest on your transcript and let the colleges decide** what they want to do with the information. You just need to write it down to the best of your ability. Know that all high schools calculate credits differently, and you are doing it differently just like they are! However, if you are trying to reconcile college credits onto a high school transcript, you may want to consider this formula: **5 or 6 college credits = 1 high school credit**.

In this chapter, I have described each full high school course as 1 credit, and a half as 0.5 credit. Just so you know, in some parts of the country, public schools have a different credit scale. Some schools say that a whole class is ten credits, and half of that would be five credits.

I know that can be confusing, and that's why I waited to mention it. Just know that colleges are used to seeing it both ways, and whichever you choose will be fine. If you don't have a preference, I recommend using one credit per high school class, not ten. That is what I usually see in the reference materials and on college websites.

Chapter 7

How to Assign Grades

My son thought homeschool grades were bogus. *"Who's going to believe the grades my Mom gives me?"* he would say. Then he took classes at community college. The professors factored in credit for class attendance, participation, discussion, and homework. If the students scored poorly on a test, they were allowed to "drop" it. One teacher declared that the highest grade on each test was the "100%" grade, and all the other students were graded on a sliding scale. My son became convinced: *"You were right, Mom! Your grades were a lot tougher than college!"*

Grades are one of the things that scare parents of high school students the most. I want you to feel completely at ease about grades. **Grades are NOT scary, and you don't have to make any major changes to your homeschool** in order to provide grades for your high school transcript.

There are three steps to giving a grade. First, select a grading scale. Second, figure out how you are already evaluating your children. Third, decide on the grade you will put on their transcript.

SELECT A GRADING SCALE

Your first job is to determine what grading scale to use. That sounds simple, until you start researching the homeschool books on the market. When I was homeschooling, I would manage my stress by doing research. Since I found grades so stressful, I did a LOT of research on grades and grading scales.

I'm a person who loves having clear-cut, right-or-wrong rules to follow. When I first tried to figure out homeschool grades, I wanted a  mathematical formula by which I would always know the grade of my child. Unfortunately, much like credits, none of the books seem to agree. **There are many different grading scales. Some are more complicated than others, but you can choose any grading scale that you like.** Decide which one works for your homeschool and for your educational philosophy. Below are four of the most commonly used grading scales.

The first grading scale option is from an extremely popular homeschool website. This expert in the homeschool community recommends an extensive grading scale with a wide variety of options for each grade on the transcript. This site recommends that a high school grading scale should look like the scale on the next page.

Grading Scale Option Number 1
>93-100% is an A
>90-92% is an A-
>87-89 is a B+
>83-86% is a B
>80-82% = B-
>77-79% = C+
>73-76% = C
>70-72% = C-
>67-69% = D+
>63-66% = D
>60-62% = D-
>Less than 60% = F

I have nothing against this grading system, and I'm sure it's useful for many people. **For me, however, it looked very confusing and**

technical. So many numbers! In our homeschool, we worked on mastery. Most of this grading scale was useless to us, because we expected our children to know the subject before moving on. I wanted a grading scale that would reflect the mastery I expected from my children.

> Choose the grading scale YOU like

So I started looking in other places. In one book, I found a grading scale that was significantly different. In fact, the first two grading scales are shockingly different. The grading scale from the second book looked like this:

Grading Scale Option Number 2

A is a 4.0

B is a 3.0

C is a 2.0

D is a 1.0

F is a 0

I thought this scale also looked reasonable. It seemed so concise and uncomplicated, but I worried that is was too broad and simplistic to really represent my homeschool. Since there were no percentages attached, I wasn't sure how I could actually use the scale. And I wasn't always confident enough to just declare a paper an "A" or a "4.0" so I felt uncomfortable with this scale.

I looked at another homeschool reference book. It actually listed TWO grading scales for parents to choose from. The first grading scale looks like this:

Grading Scale Option Number 3

93-100% = A

85-92% = B

75-84% = C

70-74% = D

Below 70% = F

I liked that scale, because it was very similar to the first one I showed you, but it wasn't so intimidating for me. It had the right amount of information, it seemed to me. The second scale within that book was similar:

Grading Scale Option Number 4
    90-100% = A
    80-89% = B
    70-79% = C
    60-69% = D
    Below 60% = F

I liked that scale because it had nice round numbers, and it was easy for me to remember and understand.

In the end, I chose the grading scale that defined an A as 90-100 percent. It just seemed to fit our family. I felt like Goldilocks and the Three Bears, because this grading scale seemed just right! I worked for mastery with my children, so I was confident that most of their work would be about 90% or greater. And, truthfully, I was a little afraid of calculating a grade point average, and was hoping to avoid that problem by using this grading scale.

> Like Goldilocks and the Three Bears, this one was "just right"

Choose the grading scale that works for your children. It's probably more important that you are consistent and less important which scale you choose. Once my children started college, I saw that each professor had their own grading scale. Now that I see clients with some public school classes, I see that every school district has its own grading scale. You can use any one that feels right to you.

If for some reason you simply can't make up your mind, I suggest that you just choose one at random. **Put these grading scales on the wall and throw a dart at it!**

It doesn't matter which grading scale you choose! Just choose one, and then move on. Don't get bogged down in the choices available to you. With so many experts providing so many options, you can feel secure with any choice you make.

Once you've settled on a grading scale, you need to think about how you evaluate your child. If you give the class grade based on tests alone, then you are doing your student a disservice. In high schools, and often in college, students may never be judged based on test scores alone. **A test only measures what you DON'T know. We are trying to express what our children DO know.** A grade is usually a mix of things, and if we don't grade with a mix of things as well, we are putting our kids at a disadvantage.

Each grade on a transcript should represent the sum of all the different ways we evaluate our children. Some of the ways you evaluate may be obvious. You can give a grade for each test, quiz, paper, or lab report. Consider also these general areas for evaluating: reading, reports, discussion, research, daily work, oral presentation, composition, practice, performance, note taking, attendance, and narration. You may want to give a grade for each activity they complete within a course. For example, you could give a grade for every activity you count as PE hours: swim team, skiing, soccer, free weights, health, and softball. For music, you might want to give a grade for lessons, practice, and performance. In history, you could give a separate grade for each report, paper, or essay they wrote on historical topics.

In our homeschool, I only graded tests in math, foreign language, and science. Only 13 of our 35.5 credits were based on tests. That was mainly a matter of convenience for me. The courses with tests used textbooks that came with tests! For all of our other classes, **I used a variety of ways to evaluate my children**.

> A transcript grade is the sum of all the ways you evaluate your children, not just tests

I evaluated them based on what they did each day, instead of using tests. What did they do in their daily work? Once it was done to my satisfaction, then I gave them 100%. What assignments did I give them, and what did they do for fun that was educational. What activities did we use to supplement learning?

For English, I decided to evaluate their reading and writing. For reading, I further decided to grade on areas such as reading, discussion, analysis, and research. For writing, I evaluated them on every paper, so I listed each paper by title or topic (Emancipation Proclamation, for example.) I didn't officially "grade" the paper. I just edited it after they wrote it, and sent it back to them for corrections. Again, **when it was done to my satisfaction, I gave them 100%.** Other times, I didn't list the actual titles of the papers they had written. Instead, I would list the KIND of papers they had written: essay, research report, short story, or poetry. Finally, I decided the testing they did each year for their annual assessment was also an evaluation. The areas on those tests were "vocabulary, comprehension, spelling, mechanics, and expression." For everything they did, when they scored grade level or above, they met my expectations and received 100 %.

One class where I did keep traditional grades was Biology. Even so, **my students did more than just take tests, and I wanted that reflected in their grade.** I supplied a numer-

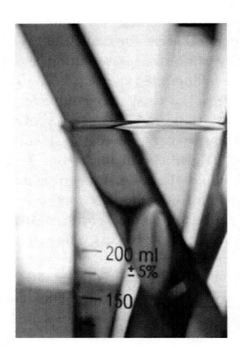

ical percentage grade for each test, grading as suggested by the curriculum supplier. The other major activity in Biology was their science lab. I decided to give them a grade for every science lab they completed. If they met expectations, their grade was 100%. They didn't always meet my expectations, however. When my kids did a lab write-up, I expected them to give me a paragraph describing what they did, along with a diagram, chart, or sketch of the experiment. There were times I felt they hadn't done their best. At times, I would give them 80%, or 90%, depending on my mood. Yes, it was sometimes a bit arbitrary! But they had NOT met my expectations, and I wanted their grade to reflect it.

There are other ways we evaluate our kids that are not quite as obvious. Just between you and me (don't tell!) **the way we evaluate is often revealed by the things we nag about.** Consider

> Annoyance (nagging) may show us the ways we evaluate our children.

these phrases: *"Are you done with your reading yet?"* (Yes? Reading, 100%) Or *"have you finished your spelling words yet?"* (Yes? Spelling Practice, 100%)

How to Assign Grades

Sometimes the things that we nag them NOT to do are also ways that we evaluate. In our home, I would sometimes get frustrated (not that frustration would ever happen to other homeschool parents!). I would think back on my frustrations to consider how I evaluated my children. For example, *"Kevin, will you PLEASE leave that chessboard alone!"* meant "Daily Chess Practice, 100%." And *"Alex, get away from the piano!"* meant "Piano Practice, 100%."

As homeschoolers, we tend to move on after our kids have mastered the material. If you are a parent who gives math problems, English papers or tests back to your student with "please correct this" messages, then you have high expectations. **I recommend when your student does "meet expectations" that you give them 100%** for that test or assignment. If it means you're giving them a 4.0 in every class, that's fine - as long as they meet your high expectations.

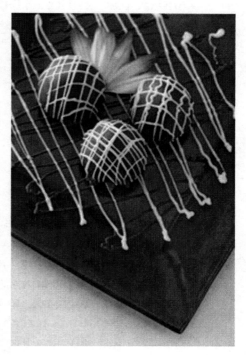

How do you grade non-test subjects like PE, culinary arts, or occupational education? Some courses don't come with a textbook, and grading doesn't involve tests or written work. Ask yourself *"How do I evaluate whether or not they are doing this?"* It can be as simple as recognizing that they are meeting your expectations, doing what is required, and completing their work. If they do those things, you can feel comfortable giving them an "A" for their work. In public school, these types of classes may be graded in terms of "effort" and I think it is fine for homeschoolers to do this as well. If you are pleased with the results in culinary arts, give them a good grade.

I put a grade for PE and Occupational Education on my transcript, but you don't have to. You can't be sure that a college will use non-academic grades you provide, because some colleges do and some colleges don't. I felt like it was my job to provide grades on the classes I taught, and my evaluations had as much credibility as any other school's evaluations. I put it on the transcript and let the colleges use it or not at their discretion.

Not all homeschoolers get all A's! "Mom knows best" sometimes means that a grade will be a "B" or lower. When you honestly know that your child has performed at a lower than "A" level, don't be afraid of how it will look on a transcript. **Honesty will always serve our children best, and a "B" can demonstrate thoughtful consideration of your grades.**

It says that all your grades are real, and you have considered each one carefully. I think that college admissions departments know that homeschool parents are harder graders than our counterparts, so they know if a parent gives a 3.5 that was probably a pretty tough 3.5 to earn.

There are times when your honest grade will include a "B" (or lower) on a test, or paper. Make sure that **the total grade on the transcript will accurately reflect everything your student does, and every area you evaluate their work.** If they have an "A" for effort in a variety of ways (discussion, daily work, narration, research, lab work, etc.) be sure to include everything they do. In the end, if the transcript grade is still less than an "A" then go ahead and write it down. There is no permanent damage from that! If it's honest, write it down.

> Not every homeschool student will get straight A's.
>
> Make sure their transcript grade reflects every way you have evaluated them!

I know **my grading system is only one of many "right ways"** to do things. As the parent, you can decide the "right way" to grade your homeschool. I'm giving you this glimpse into my homeschool evaluations because I think it really helps to see what someone else has done. These are just samples, for you to look at and adapt for yourself.

When I started thinking about transcripts, I loved seeing every sample I could find! If you want more samples, there are many transcript templates in the appendix.

There are samples of course descriptions in the appendix as well. You can see every class, every course description, and all the grading criteria for each high school class in my homeschool. In the description of each class, I carefully itemized how I arrived at each grade. These calculations are not part of the actual transcript; they are just useful in determining which grade you actually write on the transcript.

As you think through your transcript grades, it may be helpful to see the grading criteria I used with my children. **Look over the following charts, and consider all the ways you evaluate your own children.**

This will give you the opportunity to consider what the sum of your evaluations can be for your own transcript grades.

The HomeScholar Sample Grading Criteria ™

ENGLISH IDEAS:

Research & Reading ——1/3 grade——		Mechanics ——1/3 grade——		Composition & Analysis ——1/3 grade——	
Research	100%	Vocabulary	100%	Quick Essays	100%
Completed Reading	100%	Comprehension	100%	Literature Analysis	100%
		Spelling	100%	Research Report	100%
		Mechanics	100%	Short Story	100%
(Workbooks?)		Expression	100%	Poetry	100%
(List each text?)		(Annual assessments)		(Names of individual papers?)	

MATH IDEAS:

Tests ——1/3 grade——		Daily Work ——1/3 grade——		Midterm and Final ——1/3 grade——
Chapter 1	89%	Chapter 1	100%	(Add third column if it helps to improve their grade)
Chapter 2	82%	Chapter 2	100%	
Chapter 3	94%	Chapter 3	100%	

SCIENCE IDEAS:

Tests ——1/2 grade——		Lab Work ——1/2 grade——	
Chapter 1	100%	Lab 1.1	100%
		Lab 1.2 Microscopy	100%
Chapter 2	93%	Lab 2.1	100%
		Lab 2.1 Microscopy	80%
(Consider adding a third column to include daily work, or for their midterm and final grade)			

SOCIAL STUDIES IDEAS:

Reading ——1/3 grade——		Daily Work ——1/3 grade——		Reports ——1/3 grade——
Semester 1	100%	Semester 1	100%	Emancipation Proclamation 100%
				Dialog: Interview a Slave 100%
Semester 2	100%	Semester 2	100%	War in Iraq 100%
(Add a column for tests or quizzes if you use them)				(name of each report, perhaps)

MUSIC IDEAS:

Daily Work ——1/2 grade——		Performance ——1/2 grade——	
Piano Practice	100%	Performance	100%
Completed Assignments	100%	Competition	100%
		Worship Practice	100%
(Consider listing individual pieces or performances)			

ART IDEAS:

Reading ——1/3 grade——		Participation ——1/3 grade——		Analysis ——1/3 grade——	
Reading	100%	Discussion	100%	Georgia O'Keefe	100%
(list books?)		Pottery Class	100%	Norman Rockwell	100%
(Oral reports?)		(List of projects?)		MC Escher	100%
				(Compositions?)	
(Consider listing every experience or project separately)					

. . . .

How to Assign Grades

PE IDEAS:

Health ——1/3 grade——		Individual Sports ——1/3 grade——		Team Sports ——1/3 grade——	
Health 2	100%	Swimming	100%	Soccer	100%
CPR	100%	Skiing	100%	Sportsmanship	100%
		(List each activity?)		(Nutrition instead?)	

OCCUPATIONAL EDUCATION IDEAS:

Daily Work ——1/2 grade——		Preparation ——1/2 grade——	
Internship Position	100%	Income Tax Preparation	100%
Yard Maintenance	100%	Write Resume	100%
Typing Skills	100%	Preparation for Work	100%
(List every job or skill?)			

DRIVER EDUCATION IDEAS:

Preparation ——1/3 grade—		Participation ——1/3 grade——		Exam ——1/3 grade——	
Reading	100%	Narration and Discussion	100%	Classroom grades	Pass
		Daily Work	100%	Department of Licensing	Pass

ELECTIVES IDEAS – WHEN THEY LEARN SOMETHING "JUST FOR FUN"

Reading ——1/3 grade——		Daily Work ——1/3 grade——		Reports ——1/3 grade——	
Semester 1	100%	Semester 1	100%	Research Report	100%
Semester 2	100%	Semester 2	100%		
(Include a test score to show mastery? SAT 2, AP or CLEP exam?)					

WILL COLLEGES ACCEPT HOMESCHOOL GRADES?

Every college will decide which grades they will accept from your transcript and which ones they will not. For example, some may accept driver education, and not physical education. Others might do the reverse. They will merely circle the grades they will accept and make their calculations based on those. This doesn't apply just to homeschoolers, either. They do this kind of readjustment with all applicants.

Some colleges will adjust the grades based on the difficulty of the class. If you take math at a certain level and up, some colleges may give you five credits instead of a 4.0, and if you include an AP course, they may give you a whole extra credit for every AP test. **No college**

How to Assign Grades

operates exactly the same way. Therefore, it really doesn't matter which method you choose. You have the freedom to record what best represents your homeschool, because no matter what you do, each college will make their own calculations. How they figure your student's grade point average becomes just one factor in their admission and financial aid decision.

At times it's appropriate to show the nuances of your grades to a college, and you want to demonstrate your "homeschool 4.0" is not a number pulled out of thin air. This is the opportunity to demonstrate that you gave thoughtful consideration to the methods you used to evaluate your student. Show your standards and your methods of grading. Then let the college decide how

> If your student has good SAT or ACT scores, colleges may accept a homeschool 4.0 grade point average at face value.

they will use the grades, knowing that you've done your very best to provide them with the information they need.

If your student has good SAT or ACT scores, colleges may accept a homeschool 4.0 grade point average without question. One admissions official told me that he usually sees 4.0's from homeschoolers, and he is used to it. In many homeschools, if the student doesn't understand the subject, they repeat the material until it is mastered. **Mastery of the information certainly qualifies as a 4.0, right?** Don't shy away from a 4.0 if you know it is an accurate evaluation. Put down the grades you know to be true, and let the colleges decide how they will use that information.

Colleges love to see homeschool grades, and I encourage you to include your own parent-made grades on your homeschool transcript. There is value in making your own homeschool grades. There is no harm in putting your grades on a transcript. Remember that your job is to be honest, and write it down. If a college does not use your grades, you may never know it. But if the college wants to use your grades, then by all means, give them the grades!

Remember: homeschool grading is an art, not a science. There are many options available to you, and you don't have to do everything exactly the way I did. Mom and Dad know best - especially when it comes to evaluating their own children. You know better than anyone the grades your child deserves.

Chapter 8

Calculating Grade Point Average

The next step in creating your transcript is to determine your student's grade point average. Although this terrified me at first, over time I've become pretty comfortable with these calculations. In fact, it's really pretty simple!

Think first about just one class. Multiply the credit awarded times the grade given to get the "grade points" of each class. For example, if you have a one credit class and the student got a grade of 3.8, then they have 3.8 grade points for that class. Find the grade point for every class individually.

Add all the "grade points" together. Once you get the total number of grade points, divide this by the total number of credits on the transcript. That number is the grade point average.

In other words, the cumulative GPA is calculated by adding all of the grade points together and dividing by the total number of credits awarded. For those of you who think better with bullet points, here are the steps again.

HOW TO CALCULATE GRADE POINT AVERAGE:

1. Give each class a credit value and a grade (i.e. 1 credit, and 4.0 grade)
2. Work on one class at a time
3. Multiply the numerical grade of the class by the credit value of the class to find the class "grade points" (4.0 grade x 1 credit = 4.0 grade points)"

. . . .

4. Find the grade points for each class
5. Add all the grade points together
6. Divide the total number of grade points by the total number of credits
7. The result is the grade point average

> GPA is calculated by adding all of the grade points together and dividing by the total number of credits

ELEVATED GRADE POINT AVERAGES

I'm often asked about the new trend toward grade point averages that are HIGHER than a 4.0. Back in the good ol' days, giving 100% meant giving it your all. And back in the good ol' days, getting a 4.0 in high school was a perfect score, and you couldn't do any better than that. Now, it's different. You've heard about football players **"giving it 110%?"**

That's starting to happen on transcripts, too! Some high schools around the nation are giving a 5.0 in certain classes. A perfect score in high school can now be 5.0. **Some high schools will give a 5.0** for a student that receives an "A" grade in an Advanced Placement or International Baccalaureate class (That's AP or IB, to you and me.) Some high schools will even give a 5.0 for an "A" grade in honors classes, even if they don't have AP or IB classes. To further confuse things, other schools calculate the old fashioned way and give a 4.0 to AP classes.

It's as if some people measure GPA in "feet" and others measure in "meters." There is no single standard for weighting secondary school grades. They aren't using the same scale. But 100% is still 100%, and you can't really give more than that, even if you are running really, really fast!

So how does a college evaluate grade point average, if schools aren't using the same scale? Usually a college will pick and choose classes to make certain determinations. **A college may change the credit values to the standard scale** they use. One college may drop Driver's Ed from a transcript GPA, and another may only calculate the GPA from a select group of rigorous courses and leave off "fluff" grades. Be aware, they do this for public school students too! **It's not a homeschool issue - this is a HIGH SCHOOL issue.**

My advice is to choose a grading system YOU like, and be consistent with it. I'm sure somewhere in the United States, another school is doing it that way as well. If you choose to grade an AP class with a 5.0, then grade ALL your AP classes with a 5.0 grading scale. It may help to emphasize the rigorous nature on the transcript, to make sure the class doesn't get lost in a sea of grades. On the other hand, since those scores are going to be re-calculated by colleges anyway, **it probably doesn't really matter whether you choose a 4.0 scale or a 5.0 scale.** In our homeschool, we used a 4.0 scale and it seemed to work out just fine for us. Colleges will take the necessary steps to convert the meters to feet, and vice versa. Just be consistent throughout your whole transcript.

HONORS CLASS VS. REGULAR CLASS

An honors designation reflects the depth and breadth of your student's work in their study. Any course could be an honors course for a student who goes above and beyond the usual high school level. Some parents wonder how grades for honors classes should be reflected on a transcript. How do you decide whether your student should have a grade of B or C for an honors class, or an A or B without the honors designation?

It helps to keep your goal in mind: well-educated children. Your goal is to teach your child at their level. Teach them so they achieve success. It doesn't matter what the course is, or what the book is. There is no shame in a transcript full of regular courses. In "Lake Wobegon" all the children are above average, but the real world isn't like that. **You want your children to be successful.** You want them to learn according to their abilities. If it takes a class without an "honors" designation for them to be successful, then that is just fine.

Chapter 9

Academic Clearing House

As a homeschool parent, you are the clearing house for all your student's academic achievements. Whether they take a community college course, co-op class or public school band, all high school academics can be included in a homeschool transcript. You are the collector of all these treasures – a clearinghouse for every educational experience that is recorded on their transcript.

YOU ARE THE CLEARING HOUSE
FOR COMMUNITY COLLEGE GRADES

As the clearing house, your job is to clarify where each class took place. Use different symbols to indicate where they took classes. You can use the abbreviation of the school. For example, classes taken at Highline Community College may have "HCC" by the course title. Courses that are included on a CLEP transcript may have "CLEP next to the course. You can signify which classes are taken with a tutor or co-op support as well. On my transcripts, I put an asterisk by the classes that were included on their CLEP transcript, signifying that I had granted them "honors" credits for those classes. If you are using outside grades, it may look something like this, taken from my own homeschool transcript:

> Make sure to accurately represent grades from other sources.

Topic	Course Title	Completion Date	Credits	Grade
English	English 1: World Literature	06/04	1.0	4.0
	English 2: American Literature	06/05	1.0	4.0
	HCC* WRIT 101: Writing	06/06	1.0	2.8
	HCC+ WRIT 145: Communications	12/06	TBD+	TBD+
Math	Geometry	06/04	1.0	4.0
	Trigonometry	12/05	0.5	4.0
	HCC* MATH 115: Pre-Calculus	06/06	1.0	2.6
	HCC+ MATH 112: Calculus	12/06	TBD+	TBD+

*HCC Classes taken at Highline Community College
+Classes to be completed next term

Accurately representing the grades from other sources will reinforce the validity of your own homeschool grades. **It's extremely important that the information on your transcript exactly matches the information on the transcripts received from other sources**.

In the example above, you can see that English, the first two classes listed, were classes taught at home. The second two classes were taken at "HCC" or Highline Community College. You can see the second example under math is similar. On these samples, you can see that some classes are still in process, without a final grade. When classes had not yet been completed, I listed "TBD" for "to be determined" in the grade column.

Use the same strategy for all of your supplemental courses, no matter where they are taken. Assign an acronym or symbolic designation, with a key to what each one means.

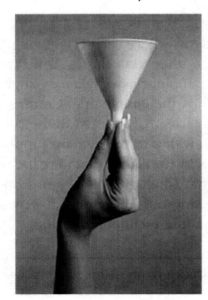

Then symbolize each class on your transcript. **You are the funnel – all classes are collected by you. They all go through you onto the homeschool transcript.**

You don't have to add symbols to classes unless you want to, but providing a quick explanation if some classes have outside grades can help colleges understand your homeschool. Outside documentation, in the form of extra tests or outside courses, can also strengthen your college application.

Once you become comfortable in your role as gate keeper, you may identify a problem that is common among homeschoolers. What if your student has too many credits for a high school transcript? Sometimes parents worry because their child has more than 24 credits. Other parents stress because their student has over 40 credits! Parents are worried because they fear this looks like bragging, and others are just concerned about how to actually fit all the classes onto one sheet of paper. If you fear your student has "too many" credits, there are several options to choose from.

(Solutions for "Too Many Credits")

- You can decide that there is no such thing as "too many credits."
- You can keep only the most recent credits.
- You can lower the credit value of all classes.
- You can eliminate some classes from the transcript and list them as an "activity" instead (ballet might be an activity instead of a PE class).
- You can pick and choose some classes to drop off the transcript if you have more than the usual requirements (drop the 5th history class).
- You can combine classes together (combine British Literature and Ancient Literature to make one European Literature class).
- Your student could explain the situation in their college application, and tell the college why they have so many credits.
- Document their high school level classes with tests (SAT Subject Tests, AP or CLEP exams) so that you can prove many of the credits.

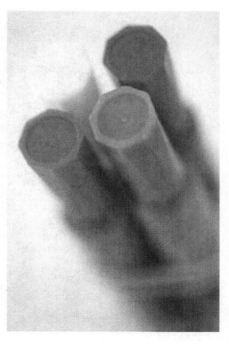

YOU ARE THE CLEARING HOUSE FOR HOMESCHOOL CO-OP GRADES

Do not assume that the grade your student receives in co-op represents the sum total of what your child has learned. A co-op grade only represents the classroom experience, and the co-op teacher is giving just a portion of a course grade. **It does not take into account how much they do at home.** Usually, co-op grades aren't official in the usual sense – they are just another mother's opinion. You can safely say their co-op grade would represent a portion of their transcript grade. Co-op grades are usually based solely on the test scores and that puts children at a disadvantage when compared to children from other schools where grades are based on other aspects in addition to tests. Not every homeschool cooperative will award a grade to students, but when they do, make sure their transcript grade includes all the educational experiences for that course.

YOU ARE THE CLEARING HOUSE FOR "MOMMY" GRADES

A common stress for parents is the high grade point average of their students. "Do my grades mean anything if I give my child all A's?" The underlying question: **are "Mommy Grades" worth anything?** They are worth a LOT! Just because you are the parent doesn't mean you don't evaluate your children accurately. **I believe parents are in a position to give a MORE accurate grade to their children.** Just because you don't give tests doesn't mean you don't evaluate your children! Give an accurate and full representation of what your "mommy grade" contains, and those grades will really count. We included a full explanation of our

grades within our course descriptions. Together, the course descriptions and grading criteria completely described every class in our transcript.

Some colleges accept "mommy grades" as is, and others want an explanation. Some colleges want test scores to corroborate our grades, and some colleges will only use grades from outside classes. Again, our job is to put on the transcript what we know to be true. Colleges will use the details they want to use!

In my homeschool, we did about one-half of our subjects in the traditional textbookish way. In fact, we only used tests for math, science and foreign language - and we only did tests in those subjects because the curriculum CAME with tests. The other part of our school was not graded with tests. I gave grades based on what they did, what they knew, and what they produced, instead. I put those "mommy grades" proudly on my transcript! Do you know what happened with those mommy grades? My children were accepted to all four colleges they applied to. My children were given good scholarships even to selective schools. Best of all, my children were given full tuition scholarships to their first choice university!

The colleges could tell that the mommy grades were most likely accurate, because my students had good SAT scores. We also had CLEP exam scores to document some of the other subjects. **You don't have to change how you homeschool your children or spend a lot of money to get grades made by someone else.** Display your mommy grades proudly!

If you remain unconvinced, or for some reason you feel you simply must have some other validation for each grade you give, I have a suggestion. Continue to homeschool the way you prefer, but list your source of the grade documentation on your transcript. One mother insisted on listing sources for all her grades. She decided to include the source of validation along with the completion date, as shown here.

Course	Class Title	Completion Date and Validation	Credit	Grade
English	Essay Writing	05/08 Certified Teacher	1.0	4.0
	Literature & Composition	06/08 SAT 2 Literature	1.0	4.0
Math	Algebra 1	09/08 Homeschool	1.0	4.0
Science	Biology with Lab	07/07 University Summer Stretch	1.0	3.5
	Advanced Biology	06/08 AP Biology Exam	1.0	4.0
	Chemistry with Lab	08/08 University Summer Stretch	1.0	3.0
Social Studies	Ancient World History	06/07 Jewish School	1.0	4.0
Foreign Language	Biblical Hebrew	06/08 Jewish School	1.0	3.7

To reiterate, I don't believe that providing validation for all our grades is important. Our homeschool grades are as likely to represent our students as any other school! But if you decide that best represents your homeschool, this is one way to include that information.

YOU ARE THE CLEARING HOUSE FOR GRADES FROM OUTSIDE CLASSES

If you supplement your homeschool transcript with outside classes, you become the clearing house for those as well. Some homeschoolers access public school classes for music, science, and math. Others

take a class or two with a private school, or with a tutor. Whatever the situation, you are the catch-all for those educational experience. By carefully labeling each one, and accurately reflecting all accredited grades, you become the "one stop shop" for colleges to understand everything your student has done academically. Yours are the FIRST credits they see. The other transcripts are below yours, merely provided as additional documentation for your homeschool.

Chapter 10

Delight Directed Learning

Some people just aren't textbook people! What do you do if your home-schooler learns by living, instead of studying textbooks? What if your child soaks up knowledge like a sponge, without being directed in any way? **Can you still create a serious-looking high school transcript?**

My son Alex was a self-motivated extreme learner. If only it were an Olympic event, like extreme sports! He learned novel writing for fun, and wanted to take a third year of French even though I didn't have a curriculum for him. He asked for an American Government curriculum for Christmas, and read every economics book he could get his hands on. Although his "love language" is reading, he was still a delight-directed learner. When it was time to make his transcript, I still had to figure out how to translate his experiences onto a piece of paper.

For our family, the problem seemed huge. What should I do with all the experiences that cover a wide range of subject? Was that report on Jean Baptiste Say (the French Economist) a paper on history, economics, or foreign language? Was my son Kevin's enjoyment of Russian History just part of World History, or could it be a course by itself? We had SO many papers that my children wrote, but I didn't know what subject I should attribute them to! Where should I file each of them?

· ·

I eventually found a system that could help me sort out all their delight directed learning, using my understanding of traditional grades and credits. It's not difficult once you get the hang of it. Before I go further, please make sure you have read the section on grades and credits first. Think about any textbooks that you happen to use. Once you understand how to calculate grades and credits with a book it's easier to understand how to do it with delight-directed learning.

THE "STICKY NOTE" STRATEGY

Once I figured out how to do it, I realized that my system would work for ALL delight-directed learners, not just "book learners." I also realized that it could help parents who are themselves kinesthetic learners. My strategy is simple, fun, and only requires one small purchase. Sticky notes. Yup. Those small square notes save the day again! You can determine what to do with each experience using a simple sticky note.

For each activity your student is involved in, there are five pieces of information you need to remember Write those five things on the sticky note, and save it with your homeschool records. At the end of each year, group those sticky notes together, and combine them to create high school courses.

I recognize that it's hard to determine where each experience will fall on a transcript, so keep each sticky note very simple. Here is what I suggest. On each note paper, indicate each of the following items:

Name the Experience. In the middle, write the experience. What did you do? "Perform Nutcracker." Do you have any course title ideas? Like "Theatrical performance" or "economics?" Just guess – and feel free to guess many times on each sticky note!

Note the year. What school year did you do this? Sometimes it will be a school year, like 2010-1011, and other times it will be for a short duration, like a play in November of 2012.

Year Completed		Grade for Experience
	Experience Or course title ideas	
Credits or hours spent		Possible Subject areas

Grade the experience. Did your student complete the project to your expectations? Were they successful, did they receive positive feedback, or learn something? Review the chapter on grading, if you need help. Remember that you don't have to test in order to give a grade. Instead, you can evaluate them in other ways.

Note credits earned or hours spent. Count or estimate the number of hours you spent on the project. A total of 75-90 hours could be recorded as "1/2 credit" when you are done with the experience. If you have more than 180 hours, you could consider it a very full credit, or you might choose to divide up your experiences into smaller bite-sized pieces and then regroup them into other courses with 180 hours apiece. If you have less than 75 hours, you will be grouping the sticky notes together, and I'll describe that in a moment. Keep sticky notes even when the activity required very few hours. You can use those experiences no matter how many hours they spend.

Suggest possible subject areas. You may not know which subjects you will use for each experience, but it's good to record the possibilities. With all our reports and papers, I would often put several ideas on each note. One paper might be regarded as English or history or economics or French. By making a note of it, I could decide later which course needed that experience to make up a full credit. If history was already packed, then perhaps I would use another subject area.

Spread them out and group them together. Once you have your sticky notes, don't review them until you are actually working on the transcript. Checking them too often can cause frustration and insecurity, so only review them when you update your transcript. This will help you keep the big picture in mind. When you are ready to work on your transcript, **spread all the sticky notes on the table or floor.** Then put them into "affinity groups," or groups of similar things. As you combine these activities, work to combine them into groups that ultimately add up to 1 credit or ½ credit subjects. **Once you have made a decision, put the course on your transcript.**

You can make a note of the experiences you included on the transcript, if you want to. This will really help you if you decide later to add course descriptions to your homeschool record. But once you've decided on a credit, try not to stress about it again. It's easy enough to change when you need to, but just putting those experiences into groups is a success in itself. You have successfully grouped your delight-directed learning into high school level courses!

This whole process of spreading notes out on the floor and manually grouping and regrouping experiences is a great technique for any parent who is a kinesthetic learner. Even if you don't use a hands-on curriculum, **this hands-on transcript process can help kinesthetic parents** understand the nuances of their child's transcript, and the process can ultimately help you remember what was included in what course – and even help you write your course descriptions! Make sure you keep the information with your homeschool records.

> This Sticky Note Strategy works well for kinesthetic learners as well as kinesthetic parents!

THE SUBJECT TEST STRATEGY

Another way to quantify delight-directed learning is to give subject tests. This doesn't work for every subject or every child, but it's an option to consider. Instead of testing your children as they are learning, you allow them to learn a subject naturally. When they are done, you can give them a sample test from a major test provider. If they pass the sample test at home or at the testing center, you will know how much they have learned, and will have a grade to put on their transcript. There are three tests available that will help you with this strategy. All three tests I'm going to describe are administered by The College Board. You can get more information at http://www.collegeboard.com/.

HIGH SCHOOL LEVEL TESTS: SAT SUBJECT TESTS

The easiest subject test is the SAT 2 Subject Test. These tests measure knowledge in a single subject. There are tests available in the following subject areas:

- Literature
- U.S. History
- World History
- Mathematics Level 1
- Mathematics Level 2
- Biology
- Chemistry
- Physics
- Chinese
- French
- German
- Spanish
- Modern Hebrew

- Italian
- Latin
- Japanese
- Korean

If your child knows a high school amount of information in any of these areas, give them a sample test first, to see if they might pass the test. It's important to do it at home first, so that you know they can succeed when they take the test. If their sample test scores at home are above 500, then you can give them a high school credit in that area, and there is no "counting hours" involved. If they pass the test, they should be awarded one whole high school credit.

> Use the SAT 2 Subject Tests to demonstrate delight-directed learning at a high school level.
>
> 1 Test = 1 Credit

COLLEGE LEVEL SUBJECT TESTS: AP AND CLEP EXAMS

If your child seems to know MORE than a high school amount of information, then you have several choices. Two tests can be used to measure college level learning: the Advanced Placement exam (AP) and the College Level Exam Program (CLEP).

AP exams are based on a set curriculum that your child may or may not be exposed to with a delight-directed approach. The AP offers exams in the following subject areas:

- Art History
- Biology
- Calculus AB
- Calculus BC
- Chemistry
- Chinese Language and Culture

- Computer Science A
- Computer Science AB
- Macroeconomics
- Microeconomics
- English Language
- English Literature
- Environmental Science
- European History
- French Language
- French Literature
- German Language
- Comp Government & Politics
- U.S. Government & Politics
- Human Geography
- Italian Language and Culture
- Japanese Language and Culture
- Latin Literature
- Latin: Vergil
- Music Theory
- Physics B
- Physics C
- Psychology
- Spanish Language
- Spanish Literature
- Statistics
- Studio Art
- U.S. History
- World History

Advance Placement Tests (AP tests) demonstrate college understanding.

1 Test = 1 Credit

The AP is partially an essay exam. If your child is a bookish learner, this test could be a good fit. Always give them a sample test at home FIRST, before taking them to the official exam at a school, as it can be difficult to know if they will pass just by guessing. You only want them to take the test for real if they are going to pass.

CLEP EXAMS ASSUME LEARNING OCCURRED NATURALLY

Finally, you could give your student credit through testing using CLEP exams (College Level Examination Program exams.) These may be a better fit for unschoolers, because on the CLEP website it says, **"Earn credit for knowledge you've acquired through independent study, prior course work, on-the-job training, professional development, cultural pursuits, or internships."** That's why it is often a perfect fit for delight directed learning. Learn first, take a quick multiple-choice exam, and voila! You have documented that your child learned a college amount of material through delight directed learning! CLEP offers tests in the following subject areas:

> CLEP exams demonstrate college learning.
>
> 1 Test = 1 Credit

- American Literature
- Analyzing and Interpreting Literature
- English Composition
- English Literature
- Freshman College Composition
- Humanities
- French Language (Levels 1 and 2)
- German Language (Levels 1 and 2)
- Spanish Language (Levels 1 and 2)
- American Government
- Human Growth and Development
- Introduction to Educational Psychology
- Introductory Psychology
- Introductory Sociology
- Principles of Macroeconomics
- Principles of Microeconomics
- Social Sciences and History

- U.S. History I: Early Colonization to 1877
- U.S. History II: 1865 to the Present
- Western Civilization I: Ancient Near East to 1648
- Western Civilization II: 1648 to the Present
- Biology
- Calculus
- Chemistry

Parents don't always know what their children are learning. There is so much life that goes on – and so many books! It's amazing what children will learn when we aren't looking! Using CLEP exams, I found out just how true that could be! I told my students to look over the exams "just to see what they were like." One son was able to pass an exam in Business Law, even though I had never seen a Law book in my home. He passed  the Principles of Marketing test, even though I had never seen a Marketing book in my home. He passed both Microeconomics AND Macroeconomics, even though I still don't know exactly what those two words mean. By testing them, I was able to put some courses on the transcript that were a surprise even to me!

When using tests to document delight-directed learning, be sure to avoid failure. Purchase a book with sample tests in it, and give the exam at home first. Only take your student to an official test if you are reasonably sure they can pass the test. Your goal is to find out what they have learned, not demonstrate what they have NOT learned.

> For more information on SAT 2 Subject Tests, AP exams, or the CLEP test, please see www.CollegeBoard.com.

Again, all the tests are available through the company that produces the college admission SAT exam. For more information on SAT 2 Subject Tests, AP exams, or the CLEP test, please see CollegeBoard.com.

I just want to give a "shout out" to all the parents with an eclectic, delight-directed homeschool! It's a great way to prepare teenagers for a career, because exploring interests can mold and shape them as they move toward college and choosing a college major. When we were

homeschooling, we incorporated delight-directed learning into gift-giving occasions. When thinking about Christmas or Birthday presents, remember that these are not just "gift" opportunities. These are learning opportunities! Instead of the Toys R Us catalog, give your child a science curriculum catalog, and see what experiments they would like. Or have them choose a course from The Teaching Company just for fun! The Teaching Company offers college-level lectures on audio and video. Their lectures are wonderful ways to encourage the love of learning for both teenagers and adults.

Chapter 11

Transcripts: A Work in Progress

They say the opera isn't over until the fat lady sings. With a homeschool transcript, it's not over until your child has graduated. Until then, a transcript can change dramatically! They will morph over time, and nothing becomes official until it is submitted somewhere official.

My transcript changed a lot over the high school years. The change was so dramatic it's difficult to even recognize some of the classes. This was because I learned more about transcripts each year. I encourage you to keep listening to conversations about transcripts, and continue your own education. Read more every year, and take classes at conventions and online. As things changed, and my knowledge about transcripts changed, so did my transcript. Stay up to date on your own transcript. It's not over until it's over, and until then it's just a work in progress.

> Transcripts can be changed and modified until they are submitted to a college. From then on, you can only add to the transcript.

In the following section, you will see my transcript and how it changed over time. I'm sure the first thing you'll notice is that as my classes filled the page, I had to use a smaller and smaller font to fit it all in! By the end of 11th grade, I realized I couldn't squeeze in anything else. For 12th grade I finally had to switch to a two-page format, just to fit in all the classes.

When you submit your transcript to a college, it will be in the middle of the school year and some classes will not be complete. List the classes they are currently working on, but do not list the unfinished grades. Where a grade is normally placed, indicate that the class is not finished by inserting the acronym "TBD" for "To Be Determined, or "IP" for "In Process." Only include completed classes in your GPA calculation. When all classes are complete, fill in the remaining grades, recalculate the GPA, and send the transcript to the colleges again.

The first few sections are the homeschool transcripts for my son Kevin. Kevin loves history and math, and loves studying chess. You can  see how he exceeded the usual classes in those areas – not because YOU have to do that, but because that's what Kevin wanted to do! Notice how the chess study changed over time, from Critical Thinking to Public Speaking, and then to Occupational Education. You can see we didn't finish Novel Writing when we expected. Notice how I didn't hold him back once he had plenty of math and history, but let him pursue his interests even though they were over my head!

OFFICIAL TRANSCRIPT
~Homeschool Senior High~

Homeschool Senior High
*Home Address * Our Town, WA Zip Code*

Student: Binz, Kevin   **Gender: Male**   **Birth Date: 01/01/00**
Parents: M/M Matthew Binz   **Address: Home Address, Town, WA, Zip**

Academic Record

Course	Class Title	Completion Date	Credits	Grade
English	American Literature & Composition Novel Writing	06/03	1.0	
Math	Algebra 1	06/01	1.0	
	Geometry	06/02	1.0	
	Algebra 2	06/03	1.0	
Science	Health 1	09/02	0.5	
	Biology with Lab	06/03	1.0	
Social Studies	American History	06/03	1.0	
Foreign Language	Latin 1	06/01	1.0	
	Latin 2	06/02	1.0	
	Latin 3	06/03	1.0	
	French 1	11/02	1.0	
	French 2	06/03	1.0	
Physical Education	Soccer, Swimming, Weights	08/03	1.0	
Electives	Music: Piano 2 with Performance	06/03	1.0	
	Art: American Art Appreciation	06/03	0.5	
	Bible: Christian Manhood	06/03	0.5	
	Critical Thinking in Chess	06/03	1.0	
	Public Speaking	06/03	0.5	

Activities	Soccer Team 2nd Place in Division, Swim Team, Competitive Chess, Student Teacher, Chess Tutor, Youth Worship Band

Grade Point Equivalents		Testing	Summary	
A=4.0 A-=3.7 B+=3.3 B=3.0 B-=2.7 C+=2.3 C=2.0			Credits 16	GPA

OFFICIAL TRANSCRIPT
~Homeschool Senior High~

Homeschool Senior High
* Home Address * Our Town, WA, Zip Code *

Student: **Binz, Kevin** Gender: **Male** Birth Date: **01/01/00**

Parents: **M/M Matthew Binz** Address: **Home Address, Our Town, WA, Zip**

Academic Record				
Course	Class Title	Completion Date	Credits	Grade
English	American Literature & Composition	06/03	1.0	4.0
	Novel Writing		1.0	
	World Literature & Composition	06/04	1.0	
Math	Algebra 1	06/01	1.0	4.0
	Geometry	06/02	1.0	4.0
	Algebra 2	06/03	1.0	4.0
	Pre-Calculus	06/04	1.0	
Science	Biology with Lab	06/03	1.0	4.0
	Chemistry with Lab	06/04		
Social Studies	American History	06/03	1.0	4.0
	Ancient & Medieval World History	06/04	1.0	
	Washington State History	06/04	0.5	
Foreign	Latin 1	06/01	1.0	4.0
Language	Latin 2	06/02	1.0	4.0
	Latin 3	06/03	1.0	4.0
	French 1	11/02	1.0	4.0
	French 2	05/03	1.0	4.0
	French 3	06/04	1.0	
Electives	Music: Piano 2 with Performance	06/03	1.0	4.0
	Music: Piano 3 with Performance	06/04	1.0	
	Fine Arts 1	06/03	0.5	4.0
	Fine Arts 2	06/04	0.5	
	Bible: Christian Manhood	06/03	0.5	4.0
	Bible: Apologetics	06/04	0.5	
	Critical Thinking in Chess	06/03	1.0	4.0
	Public Speaking	06/03	1.0	4.0
	Occupational Education	06/04		
	Driver's Education		0.5	
	Russian History	06/04	0.5	
Physical	PE 1	06/03	1.0	4.0
Education	PE 2	06/04	1.0	
Activities:	Soccer Team 9, 10: Swim Team 9,10, Coaches Award 10: Competitive Chess 9, 10: Student Teacher 9,10: Youth Worship Band 9			

Grade Point Equivalents	Testing	Summary	
		Credits	G.P.A.
A=4.0 A-=3.7 B+=3.3 B=3.0 B-=2.7 C+=2.3 C=2.0		14	4.0

Transcripts: A Work in Progress

Kevin's transcript at the end of 11th grade

OFFICIAL TRANSCRIPT
~Homeschool Senior High~

Homeschool Senior High
Home Address * Our Town, WA, Zip

Student: **Binz, Kevin**   Gender: **Male**   Birth Date: **01/01/00**
Parents: **M/M Matthew Binz**   Address: Home Address, Our Town, WA Zip Code

Academic Record by Year				
Year	Class Title	Completion Date	Credits	Grade
Early High School	Algebra 1	06/01	1.0	4.0
Credits	Geometry	06/02	1.0	4.0
	Latin 1	06/01	1.0	4.0
	Latin 2	06/02	1.0	4.0
2002-2003	English 1: American Literature & Composition	06/03	1.0	4.0
	Algebra 2	06/03	1.0	4.0
	Biology with Lab	06/03	1.0	4.0
	**American History	06/03	1.0	4.0
	Latin 3	06/03	1.0	4.0
	French 1	11/02	1.0	4.0
	French 2	05/03	1.0	4.0
	Music: Piano 2 with Performance	06/03	1.0	4.0
	Fine Arts 1: American Art	06/03	0.5	4.0
	Bible: Christian Manhood	06/03	0.5	4.0
	Critical Thinking in Chess	06/03	1.0	4.0
	Public Speaking	06/03	1.0	4.0
	PE 1	06/03	1.0	4.0
2003-2004	English 2: World Literature & Composition	06/04	1.0	4.0
	Novel Writing	06/04	1.0	4.0
	Pre-Calculus	06/04	1.0	4.0
	Chemistry with Lab	06/04	1.0	4.0
	**Ancient & Medieval World History	06/04	1.0	4.0
	Washington State History	06/04	0.5	4.0
	French 3	06/04	1.0	4.0
	Music: Piano 3 with Performance	06/04	1.0	4.0
	Fine Arts 2: History of Art	06/04	0.5	4.0
	Bible: Apologetics	06/04	0.5	4.0
	Occupational Education	06/04	0.5	4.0
	Russian History	06/04	0.5	4.0
	Formal Logic	06/04	0.5	4.0
	PE 2	06/04	1.0	4.0
	Driver's Education	07/04	0.5	4.0
2004-2005	**English 3: World Literature & Composition	06/05	1.0	4.0
	Calculus	06/05	1.0	4.0
	Physics with Lab	06/05	1.0	4.0
	**Modern World History	06/05	1.0	4.0
	**American Government	06/05	1.0	4.0
	Music: Piano 4 with Performance	06/05	1.0	4.0
	Fine Arts 3: Art and Music Appreciation	06/05	0.5	4.0
	Bible: World View	06/05	0.5	4.0
	PE 3	06/05	1.0	4.0
Activities:	Soccer Team 9, 10,11: Swim Team 9,10, 11 Coaches Award 10: Competitive Chess 9, 10, 11 Student Teacher 9,10, 11: Youth Mission Team 10: Youth Group 9, 10, 11: Worship Team 11			

SAT Results	Grade Point Equivalents	
March 2005: Reading 740, Math 710, Writing 760, Total 2210	A =90-100% =4.0	Summary
June 2005: Reading 790, Math 770, Writing 690, Total 2250	B=80-89% = 3.0	Credits GPA
**Denotes Honors course, documented by passing CLEP exam	C=70-79% = 2.0	35.5 4.0
	D = 60-69% = 1.0	

OFFICIAL TRANSCRIPT
~Homeschool Senior High~

Homeschool Senior High
Home Address * Our Town, WA, Zip Code
HIGH SCHOOL DIPLOMA AWARDED JUNE 11, 2006
Student: Binz, Kevin   **Gender**: Male   **Birth Date**: 01/01/00
Parents: M/M Matthew Binz   **Address**: Home Address, Our Town, WA Zip Code

Academic Record by Subject

Course	Class Title	Completion Date	Credits	Grade
English	English 1: American Literature & Composition	06/03	1.0	4.0
	Novel Writing	06/04	1.0	4.0
	English 2: World Literature & Composition	06/04	1.0	4.0
	**English 3: Honors Literature & Composition	06/05	1.0	4.0
	HCC SPCH 100: Basic Oral Communication	12/05	1.0	4.0
Math	Algebra 1	06/01	1.0	4.0
	Geometry	06/02	1.0	4.0
	Algebra 2	06/03	1.0	4.0
	Pre-Calculus	06/04	1.0	4.0
	Calculus	06/05	1.0	4.0
	HCC MATH 124: Calculus	12/05	1.0	4.0
	HCC MATH 125: Calculus	03/06	1.0	3.8
	HCC MATH 126: Calculus	06/06	1.0	3.9
	HCC MATH 220: Linear Algebra	06/06	1.0	3.7
Science	Biology with Lab	06/03	1.0	4.0
	Chemistry with Lab	06/04	1.0	4.0
	Physics with Lab	06/05	1.0	4.0
	HCC PHYS 201: Mechanics	03/06	1.0	4.0
	HCC PHYS 202: Electricity and Magnetism	06/06	1.0	4.0
Social Studies	**American History	06/03	1.0	4.0
	**Ancient World History	06/04	1.0	4.0
	Washington State History	06/04	0.5	4.0
	**Modern World History	06/05	1.0	4.0
	**American Government	06/05	1.0	4.0
	HCC POL S 180: Critical Issues/ World Politics	12/05	1.0	4.0
Foreign Language	Latin 1	06/01	1.0	4.0
	Latin 2	06/02	1.0	4.0
	Latin 3	06/03	1.0	4.0
	French 1	11/02	1.0	4.0
	French 2	05/03	1.0	4.0
	French 3	06/04	1.0	4.0
Fine Arts	Music: Piano 2 with Performance	06/03	1.0	4.0
	Music: Piano 3 with Performance	06/04	1.0	4.0
	Music: Piano 4 with Performance	06/05	1.0	4.0
	Fine Arts 1: American Art	06/03	0.5	4.0
	Fine Arts 2: History of Art	06/04	0.5	4.0
	Fine Arts 3: Art and Music Appreciation	06/05	0.5	4.0
	HCC ART 100: Introduction to Art	03/06	1.0	4.0
Bible	Bible: Christian Manhood	06/03	0.5	4.0
	Bible: Apologetics	06/04	0.5	4.0
	Bible: World View	06/05	0.5	4.0
Electives	Critical Thinking in Chess	06/03	1.0	4.0
	Public Speaking	06/03	1.0	4.0
	Occupational Education	06/04	0.5	4.0
	Driver's Education	07/04	0.5	4.0
	Russian History	06/04	0.5	4.0
	Formal Logic	06/04	0.5	4.0
	HCC ENGR 100 Orientation to Engineering	12/05	0.5	4.0
Physical Education	PE 1	06/03	1.0	4.0
	PE 2	06/04	1.0	4.0
	PE 3	06/05	1.0	4.0
Activities:	Soccer Team 9, 10,11: Swim Team 9, 10, 11,12 Coaches Award 10: Competitive Chess 9, 10, 11, 12 Student Teacher 9, 10, 11,12: Youth Mission Team 10: Youth Group 9, 10, 11, 12: Worship 9, 11			

SAT Results	Grade Point Equivalents	Summary
March 2005: Reading 740, Math 710, Writing 760, Total 2210	A =90-100% =4.0	
June 2005: Reading 790, Math 770, Writing 690, Total 2250	B=80-89% = 3.0	Credits GPA
	C=70-79% = 2.0	45 3.99
**Denotes Honors course, documented by passing CLEP exam	D = 60-69% = 1.0	
HCC denotes courses taken at Highline Community College		

OFFICIAL TRANSCRIPT	
~Homeschool Senior High~	

Homeschool Senior High
*Home Address * Our Town, WA, Zip Code*
HIGH SCHOOL DIPLOMA AWARDED JUNE 11, 2006

Student: Binz, Kevin   **Gender:** Male   **Birth Date:** 01/01/00
Parents: M/M Matthew Binz   **Address:** Home Address, Our Town, WA Zip Code

	Academic Record by Year			
Year	Class Title	Completion Date	Credits	Grade
Early High School	Algebra 1	06/01	1.0	4.0
Credits	Latin 1	06/01	1.0	4.0
	Geometry	06/02	1.0	4.0
	Latin 2	06/02	1.0	4.0
	French 1	11/02	1.0	4.0
2002-2003	English 1: American Literature & Composition	06/03	1.0	4.0
	Algebra 2	06/03	1.0	4.0
	Biology with Lab	06/03	1.0	4.0
	**American History	06/03	1.0	4.0
	Latin 3	06/03	1.0	4.0
	French 2	05/03	1.0	4.0
	Music: Piano 2 with Performance	06/03	1.0	4.0
	Fine Arts 1: American Art	06/03	0.5	4.0
	Bible: Christian Manhood	06/03	0.5	4.0
	Critical Thinking in Chess	06/03	1.0	4.0
	Public Speaking	06/03	1.0	4.0
	PE 1	06/03	1.0	4.0
2003-2004	English 2: World Literature & Composition	06/04	1.0	4.0
	Novel Writing	06/04	1.0	4.0
	Pre-Calculus	06/04	1.0	4.0
	Chemistry with Lab	06/04	1.0	4.0
	**Ancient World History	06/04	1.0	4.0
	Washington State History	06/04	0.5	4.0
	French 3	06/04	1.0	4.0
	Music: Piano 3 with Performance	06/04	1.0	4.0
	Fine Arts 2: History of Art	06/04	0.5	4.0
	Bible: Apologetics	06/04	0.5	4.0
	Occupational Education	06/04	0.5	4.0
	Russian History	06/04	0.5	4.0
	Formal Logic	06/04	0.5	4.0
	PE 2	06/04	1.0	4.0
	Driver's Education	07/04	0.5	4.0
2004-2005	**English 3: Honors Literature & Composition	06/05	1.0	4.0
	Calculus	06/05	1.0	4.0
	Physics with Lab	06/05	1.0	4.0
	**Modern World History	06/05	1.0	4.0
	**American Government	06/05	1.0	4.0
	Music: Piano 4 with Performance	06/05	1.0	4.0
	Fine Arts 3: Art and Music Appreciation	06/05	0.5	4.0
	Bible: World View	06/05	0.5	4.0
	PE 3	06/05	1.0	4.0
2005-2006	HCC ENGR 100: Orientation to Engineering	12/05	0.5	4.0
	HCC MATH 124: Calculus	12/05	1.0	4.0
	HCC POL S 180: Critical Issues/ World Politics	12/05	1.0	4.0
	HCC SPCH 100: Basic Oral Communications	12/05	1.0	4.0
	HCC ART 100: Introduction to Art	03/06	1.0	4.0
	HCC MATH 125: Calculus	03/06	1.0	3.8
	HCC PHYS 201: Mechanics	03/06	1.0	4.0
	HCC MATH 126: Calculus	06/06	1.0	3.9
	HCC MATH 220: Linear Algebra	06/06	1.0	3.7
	HCC PHYS 202: Electricity/ Magnetism	06/06	1.0	4.0
Activities:	Soccer Team 9, 10,11: Swim Team 9, 10, 11,12 Coaches Award 10: Competitive Chess 9, 10, 11, 12			
	Student Teacher 9, 10, 11,12: Youth Mission Team 10: Youth Group 9, 10, 11, 12: Worship 9, 11			

SAT Results	Grade Point Equivalents		
March 2005: Reading 740, Math 710, Writing 760, Total 2210	A =90-100% =4.0	**Summary**	
June 2005: Reading 790, Math 770, Writing 690, Total 2250	B=80-89% = 3.0	Credits	GPA
**Denotes Honors course, documented by passing CLEP exam	C=70-79% = 2.0	45	3.99
	D = 60-69% = 1.0		
HCC denotes courses taken at Highline Community College			

Kevin's transcript when we applied to college (Dual Enrollment)

OFFICIAL TRANSCRIPT
~Homeschool Senior High~

Homeschool Senior High
*Home Address * Our Town, WA, Zip Code*
HIGH SCHOOL DIPLOMA AWARDED JUNE 11, 2006

Student: Binz, Kevin   **Gender:** Male   **Birth Date:** 01/01/00
Parents: M/M Matthew Binz   **Address:** Home Address, Our Town, WA Zip Code

Academic Record of Dual Enrollment

Year	Class Title	Completion Date	Credits	Grade
Summer 2005	American Government**	7/13/05	TBD	52 Pass
CLEP exams	English Composition**	7/20/05	TBD	68 Pass
	Western Civilization I**	7/20/05	TBD	68 Pass
	History of the US II	8/03/05	TBD	55 Pass
	Western Civilization II**	8/03/05	TBD	63 Pass
	History of the US I**	8/17/05	TBD	64 Pass
2005-2006	Math 124: Calculus	12/08/05	5.0	4.0
Highline	Political Science 180	12/08/05	5.0	4.0
Community	Speech 100	12/08/05	5.0	4.0
College	Engineering 100	12/08/05	1.0	4.0
	Math 125: Calculus	03/15/06	5.0	3.8
	Physics 201: Mechanics	03/15/06	5.0	4.0
	Art 100: Intro to Art	03/15/06	5.0	4.0
	Math 126: Calculus	06/23/06	5.0	3.9
	Math 220: Linear Algebra	06/23/06	5.0	3.7
	Physics 202: Electricity/Magnetism	06/23/06	5.0	4.0
	Cumulative GPA at Highline CC			**3.93**

Activities:	Soccer Team 9, 10,11: Swim Team 9,10, 11 Coaches Award 10: Competitive Chess 9, 10, 11 Student Teacher 9,10, 11: Youth Mission Team 10: Youth Group 9, 10, 11: Worship 9, 11
Awards:	National Merit Scholarship Program: Commended Student President's List: Highest Scholastic Achievement. Awarded by Highline Community College
*	Classes currently registered. Remaining Classes are projected.
**	High School Honors Course awarded by passing CLEP exam

You can do this! **It may look complicated when you see the end result, but if you look at it one step at a time, it's not that hard**. Work on your transcript each year, and it will gradually look more complete as you go along. Just remember that it doesn't start out complete – it's a process.

By the end of high school, I still couldn't decide whether I wanted a transcript by subject or by year. Some colleges prefer a transcript by subject, so they can easily determine if the applicant has enough math classes, or has the right number of science credits. Other colleges want a transcript by year, so they can see if the student worked hard during their senior year, or just goofed off. Ultimately, **I decided to provide both types of transcripts–** one by subject, one by year, and for the final year of high school, a transcript of dual enrollment in community college.

Finally, I've included a copy of my other son's homeschool transcript. He has his own unique interests and specialization, and it's interesting to see two different transcripts from the same family. You can tell that both students studied many subjects together, but I hope you can also see that each child was allowed to pursue their own interests.

OFFICIAL TRANSCRIPT
~Homeschool Senior High~

Homeschool Senior High
*Home Address * Our Town, WA, Zip Code*
HIGH SCHOOL DIPLOMA AWARDED JUNE 11, 2006

Student: **Binz, Alex**　　　　Gender: **Male**　　　　Birth Date: 01/01/01
Parents: M/M Matthew Binz　　　**Address**: Home Address, Our Town, WA Zip Code

Academic Record by Subject

Subject	Class Title	Completion Date	Credits	Grade
English	**English 1: American Literature & Composition	06/03	1.0	4.0
	Novel Writing	06/04	1.0	4.0
	**English 2: Literature & Composition	06/04	1.0	4.0
	**English 3: Literature & Composition	06/05	1.0	4.0
	HCC SPCH 100: Basic Oral Communication HONORS	12/05	1.0	4.0
	HCC SPCH 213: Presentation Skills HONORS	06/06	1.0	4.0
Math	Algebra 1	06/03	1.0	4.0
	Geometry	06/04	1.0	4.0
	Algebra 2	01/05	1.0	4.0
	Pre-Calculus	08/05	1.0	4.0
	HCC MATH 124: Calculus	12/05	1.0	4.0
	HCC MATH 125: Calculus	03/06	1.0	3.9
	HCC MATH 126: Calculus	06/06	1.0	4.0
	HCC MATH 220: Linear Algebra	06/06	1.0	4.0
Science	**Biology with Lab	06/03	1.0	4.0
	Chemistry with Lab	06/04	1.0	4.0
	Physics with Lab	06/05	1.0	4.0
	HCC PHYS 201: Mechanics	03/06	1.0	4.0
Social Studies	**American History	06/03	1.0	4.0
	**Ancient World History	06/04	1.0	4.0
	Washington State History	06/04	0.5	4.0
	**Modern World History	06/05	1.0	4.0
	Civics	06/05	0.5	4.0
	HCC POL S 180: Critical Issues/World Politics HONORS	12/05	1.0	4.0
Foreign Language	Latin 1	06/01	1.0	4.0
	Latin 2	06/02	1.0	4.0
	Latin 3	06/03	1.0	4.0
	French 1	11/02	1.0	4.0
	French 2	05/03	1.0	4.0
	French 3	06/04	1.0	4.0
Fine Arts	Music: Piano 3 with Performance	06/03	1.0	4.0
	Music: Piano 4 with Performance	06/04	1.0	4.0
	Music: Piano 5 with Performance	06/05	1.0	4.0
	Fine Arts 1: American Art	06/03	0.5	4.0
	Fine Arts 2: Art History	06/04	0.5	4.0
	**Fine Arts 3: Art and Music Appreciation	06/05	1.0	4.0
Bible	Bible: Christian Manhood	06/03	0.5	4.0
	Bible: Apologetics	06/04	0.5	4.0
	Bible: World View	06/05	0.5	4.0
Electives	**American Government 1	06/03	1.0	4.0
	Economics 1	06/03	1.0	4.0
	**Economics 2	06/04	1.0	4.0
	**Economics 3	06/05	1.0	4.0
	HCC GEOG 207: Economic Geography HONORS	03/06	1.0	4.0
	Formal Logic	06/04	0.5	4.0
	Occupational Education	06/05	0.5	4.0
	Driver Education	09/05	0.5	4.0
Physical Education	PE 1	06/03	1.0	4.0
	PE 2	06/04	1.0	4.0
	PE 3	06/05	1.0	4.0
Activities:	Research Intern at Discovery Institute Public Policy Think Tank, YMCA Youth And Government, Soccer Team, Swim Team, Competitive Chess, Piano Performance, Choir			

PSAT October 2005: Reading 72, Math 69, Writing 76, Percentile 99	**Grade Point Equivalents**	
SAT March 2005: Reading 800, Math 740, Writing 750, Total 2290	A =90-100% =4.0	**Summary**
SAT June 2005: Reading 750, Math 790, Writing 790, Total 2330	B=80-89% = 3.0	Credits　GPA
**Denotes Honors course, documented by passing CLEP exam	C=70-79% = 2.0	45　　4.0
HCC denotes course taken at Highline Community College	D = 60-69% = 1.0	

Alex's transcript when we applied to college (By Year)

OFFICIAL TRANSCRIPT
~Homeschool Senior High~

Homeschool Senior High
Home Address * Our Town, WA, Zip Code
HIGH SCHOOL DIPLOMA AWARDED JUNE 11, 2006

Student: **Binz, Alex**   Gender: **Male**   Birth Date: 01/01/01
Parents: M/M Matthew Binz **Address**: Home Address, Our Town, WA Zip Code

Academic Record by Year

Year	Class Title	Completion Date	Credits	Grade
Early High School	Latin 1	06/01	1.0	4.0
Credits	Latin 2	06/02	1.0	4.0
	French 1	11/02	1.0	4.0
2002-2003	**English 1: American Literature & Composition	06/03	1.0	4.0
	Algebra 1	06/03	1.0	4.0
	**Biology with Lab	06/03	1.0	4.0
	**American History	06/03	1.0	4.0
	Latin 3	06/03	1.0	4.0
	French 2	05/03	1.0	4.0
	Music: Piano 3 with Performance	06/03	1.0	4.0
	Fine Arts 1: American Art	06/03	0.5	4.0
	Bible: Christian Manhood	06/03	0.5	4.0
	**American Government 1	06/03	1.0	4.0
	Economics 1	06/03	1.0	4.0
	PE 1	06/03	1.0	4.0
2003-2004	Novel Writing	06/04	1.0	4.0
	**English 2: Literature & Composition	06/04	1.0	4.0
	Geometry	06/04	1.0	4.0
	Chemistry with Lab	06/04	1.0	4.0
	**Ancient World History	06/04	1.0	4.0
	Washington State History	06/04	0.5	4.0
	French 3	06/04	1.0	4.0
	Music: Piano 4 with Performance	06/04	1.0	4.0
	Fine Arts 2: Art History	06/04	0.5	4.0
	Bible: Apologetics	06/04	0.5	4.0
	**Economics 2	06/04	1.0	4.0
	Formal Logic	06/04	0.5	4.0
	PE 2	06/04	1.0	4.0
2004-2005	**English 3: Literature & Composition	06/05	1.0	4.0
	Algebra 2	01/05	1.0	4.0
	Pre-Calculus	08/05	1.0	4.0
	Physics with Lab	06/05	1.0	4.0
	**Modern World History	06/05	1.0	4.0
	Civics	06/05	0.5	4.0
	Music: Piano 5 with Performance	06/05	1.0	4.0
	**Fine Arts 3: Art and Music Appreciation	06/05	1.0	4.0
	Bible: World View	06/05	0.5	4.0
	**Economics 3	06/05	1.0	4.0
	Occupational Education	06/05	0.5	4.0
	Driver Education	09/05	0.5	4.0
	PE 3	06/05	1.0	4.0
2005-2006	HCC MATH 124: Calculus	12/05	1.0	4.0
	HCC POL S 180: Critical Issue/World Politic HONORS	12/05	1.0	4.0
	HCC SPCH 100: Basic Oral Communication HONORS	12/05	1.0	4.0
	HCC GEOG 207: Economic Geography HONORS	03/06	1.0	4.0
	HCC MATH 125: Calculus	03/06	1.0	3.9
	HCC PHYS 201: Mechanics	03/06	1.0	4.0
	HCC MATH 126: Calculus	06/06	1.0	4.0
	HCC MATH 220: Linear Algebra	06/06	1.0	4.0
	HCC SPCH 213: Presentation Skills HONORS	06/06	1.0	4.0
Activities:	Research Intern at Discovery Institute Public Policy Think Tank, YMCA Youth And Government, Soccer Team, Swim Team, Competitive Chess, Piano Performance, Choir			

PSAT October 2005: Reading 72, Math 69, Writing 76, Percentile 99	Grade Point Equivalents	Summary
SAT March 2005: Reading 800, Math 740, Writing 750, Total 2290	A =90-100% =4.0	Credits GPA
SAT June 2005: Reading 750, Math 790, Writing 790, Total 2330	B=80-89% = 3.0	
**Denotes Honors course, documented by passing CLEP exam	C=70-79% = 2.0	45 4.0
HCC denotes course taken at Highline Community College	D = 60-69% = 1.0	

Alex's transcript when we applied to college (Dual Enrollment)

~Homeschool Senior High~

Homeschool Senior High
*Home Address * Our Town, WA, Zip Code*
HIGH SCHOOL DIPLOMA AWARDED JUNE 11, 2006

Student: Binz, Alex   **Gender:** Male   **Birth Date**: 01/01/01
Parents: M/M Matthew Binz   **Address**: Home Address, Our Town, WA Zip Code

Academic Record of Dual Enrollment

Year	Class Title	Completion Date	Credits	Grade
Summer 2005	American Government**	6/29/05	TBD	69 Pass
CLEP Exams	History of the US I**	6/29/05	TBD	70 Pass
	Western Civilization I**	7/06/05	TBD	71 Pass
	Western Civilization II**	7/06/05	TBD	67 Pass
	Principles of Microeconomics**	7/13/05	TBD	69 Pass
	Principles of Macroeconomics**	7/13/05	TBD	69 Pass
	History of the US II	7/20/05	TBD	68 Pass
	English Composition**	7/20/05	TBD	70 Pass
	Principles of Marketing	7/20/05	TBD	68 Pass
	Introduction to Business Law	7/27/05	TBD	52 Pass
	Humanities**	7/27/05	TBD	70 Pass
	English Literature**	8/03/05	TBD	62 Pass
	Biology**	8/03/05	TBD	63 Pass
	Introductory Psychology	8/10/05	TBD	64 Pass
	American Literature**	8/17/05	TBD	61 Pass
2005-2006	Math 124: Calculus	12/08/05	5.0	4.0
Highline	Political Science 180 - Honors	12/08/05	5.0	4.0
Community	Speech 100 - Honors	12/08/05	5.0	4.0
College	Math 125: Calculus	03/15/06	5.0	3.9
	Physics 201: Mechanics	03/15/06	5.0	4.0
	Geography 207: Economic Geography - Honors	03/15/06	5.0	4.0
	Math 126: Calculus	06/14/06	5.0	4.0
	Speech 213: Presentation Skills - Honors	06/14/06	5.0	4.0
	Math 220: Linear Algebra	06/14/06	5.0	4.0
	Cumulative GPA at Highline CC			**3.99**

Activities:	Research Intern at Discovery Institute Public Policy Think Tank, YMCA Youth And Government, Soccer Team, Swim Team, Competitive Chess, Piano Performance
Awards:	President's List: Highest Scholastic Achievement Highline Community College Fall 2005
	Vice President's List: Highline Community College Winter 2006
	President's List: Highest Scholastic Achievement Highline Community College Spring 2006
**	Denotes Honors course high school credit given.

Chapter 12

Course Descriptions Demystified

When I arranged to visit our favorite college for the first time, I asked if they wanted me to bring my homeschool records. I received an enthusiastic reply. "Yes! **Please bring ALL your homeschool records** – that would be great!"

So my husband took the day off work to help me carry in our homeschool records. I had a large three-ring binder for each year of school, and for each child. We brought in six heavy binders. The college admission representative looked at the binders and politely said, "Thank you for bringing in your records." He didn't appear to have any plan to look at them, however. After all the energy and effort of making all the course descriptions, I was pretty frustrated. **"Don't you even want to see them?" I whined.** It seemed like they  were more interested in knowing that I actually HAD homeschool records. They seemed less interested in actually reading them!

When we were visiting another college, **I asked the admission staff what kind of records they wanted to see from homeschoolers.** I showed them a sample page from my Comprehensive Record. I was surprised when they told me that they wanted this kind of documentation for every class I taught.

One admission advisor went even further. She said that she wished every applicant would provide this kind of information, even public school students. "The transcript will say English each year, but when they come to our college we find out the student can't read or write well. I would love to see what they are supposed to be learning in their English class!"

I often think about these events when I talk about writing course descriptions. The variety of responses revealed something significant.

Course descriptions are important to write, but you may never know how they will be used. They may be read thoroughly and for detail, or **they may be "viewed" but not read.** While we may stress about the details of our wording and expression, that may not be what is important. Think about these stories when you are writing your course descriptions. Colleges will want to know about the classes, and they will want to know what your child learned. Beyond that, you have freedom.

Some universities prefer very long and detailed course descriptions. The 2007 article "In a Class of Their Own" in Harvard's *Crimson Magazine* describes one homeschooler's experience. "My mom wrote out exhaustive transcripts for us. Every class we took and what the class consisted of. It wouldn't just say 'English.' It was what texts we used and how the grade was determined." (http://www.thecrimson.com/article/2007/2/28/in-a-class-of-their-own/)

Writing course descriptions can help you prepare college applications that require details. Some large, public universities distrust home-

> For some colleges, providing details will help you.

school education, and may ask for course descriptions as "proof." Other small private schools may feel they need to determine academic rigor and want comprehensive documentation as evidence of college preparation. One college may want to receive homeschool records on paper, so the college can save money by not printing it themselves.

Others prefer receiving the information electronically, so they can quickly share the documents within the admission department.

It's impossible to predict how much information and detail a college will need. **It is imperative that you ask each individual university.** Their policy may change over time, so ask again immediately before your student applies. It's also difficult to predict what college your child will choose, and whether that college will require course descriptions in the future or not.

For that reason, think about how you will plan for course descriptions when you first begin high school. You can be prepared for college admission if you simply keep high school records. Keep track of what books you use and what great things you did. Save your records, and later on you will have the information necessary to create course descriptions – if you need them Plan ahead by keeping records. Even if you keep everything is a box, you can still go back later and document what is necessary.

Keep in mind that **a college may want only a transcript** from a student. Some colleges like to have a transcript and a reading list. Course descriptions and portfolio-like records, such as these, are not always necessary. You may want to check with the college before submitting this much information.

There are four situations when course descriptions are extremely important. First, of course, is when the college requires or requests course descriptions. It is important if your child wants to go to a college that is very selective or one that is a big reach for your student. It is important if you are pursuing really big scholarships from a college. Finally, if you need to compensate for something about their academic record, whether it is a poor SAT score or other perceived weakness.

College preferences and requirements vary widely on many things. It varies so widely from college to college, that it's really important for you to find out what each college wants to see from your homeschool records. My children were each admitted to all of the colleges where they applied, and they were given great scholarships from every college, including full-tuition scholarships. The Associate Director of Admissions for Seattle Pacific University wrote, **"Your transcripts and records were the best organized and documented I have seen."** I believe our thorough documentation really made a difference.

Most course descriptions have three components; a descriptive paragraph about the class, a list of the educational materials and supplements, and an explanation of how the grade was achieved.

The most common course description is a descriptive paragraph about the class. Within that definition, you have so much flexibility. A descriptive paragraph can use any verb tense; it can speak to the future or to the past. It can be formal or casual, and it doesn't require any specific educational vocabulary.

> **When course descriptions are crucial:**
>
> - The College requires them
>
> - Applying to a selective or "reach" college
>
> - Scholarships are a necessity
>
> - Compensating for a weakness

Course descriptions are a simple elementary school writing assignment. They are a single paragraph about a single topic. We taught our children to write a paragraph when they were very young, and we are capable of a simple writing assignment ourselves.

I remember when my children were in 5th grade, and how difficult it was for them to start writing. They were confused about the directions, and they didn't know how to start. They didn't want to do it "wrong" but they didn't know how to do it "right." I would patiently explain that they simply needed to start, and do their best. It was frustrating! When I started writing course descriptions, however, I started to really appreciate their feelings. I felt incompetent!

Don't beat yourself up about writing perfectly in the beginning. Instead, think about how your children learned to write a paragraph essay, and encourage yourself the same way. You simply need to start. You can do it! I was nervous about it myself, but I managed to get it done – AND it earned praise from colleges. You can do it too.

LIST OF MATERIALS

Beyond a descriptive paragraph, provide a list of what you used for the class. List the primary textbooks, supplements, activities, and events used to achieve learning. For example, a course on occupational education may list every skill your child learned, from typing and shoveling to banking and tax preparation. Each learning activity could be evaluated by "pass or fail" method or "achieve or did not achieve" standard.

DEMONSTRATE THE GRADE

Finally, provide information about how you determined a grade. Review Chapter 7 and the material about grading and grading scales. Above all, remember that transcript grades include every way you evaluate your children, and final grades are not just the grade on a test. Demonstrating thoughtful consideration of your grades can convince skeptics that your grades truly reflect what your student earned in a class.

At the core, documentation of a class involves three things. Provide a short descriptive paragraph that is no more than an elementary writing assignment. Write a list of all

> Course description components:
>
> • Descriptive paragraph
>
> • List of materials
>
> • Explanation of grades

the wonderful things you used and did. List the multitude of ways you evaluated your children in the normal course of your homeschool.

There are many different ways to write course descriptions – and even many ways to avoid writing course descriptions.

Chapter 13

How to Write a Course Description

One of the most intimidating requirements of homeschool parents can be course descriptions. We know we are supposed to have them, and that colleges may require it. However, parents rarely know what a course description is, or how to make one.

As a homeschool mother, I felt that intimidation. I mentioned earlier that I cope with stress by doing research, and course descriptions caused me a LOT of stress, so I did a LOT of research. As my children were involved in their activities, and I was waiting for them endlessly in coffee shops and in the car, **I read every book I could find.**

There are many homeschool books that have course descriptions in them. They all looked different. Every book had a different way and a different look. Some even called it by different names; portfolio, comprehensive record, exhaustive transcript, etc. Even course descriptions in the same book would look different from one another. After reading all the books, **I was able to identify strategies for making course descriptions almost painless.**

There is freedom to write course descriptions in a variety of different ways. No two parents do it the same. **There is no single "right way" to do it, and everything else is the "wrong way."** Instead, everyone has a different method. It's not necessary to feel overwhelmed with the choices. Instead, revel in the amount of freedom! You can make a course description your own way, and it WILL be the right way.

The easiest way to begin is by avoiding writing course descriptions yourself – at least in the beginning.

DESCRIPTIONS WRITTEN BY OTHERS

BOOKS WITH COURSE DESCRIPTIONS

One of the easiest ways to start is to use a description written by someone else. I have written a huge number of course descriptions for you,

that are included in an appendix of this book, and you are free to use them. There are other **homeschool books that provide course descriptions that are intended for parents to use** or modify to fit their homeschool.

When I was writing course descriptions, I brought home every homeschool high school book in our library. I opened each one to the section on course descriptions. I looked over their descriptions until I found a class we had done in our own homeschool. Comparing similar course descriptions in the various books, I determined which example I preferred. I used that example when I began writing each course.

Course descriptions written by others:
- Homeschoolers' College Admissions Handbook by Cafi Cohen
- Homeschooling High School by Jeanne Gowen Dennis
- The High School Handbook by Mary Schofield
- Senior High: A Home-Designed Form+U+La by Barbara Edtl Shelton

In the process of reading course descriptions written by others, it becomes easier to create course descriptions yourself. **Like reading**

quality literature can make good writers, reading completed course descriptions can help you write better as well. As I read the information in the books, I would use what I could, and modify or vary courses to best represent out homeschool.

COURSE DESCRIPTIONS FROM FRIENDS

Friends may be a wonderful source of course descriptions. Homeschoolers who use the same or similar curriculum may share course descriptions. Sharing the intimate details of your homeschool and your descriptive paragraphs can be very scary. Even when I was finished homeschooling, with children successful through the college admission process, I still felt funny about other parents seeing my homeschool details. Homeschoolers tend to be very private people, and I will admit that can be a huge emotional hurdle. If your homeschool friends feel insecure sharing their work, consider me your friend – you can look at my work. The course descriptions I wrote for my children are all in the appendix, and you can see every last detail of my homeschool for yourself.

COURSE DESCRIPTIONS FROM OUTSIDE CLASSES

There is another source for course descriptions written by others. When classes are taken outside the home, course descriptions may be provided. An organized **homeschool co-op may have course descriptions available**, and you can use the description of the classes taken there. Be sure to add details about supplements you included at home. In general, those descriptions can be easily used exactly as they were written, with little effort or aggravation.

Classes taken at a public school, private school, community college, or online may also have **online course descriptions**. Again, when your child is registered for these classes, the descriptions may be simple to cut and paste from the internet. Look for a description of the course when registering. Save those course descriptions electronically, or print them and keep that information with your homeschool records.

Keep the course descriptions provided from community college, if your child utilizes dual enrollment. Community college requirements vary, and a title alone does not clearly explain courses. University admission representatives will appreciate having details about community college course, so that your student can be accurately placed into the correct courses when they begin at the university. It can surprise parents, but universities may be cautious about community college classes, so documentation of those classes may help.

CURRICULUM PROVIDERS

When choosing curriculum to use, a homeschool parent may spend hours on the internet and pouring over books trying to find just the right resource for their courses and students. Curriculum descriptions can provide great raw material for a course description. There are a variety of sources for this kind of information.

Textbook publishers and curriculum authors will provide information you can use. Read about the book on their website, looking for concepts. Read about your math or science textbook on the Apologia or Saxon website for example, and see what they say the course contained. If a textbook was the sole source for a class, then a paragraph provided from the author may be the only thing required.

Catalogs from curriculum suppliers may have a detailed description of their product. These paragraphs are perfect for use as course descriptions. Read about your curriculum in the catalog where you initially decided on the book, or use other catalogs describing the same product.

Product reviews provide additional information. Simply search the internet for the curriculum name, along with the word "review" to see what others have said. My favorite reviewer is Cathy Duffy, and she has some wonderful product evaluations in her books that you can purchase or find in the library. *100 Top Picks For Homeschool Curriculum* and *The Christian Home Educators' Curriculum Manual* are both excellent resources by Cathy Duffy.

> Where to find content
>
> - Homeschool books
> - Outside Classes
> - Online searches
> - Curriculum authors
> - Homeschool Catalogs
> - Table of Contents

A textbook table of contents can be your best friend. Using words from a table of contents can provide a huge amount of information about a course. For that reason, keeping information about textbooks can be invaluable when it is time to describe classes. Copy the textbook cover and the table of contents for your homeschool records. You don't have to keep the book forever, but the information in the table of contents will be available when you need it.

AVOID PLAGIARISM

Many sources will allow you to copy course descriptions directly. If you do not have permission to use course descriptions written by others, the information may still be very useful. Avoid plagiarism with some simple steps. Read the material, with or without taking notes. Close the book and take a short break. Sip coffee, take a deep breath, or put the book aside for a second. Write about what you have read using your own words. It is not gener-

ally considered plagiarism when you write down your ideas after reading them, without quoting the source word for word.

Homeschoolers are a pretty unique crowd, and some courses will be so unique that you'll be left high and dry. Nobody else has ever written a course description like it. There were no formal classes or textbooks. For those situations and others, there is the Template Strategy.

How to Avoid Plagiarism

- Read
- Take Notes
- Close Book
- Sip Coffee
- Write

DEVELOP A TEMPLATE

I remember writing thank-you notes for our wedding gifts years ago. I was on the airplane on the way to Hawaii, trying to get as much done as possible during the flight. **I quickly developed an unspoken template**

for my thank you cards, writing the notes in a similar way each time. After a while, my unspoken template was ingrained and even now my husband still teases me about it! "This will come in handy in starting our new home," he says to me. You can develop a template for your course description as well. Your template can get you started if you get stuck.

For some parents, choosing a template will mean deciding on a writing style. Look at a course description that you like. Why do you like it? How is it written? Is it in the first person, using the pronoun "I"? Is it in the third person, using "he" or "she?" What tense is the verb? Is it past tense, as the class has already been completed, or future tense, saying what will happen in the future? Notice what details are included first, and which details follow. What is the first sentence? Once you decide on a course description you like, it is relatively simple to imitate the style.

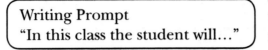

Writing Prompt
"In this class the student will…"

When I was teaching my children to write, I often used books with writing prompts. It would suggest different ways to get the children started. Sometimes the curriculum would begin a sentence, so the children just needed to complete the started paragraph.

You may want to **use a writing prompt for yourself.** If we can get children writing that way, then it must work for adults too! As I was

working on my course descriptions, when all else failed, I would resort to my own writing prompt. Feel free to use the phrase that I used! Have a beginning sentence that you like, to get you started each time. My prompt began "In this class the student will….." To be honest, I wrote all of my course descriptions after the fact. Still, having the course description in future tense sounded "right" to me. I liked that it made the classes seem so intentional, when many times I was just following after my children and writing up what they had learned naturally. **I wasn't sure what person or tense I was using. I just knew that it**

helped me to write what needed to be written. Just begin writing your course descriptions. It will get much easier as you go along.

Instead of being afraid, use simple techniques to ease into them gently. First, take some deep breaths! Plenty of ordinary homeschoolers have written course descriptions that were good enough to meet requirements. Next, become familiar with course descriptions so they don't seem so scary. Simply reading through course descriptions written by other parents can help. Third, recognize the simplicity of a course description. At the core, it is simply a one-paragraph description of how your child learned. Like transcripts, it doesn't start out complete – it's a process. Just start. You can edit later.

Chapter 14

Course Descriptions in Real Life

In my work consulting with homeschool families, I have frequently been asked for a copy of my children's Comprehensive Record. No two homeschoolers are alike, so the information is unique to my family. I know, however, that **I would have loved to see another homeschooler's records** cover-to-cover. Many homeschoolers feel insecure and long to see a successful sample they can imitate.

In my research, I saw books with only one or two course descriptions from a single parent, but never one child's records from beginning to end, exactly as submitted to a college. The parents I talk to say, "Just show me what it should look like, and I can imitate it!" That's why I have provided many examples in this book. One is mine, one is from a mom named Christine, and another from a mom named Ann. Finally, I have an example that I have shown my clients, demonstrating an expanded transcript method.

THE HOMESCHOLAR EXAMPLE:
THE SAMPLE COMPREHENSIVE RECORD

When parents started asking me for my own homeschool records, I knew I needed to provide that help for others. I have included my course description book, the "sample comprehensive record in Appendix 3" in the appendix, so you can see a child's complete record, cover to cover. Other than removing my son's personal information from each page, it is in the same format that I submitted to colleges.

Our comprehensive record contained all course descriptions, reading list, and work samples for my child. With simply his name on the front, we had the entire packet of information spiral-bound at the local office supply store.

On top of this comprehensive record, we had a transcript on a single page. My plan was to provide the transcript as a simple overview, for colleges that only wanted the basics. I provided the spiral-bound package as additional information, so colleges could choose to read it and use the information if they found it helpful, while still having a simple and clear one-page transcript for reference.

Some homeschoolers utilize classes in a school or co-op setting. At the end of my Comprehensive Record, there are also course descriptions for classes that were completed outside the home, written for other parents, so you can see how that is done.

CHRISTINE'S EXAMPLE

Christine volunteered to supply the records from her own child, so you can see a completely different example. Christine made a long comprehensive record for her own son, and was very successful in college admissions. There are many "right ways" to format course descriptions and provide them to colleges. You can find your own "right way" using the many samples I have provided. Christine's example is in Appendix 4.

ANN'S EXAMPLE

Ann has independently homeschooled her 7 children for the last 19 years. She has graduated three already, and they have been admitted to four colleges and her family has been awarded over $300,000 in scholarships thus far. Her first two children graduated debt free from their top-choice university. Ann's example is in Appendix 5.

EXPANDED TRANSCRIPT EXAMPLE

In the appendix, you will also see how to eliminate bulky course descriptions by replacing them with a simplified expanded transcript. This option is clarified in chapter 15, "How to Avoid Writing Course Descriptions." Although these are significantly shorter than full-fledged course description, they are included in the list of many options.

THINKING IT THROUGH

Here are some course descriptions I have written, so you can learn more about the process, and how to modify descriptions to meet your needs. The first example is a class guided by **delight-directed learning**. By reading about occupational education, you can begin to think of ways to write course descriptions involving things your children love to do. The second example is a class with an **unusual duration**. My son's math class ended in the middle of the year, and many parents ask me how to handle a class like that. The third example is a class **without any records at all**. The piano courses had no textbooks or written papers, and at first I was completely baffled how to handle that. Finally, in the fourth example you will see **how to utilize standardized** tests as part of your assessment. The example is an English class, but you can use the same technique with other classes as well.

EXAMPLE OF DELIGHT DIRECTED LEARNING

Occupational Education is one of the easiest courses to both teach and describe. Here are the simple steps:

1. The child becomes motivated by money
2. The child will seek employment
3. Count hours on the job
4. At 150 hours, call it a credit
5. Retroactively list individual tasks done

On the following pages, you will see our Occupational Education course description. Notice that is was FILLED with chess. My son Kevin loved chess, and his high school years revolved around chess. It was his passion – and it totally drove me crazy. Every year of high school he would study chess for hours and hours every day. **His booklist is also filled with chess.** He would spend hours every evening studying and competed in countless tournaments. He even taught chess in a variety of settings, When he would "accidentally" stray from his schoolwork, I usually found him in front of a chess board, or with a chess book in his hand.

The things that bother us often become our subconscious grading criteria. "Is that all you want to read about?" can tell you about a delight-directed course. Saying "You simply HAVE to put that down now and do some school!" can help you determine credit value for your delight-directed course. How often do you say it? Once a week? Once a day? Once an hour? It may mean your child is spending more than 5 hours a week on the activity and you might be able to make it a high school credit. (And yes, I know for some kids it's more like five hours per day!)

Chess is not a course that many students take in high school, but it does represent a unique passionate interest that a child might have. You student will have completely different interests, of course, but I hope you will see how to take ANY unique interest and turn it into a course description.

Even though I found chess annoying, I was able to include chess in his transcript each year. I figured those hundreds and hundreds of hours had to be good for something! **The course description for occupational education is on the following page.**

> What annoys you?
>
> Is it a delight-directed learning class?

Course Description
Elective: Occupational Education

Description: This is a self-directed course. The student will work to pursue their area of interest, seeking work and volunteer opportunities in that area. Within his area of interest, the student will demonstrate initiative, responsibility, reliability, and enthusiasm in the workplace. The student will demonstrate basic computer and word processing skills. Written work available on request.

Skills and Opportunities include:
➢ Teaching chess at Manhattan Homeschool Center
➢ Teaching chess at Marvista Elementary School, Normandy Park
➢ Teaching chess with individual tutorial students
➢ Teaching chess at Stella Schola Middle School, Redmond
➢ Substitute chess teacher at Issaquah Chinese Academy
➢ Experience in interviewing
➢ Experience in making resume, cover letter, and obtaining letter of recommendation
➢ Experience with handling regular pay

Course Grade
Occupational Education – Completed 06/04

Daily Work ------------------------- 1/2 grade-------------------------		Preparation -----------1/2 grade---------	
Teacher: Manhattan Homeschool Center – Volunteer Position	100%	Preparation for Class	100%
Teacher: Marvista Elementary School – Paid Position	100%	Preparation for Class	100%
Teacher: Stella Schola Middle School – Paid Position	100%	Preparation for Class	100%
Substitute Teacher: Issaquah Chinese School – Paid position	100%	Preparation for Class	100%
Private Tutor with Individual students	100%	Preparation for Students	100%
Yard Maintenance – Paid Position	100%		
Basic Computer and Typing Skills	100%		
------------ **Final grade for Occupational Education = 100% = A** ------------			
A =90-100% =4.0　　　*B=80-89% = 3.0*　　　*C=70-79% = 2.0*　　　*D = 60-69% = 1.0*			

Since children don't all learn at the same rate, sometimes you may finish a class in 5 months – or in 18 months. **Not everything will fit neatly into the regular school year**, beginning in September and ending in June. When Alex took geometry, he was able to finish it in March. I wanted him to continue with math each day, so we didn't stop all math studies in March. Instead, we continued with the next math level right away. On his course description, you can see that his Geometry class was completed on 03/04. The completion date is listed just below the class grade. The following year his Algebra 2 class was completed in 01/05. You don't have to try to force your children into the constraints of a public school schedule. They can stop and start classes when it is natural for them. It's very easy to simply **label each class with a completion date and move on.**

The grading of this course shows three columns. **I always tried to include three different kinds of grades for each class. In math, it often broke into daily work, tests, midterm and final exams.** I know it can be tempting to include only grades for tests, but that is not how children in public schools are graded. They are evaluated in multiple ways, and we can do that as well. I wanted my children to get some benefit from all their math homework each day. In high school math it's not uncommon for children to work two or more hours each day on a math lesson, and I wanted to give them the proper credit for that. I saw their public school friends get grades for turning in homework and class participation (sometimes attendance and extra credit.) To make a level playing field, I had to do something.

In the end, I decided to provide a grade for daily work for each chapter in the math book. When my children did every problem I asked them to do, and corrected the problems that we wrong as I asked them, they would receive a 100% in their daily work for that chapter. In the third column I gave a grade for tests. That's not necessary at all, and you can certainly include a midterm and final within the regular grades. I usually suggest that you separate the column if it helps your grade, and do not separate the column if it does not help your grade.

It wasn't until the following year in math, Algebra 2, that I completely lost my ability to teach and had to rely exclusively on video tutorials. Remember that **everyone gets to that "unable to teach" place at some point. It's not a sign of weakness. It's an indication that your child has become self-teaching, so it's a success!** This following course description demonstrates what you can do with classes with unusual duration.

Course Description
Math: Geometry

Course Description: This course stresses logic, deductive reasoning, and formal proofs. The value of geometry is the development of logical thinking skills. This text spends the first 9 lessons on logic, to ensure logical thinking, before moving on to geometry topics. Given the foundation in logic, students immediately begin work with proofs. Work with circles follows introductory lessons on trigonometry. Construction activities are supplemented with an additional text.

Primary Text: <u>Geometry</u> by Harold R. Jacobs

Topics include:
- Deductive reasoning and logic
- Points, lines, and planes
- Rays and angles
- Congruent triangles
- Inequalities
- Parallel lines
- Quadrilaterals
- Transformations
- Area

- Similarity
- Right Triangles
- Circles
- Concurrence Theorems
- Regular Polygons and the Circle
- Geometric Solids
- Non-Euclidean Geometries
- Coordinate Geometry

Supplement: Patty Paper Geometry by Michael Serra
Tests in student handwriting available on request.

Course Grade
Geometry – Alex Binz– Completed 03/04

Tests		Daily Work		Midterm and Final
-------------1/3 grade-------------		-------------1/3 grade-------------		-------------1/3 grade-------------
Chapter 1	100%	Chapter 1	100%	
Chapter 2	100%	Chapter 2	100%	
Chapter 3	94%	Chapter 3	100%	
Chapter 4	100%	Chapter 4	100%	
Chapter 5	91%	Chapter 5	100%	
Chapter 6	97%	Chapter 6	100%	
Chapter 7	91%	Chapter 7	100%	
Chapter 8	95%	Chapter 8	100%	Midterm Exam 96%
Chapter 9	95%	Chapter 9	100%	
Chapter 10	98%	Chapter 10	100%	
Chapter 11	93%	Chapter 11	100%	
Chapter 12	97%	Chapter 12	100%	
Chapter 13	95%	Chapter 13	100%	
Chapter 14	100%	Chapter 14	100%	
Chapter 15	100%	Chapter 15	100%	
Chapter 16	89%	Chapter 16	100%	
Chapter 17	93%	Chapter 17	100%	Final Exam 93%
Tests average 96%		**Daily work average 100%**		**Exams 95%%**
----------------------Final grade for Geometry = 97% = A----------------------				
A =90-100% =4.0	*B=80-89% = 3.0*	*C=70-79% = 2.0*	*D = 60-69% = 1.0*	

When I looked at my homeschool records folder, within the music section, I recognized something pretty quickly. I had no records for music. I couldn't write down anything about the class, because I hadn't saved any documentation. **After a couple of months with no tests, no papers, and no worksheets of any kind, I realized I had to think outside the box.**

One benefit of working on course descriptions throughout the year is that you can recognize classes that don't produce records. Once the issue is identified, changes can be made. Recognizing that records are missing is the first step towards a solution. Remember that for course descriptions you want to **specify what you used, what you did, and how you graded.** From that point, try to think creatively. Ask friends for advice, or seek help if needed.

For my son's piano class, I began by listing the books that he used for his piano lessons. I made a special note of his performance-ready pieces. "What we did" included practice, lessons, and performances. The "how we graded" section was discussed only in general terms. In case you are wondering how I decided to call the piano class "level 5" it all boiled down to the adjudication. Once we started having the piano performances judged, they assigned Alex a level. I simply counted backward, so the previous year had the previous number level, even though he was not adjudicated every year.

Creating Records

Quick Essay
Research Paper
Book List
Projects
Performances
Awards
Evaluations

Some homeschool classes don't easily provide records. Often a Physical Education class will look completely empty. Some time spent brainstorming ideas will help. For our homeschool PE class, we decided to keep ribbons from swim team, but every homeschooler will do it differently. I have consulted with others about cooking classes, and suggested they keep shopping lists, menus, and recipes. Brainstorm your own ideas, and see what you can accumulate for those blank sections. **Once a month, or once a quarter, go through your records and see what you have kept, to determine if any records are lacking.**

If you have a class that truly has no records at all, then consider making some. When we had classes with little documentation, I would encourage my children to **write a paper about the subject.** We would regularly practice writing short essays for the SAT exam. The practice was important so they would be comfortable writing a timed 25 minute essay. The content of the paper was less important.

On the following page is an example of a class without records.

Course Description
Music: Piano 5 with Performance

Description: The student will attend private professional piano lessons weekly throughout the year, and will practice piano 45 minutes daily. Students will learn practical aspects of playing the piano as well as the technical aspects such as scales and chording. Different piano playing styles, such as jazz and   classical music will be explored. Sight-reading and music theory will be studied. The student will study a variety of composers and musical styles. The student will develop musicianship and performance skills. Performances are required.

Primary Texts:
Hanon: The Virtuoso Pianist in Sixty Exercises for the Piano by Schirmer's Library
Piano Solo: The World's Favorite Classical Themes by Hal Leonard
At the Piano With Scott Joplin by Maurice Hinson
Bumble-Boogie: Adapted from the "Flight of the Bumble-Bee" by Jack Fina
Moonlight Sonata by Beethoven, G. Schirmer, Inc.
Rondo Alla Turca by Wolfgang Amadeus Mozart, Belwin Classic Library.
The Classical Period: An Anthology of Piano Music Volume 2, edited by Denes Agay.
The Romantic Period: An Anthology of Piano Music Volume 3, edited by Denes Agay.
The Library of Piano Classics by Amsco
The Library of Piano Classics 2 by Amsco
Mozart Piano Solo Complete Edition Published by Urtext, with 4 texts:
➤   Klavierstucke, Piano Pieces, Morceaux Pour Piano
➤   Variationen
➤   Sonaten, Fantasien and Rondi 1
➤   Sonaten, Fantasien and Rondi 2

Performances:
1. Winter Recital
2. National Federation of Music Clubs Junior Festival: Rated Excellent
3. Spring Recital
4. Church Offertory music

Course Grade
Piano Level 5 – Alex Binz– Completed 06/05

Daily Work		Performance	
----------------1/2 grade----------------		----------------1/2 grade----------------	
Piano Practice	100%	Performance	100%
Attend Lessons	100%	Competition	100%
--------------- Final grade for Piano Level 5 = 100% = A ---------------			
A =90-100% =4.0 B=80-89% = 3.0 C=70-79% = 2.0 D = 60-69% = 1.0			

We loved "Learn to Write the Novel Way" by Carole Thaxton. My children actually wrote a novel during the course. Like other classes we did in our home, there were no tests, and I had to think long and hard about how I was evaluating my children.

When considering different grading criteria, I recognized that **our annual assessment evaluated my children** in English, so I incorporated that assessment in our grading criteria. The middle section called "Mechanics" is taken directly from our standardized test scores. The words in that section came directly from that test.

If your children take a standardized test, you can use the test results on a portion of your evaluation. If the test measures science reasoning, include those words in your science course description. Standardized tests are one way we evaluate our children. I see parents all the time that are thrilled (or concerned) about test results, which is evidence of using it for evaluation. You aren't required to use standardized tests for your evaluation – I certainly didn't use it all the time. However, **those tests are one tool we can use in our course descriptions, and they are at your disposal.** The PSAT, SAT, and ACT may be included in course descriptions if desired. The course description below illustrates how I incorporated standardized test results in my course description.

Course Description
English: Novel Writing

The student will learn, practice and apply the research and writing skills necessary to produce a novel. By the end of this course, the student will have written an entire novel with excellent style, vocabulary, grammar, and mechanics. Credit will be awarded based on a minimum of 150 hours of research and writing, as well as completion of a finished novel. Grades will be awarded based on language mechanics and completion of the project. The student workbook and completed novel are available on request. This is a 2-year course.

Composition Objectives:

- Overview of steps for writing fiction
- Evaluate personal preferences
- Pre-writing
- Character and scene description
- Appropriate use of person and tense
- Plot and sub-plot outline
- Sequencing
- Titling
- Paragraph division
- Computers in writing
- Writer's block
- Picture writing
- Detailing
- Dialog

- Communicating abstract concepts
- Simile and metaphor
- Word choice
- Concise language
- Active voice
- Positive form
- Connecting ideas
- Sentence variety
- Word variety
- Spotlighting
- Flashbacks
- Foreshadowing
- Openings and endings

Grammar and spelling objectives:

- Whole sentences
- Subject-verb agreement
- Parallelism
- Correct use of pronouns
- Correct use of verbs
- Correct use of modifiers
- Homonyms and common mix-ups

- Spelling rules
- Capitalization rules
- Common abbreviations
- Use of numbers in writing
- Punctuation rules
- Editor's marks

Publishing objectives: Publishing terms

- Book reviews
- Title page
- Copyright page
- Dedication page acknowledgements
- Table of contents

- Author description
- Layout
- Illustrations and book cover design
- Printing and binding
- Presentation

Texts:
Learn to Write the Novel Way by Carol Thaxton. Published by Konos Connection 2001.
Building Better Plots by Robert Kernan.

Course Grade
Novel Writing – Alex Binz – Completed 06/04

Research ---------1/3 grade---------		Mechanics ---------1/3 grade---------		Composition ---------1/3 grade---------	
Research	100%	Vocabulary	100%	Novel	100%
Work text	100%	Comprehension	100%	Editing	100%
		Spelling	100%		
		Mechanics	100%		
		Expression	100%		

---------------**Final grade for Novel Writing = 100% = A** ----------

A =90-100% =4.0	B=80-89% = 3.0	C=70-79% = 2.0	D = 60-69% = 1.0

Chapter 15

How to Avoid Writing Course Descriptions

When you think about writing high school course descriptions do your palms feel sweaty? Do you break out in hives? I know that sometimes parents will have an unreasonable fear of course descriptions. If that is you, I need to let you in on a secret. **Not everyone has to write course descriptions** for their high school students. Although I work hard to help parents with course descriptions, I also want to provide **a way out, for those who simply can't cope.** Depending on your state law, you may not need course descriptions to graduate from high school. If your student will not be going to college, and state law doesn't require course descriptions, then you don't need to bother. For college-bound families there are other ways to avoid the task.

COLLEGE SEARCH STRATEGY

The good news is that not every college requires course descriptions. When they do require course descriptions, they rarely require a specific method of providing those records. Go to a college fair and ask different colleges about the record keeping they require from homeschoolers. Look at colleges that you are interested in, and ask about their homeschool admission policy.

Some colleges want only a transcript, and would prefer that you do not submit additional documentation. If you ask the right questions, you can find a college that doesn't want the extra paperwork or the hassle of reading course descriptions. On the California State University website, Paula Wasley writes about the rise of homeschooled applicants. While praising homeschool applicants in general, she describes lengthy course descriptions with disdain, "But sifting through home-made transcripts, extensive book lists, and portfolios can be unusually time-consuming for admissions officers. Eddie K. Tallent, director of admissions at George Mason University, recently received one application that contained a page of explanation for each class listed on the transcript. 'That was a bit much,' he says."

(www.calstate.edu/pa/clips2007/october/10oct/ched.shtml)

> College policies vary:
>
> Transcript only
> Reading list
> Short description
> Extreme example

Some colleges want concise records – less than a handbook, but more than a transcript. They want brief course explanations, and "short, short, short" is the name of the game. The 2008 University of Washington Admissions Policy requested a short description of each course. "Homeschooled applicants must present a homeschool transcript that includes course titles of each subject studied, duration of study, **a short description of content**, and grade or assessment of performance."

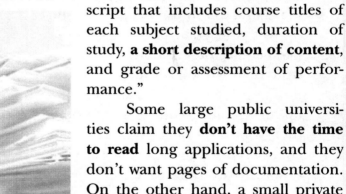

Some large public universities claim they **don't have the time to read** long applications, and they don't want pages of documentation. On the other hand, a small private college may say they have no need for course descriptions because they base **decisions solely on the home-school transcript**. On the opposite end of the spectrum, some colleges determine admission by SAT/ACT, and rarely consider any additional data. Some colleges care more about musical auditions, art portfolios or sports try-outs and scouting reports than academic records. There are colleges that don't require course descriptions for a variety of reasons.

There are two problems, however. First, college policies may change over time, as they grow accustomed to homeschool applicants. Always check with a college about their own unique requirements. Second, teenager preferences change over time, and your child may end up with a strong preference for a college that requires course descriptions.

If your child really wants to go to a college that requires course descriptions, there are some options. Before you speak to your lawyer about early emancipation, rest assured there are still ways to avoid writing them! You have other strategies available.

LIST-ONLY STRATEGY

If you want to do it yourself but you don't speak the language, then consider scrapping the term "course description" and simply write a few words about each subject - in English. **Write a shopping list** of

what you have done in your homeschool, rather than what you have to buy at the store. Like a shopping list, you don't have to use complete sentences for this method. Write a list of experiences or curriculum that you used for each class. For example:

Economics
- <u>Economics in One Lesson</u>, by Hazlitt
- <u>Basic Economics audio course</u>, by The Teaching Company
- <u>Whatever Happened to Penny Candy</u>, by Richard Maybury
- <u>Whatever Happened to Penny Candy Workbook</u>, by Richard Maybury
- Personal experience buying and selling on Ebay

It's not hard to write a list, and if you use English words you don't even have to learn the language of "educationalese." It may be an acceptable alternative to full-blown course descriptions. If you use mostly literature in your courses, then list the books. For example:

British Literature
- <u>British Literature</u>, by James Stobaugh
- <u>Pride and Prejudice</u>, by Jane Austen
- <u>David Copperfield</u>, by Charles Dickens
- <u>Jane Eyre</u>, by Charlotte Bronte

Notice that these options look like a reading list. Many colleges will say they don't need course descriptions, but they will ask for a transcript and reading list. I often wonder if those "reading list" colleges are actually just looking for a course description that is very short and in list format. This list format is certainly easier to write and read, since there is **no punctuation or grammar required**.

EXPANDED TRANSCRIPT STRATEGY

Instead of completing a comprehensive list of course descriptions as I did, you may want to keep an expanded transcript with additional details. Some parents find freedom in filling in a box, rather than writing a whole paragraph. If that describes you, then this technique may be a perfect fit for you.

Begin with your regular transcript that you have already filled in. Instead of simply listing the name of the course, add more detail. Under the course title, list as many details as you can. If you are not going to provide a comprehensive record listing everything and explaining your grading criteria, then this may provide the important additional details. Here is the information a regular transcript provides:

Subject	Class Title	Completion Date	Credits	Grade
English	English 1: American Literature	06/03	1.0	4.0

An expanded transcript can **provide as much information as you desire**.

Subject	Class Title	Completion Date	Credits	Grade
English	English 1: American Literature Sonlight Core 100 American Literature Tom Sawyer by Mark Twain Huckleberry Finn by Mark Twain The Call of the Wild by Jack London White Fang by Jack London To Kill A Mockingbird by Harper Lee	06/03	1.0	4.0

Type the key details, listing the textbook used or class location. It's a handy way to keep track of information. You can use this minimalistic resource if you decide to make a course description later. If you leave it simplistic, it is still better than no course descriptions at all.

This method will work even if you fill the boxes with a larger amount of information. The amount of information you choose to include may vary, and some families will choose to include more than others. There are examples of extended transcripts in Appendix 6. I tried to provide a few different kinds of details that you might choose to include, and you can decide for yourself what you think is best.

Some examples are simple lists. For classes taken outside the home, you may copy and paste information from the class website.

If you use the expanded transcript method, I recommend that you provide a one-page transcript as well. College admissions personnel may want to have a concise overview as well as your multi-page detailed record.

BACK DOOR STRATEGY

Another strategy for getting into colleges without writing course descriptions is to go "through the back door." Instead of going to college as high school students usually do, you can go to college the way adults continue their education after being in the work force. You may **document a general high school education by passing the GED test**. That may eliminate the need for course descriptions.

Students can also take college courses at a community college, giving them a foot in the door. Once they have proven themselves capable of college work, with adequate grades in a variety of classes, they can move into a university setting. Obtaining an Associate's Degree (AA or AS) from a community college will document the educational level of your student, instead of your homeschool transcript and course descriptions. Community college has its pros and cons, but it's certainly a viable method of avoiding intimidating homeschool paperwork.

BE PREPARED

Don't be fearful of keeping good records! There are many viable ways of getting into college. Admissions departments love homeschoolers,

and you can find the perfect college that will love your student and appreciate your homeschool.

Parents with students just beginning high school can practice writing course descriptions. Be prepared for college admission, and simply keep high school records. Keep track of books and supplements used. Keep a record of the wonderful field trips and learning experiences. Save homeschool records so you will have the information necessary to create course descriptions – if you need them. Plan ahead by keeping records. Even if you keep everything in a box, you can still go back later and document what is needed.

But be careful! Teenagers will actually change their minds about things sometimes. It can help you to be prepared. Read and review information about course descriptions so that you will be prepared for the future. Each college is unique, and each child's needs are unique. Keep your options open, and be prepared to write course descriptions if necessary.

DO THIS ... NOT THAT

The challenging aspect of record keeping is not about keeping records, because record keeping is as simple as having a box or tub to store things. The difficulty isn't the transcript, which is simply translating your great homeschool experiences into the words and numbers that colleges understand. The hard part is not writing course descriptions, because those are only elementary school writing assignments for a descriptive paragraph. **The most difficult part of making great homeschool records is actually doing the job.**

I hear from a lot of homeschool families in a variety of different situations. When parents put off record keeping until their child's senior year, they are surprised at how difficult it is. These are the words they use:

- hyperventilating
- procrastinating
- overworked
- freaked out
- worried
- tedious
- time-consuming
- stressful
- I've made a huge mistake!

It sounds terrible! Meanwhile, parents who start earlier can **work slowly and steadily** through the process and complete the task with less anxiety. They can find what they need, and they don't have a mountain to climb before a soon-coming deadline. Procrastinators all say it could have been easier if they had simply started earlier.

- I really thought it'd be no big deal
- I really thought I could do it "later"
- Boy, was I wrong

Thankfully these parents will give good advice to friends. On their blogs and social networking sites they proclaim the answer to making the best homeschool records

- I just needed to do a little research
- Simply keeping records would help
- Make transcripts from the beginning
- Why didn't I start earlier?
- I should have kept records current
- It didn't need to be so hard
- This could have been much easier!

I'm a bit of a planner by nature – I love to plan. Implementing…. not so much. But it's the real DOING of homeschooling that is the crucial part. You can plan all day long, but if you don't actually do the work, it won't matter.

Start simply, by simply keeping records. Begin making high school records by reviewing the Planning Guide on Page 20. Make your transcript, following the simple step-by-step instructions in the "Making a Transcript Guide" in the appendix. Once your transcript is up-to-date, begin to write a course description on each course. Then "Lather, Rinse, and Repeat" each year, updating your transcript and course descriptions every subsequent year.

Remember the story about "**The Tortoise and the Hare**?" The Hare ran fast, but quickly became tired and fell behind. It was the steady Tortoise that won the race. By working at a steady pace, with perseverance not panic, you will be in the best possible position. When your child is ready for college admission, you will be ready to provide the necessary records.

Keep Records
Make a Transcript
Write Course Descriptions
Later, Rinse, and Repeat Each Year!

Chapter 16

Knowledge, Wisdom and Character

Now that you've learned the easy steps to creating your homeschool records, remember to do only what works for you and fits with your homeschool. Making a transcript should not change the way you manage your homeschool. Keep in mind that there is something more important than having a transcript - the learning that stands behind the piece of paper. Learning is what it is all about. You may have  a beautiful transcript, but if your student isn't able to function well in society, that is a bigger issue.

Knowledge is important. Wisdom is more important. **But character is the most important.** Do the things that build your student's knowledge, wisdom and character and you can't go wrong!

Knowledge will help them get into college, and wisdom will help them succeed in college. Truthfully, though, character is what will help them succeed in a career and in life. Character training will mean more than a beautiful transcript can ever mean. It really is the most important thing we teach in our homeschool.

You can do this! Homeschool records do not have to be intimidating. Take it one step at a time and you will soon find yourself on the other side of high school admiring your beautiful homeschool records.

It can be a hassle, so why bother? Because transcripts are the love language of colleges and a key to college admission and scholarships. Because parents are capable of providing a quality high school education and because colleges want to hear about it.

Knowledge is important.

Wisdom is more important.

Character is the MOST important!

Parents are completely capable of creating effective course descriptions and transcripts with grades, credit value, and course titles.

What's more, parents can do it without spending thousands of dollars on accreditation agencies, complicated computer software, or certified teachers! Homeschoolers have the advantage, because parents can create transcripts and course descriptions that represent the whole student and demonstrate their unique strengths.

Now **YOU** have the tools you need to craft transcripts and course descriptions for your student. Now YOU can set the records straight.

Appendix 1: Making a Transcript Guide

Necessary on a Transcript
Transcript title, student name, gender, date of birth, parent names, name and address of school, names of courses, graduation date, TYPED

Recommended on a Transcript
Credits, grades & grading system, completion date, grade point average, class rank (some use percentile ranking) and test scores (SAT, ACT)

Grading Scale Suggestion
90-100% = A, 80-89% = B, 70-79% = C, 60-69% = D, Below 60% = F
Be sure to include ALL the ways you evaluate

Credit Value
High school level work at any age
1 credit = 120-180 hours
½ credit = 75-90 hours
5-6 college credits = 1 high school credit

Grade Point Average
Multiply class grade times class credit = grade point for that class
Add all the grade points, divide by total number of credits

Blessings,
Lee

The HomeScholar!

Appendix 2: Transcript Templates

There are a variety of "right ways" to make a transcript. On the following pages I have included a number of different transcript formats. Choose the one that best meets your needs. They can be easily created in Microsoft Word or Excel. You need no additional software.

High School Transcript Sample

Name: Student Name   Gender: M   Birth Date: 02/02/1992
Address: Street Address
            My Town, State, Zip

School Name: Homeschool High School   Graduation Date: 6/2010
Phone: 206-XXX-YYYY   Person to Contact: Dad or Mom's Name

Grade	Year	Course Title	1st Semester		2nd Semester		Final		Yearly Cumulative Totals	
			Grade	Credit	Grade	Credit	Grade	Credit	Credits	GPA
9	01-02	Algebra 2	B	0.50	B	0.50	B	1.0		
		Geography	B	0.50	B	0.50	B	1.0		
		Composition	A	0.25	A	0.25	A	0.5		
		Psychology	A	0.25	A	0.25	A	0.5		
		Biology I	C	0.50	A	0.50	B	1.0		
		Biology I Lab	B	0.25	B	0.25	B	0.5		
		Physical Education	A	0.25	B	0.25	A	0.5		
		Health	B	0.25	B	0.25	B	0.5		
		Piano	B	0.50	B	0.50	B	1.0	6.5	3.2
10										
11										
12										

Credits and Grading Scale: A 90-100; B 80-89; C 70-79; D 60- 69; F below 60
Weight for one-credit courses (120 hours): A=4; B=3; C=2; D=1; F=0   AP Courses: A=5; B=4; C=3
Activities:

Signed: Your signature here   Date: write date here

HOME SCHOOL TRANSCRIPT

Student Name:　　　　　　　　　　　　School Name:

Address:　　　　　　　　　　　　　　**Address:**

Parent's Names:
Phone:　　　　　　　　　　　　　　　**Phone:**
Birth Date:　　　　　　　　　　　　　**Fax:**
Gender:　　　　　　　　　　　　　　　**Date of Graduation:**
Social Security #:　　　　　　　　　　**Graduation G.P.A.:**

YEAR													
GRADE		9			10			11			12		
SEMESTER		1	2	CR	1	2	CR	1	2	CR	1	2	CR
English													
Math													
Foreign Lang.													
Social Studies													
Science													
Electives													
Year GPA/Total Credits													
Cumulative GPA													

TEST RECORD

Date　　Test　　　Results:

KEY TO GRADING
A:
B:
C:
D:
F:

NOTES

Administrator's Signature　　　　Name and Title　　　　Date

Homeschool High School Transcript

<table>
<tr><td>

Student Name:
Student Address:
Current Grade Level:
Gender:
Date of Birth:
Parent/Guardian Name:

</td><td>

Career Summary
Graduation Year:
Graduation Date:
Cumulative GPA:
Total Credits Earned:
Total Credits Attempted:

</td></tr>
</table>

	Course Name	Final Grade	Credit Amount
Grade 9			
Grade 10			
Grade 11			
Grade 12			

ACT or SAT Test Score Results	ACT	SAT
	Date of Test: Composite Score: English Score: Math Score: Reading Score: Science Score: Writing Score:	Date of Test: Composite Score: Reading Score: Math Score: Writing Score:

Key to Grading System

A 4.0	D+ 1.3
A- 3.7	D 1.0
B+ 3.3	D- .7
B 3.0	E .0
B- 2.7	CR/NC
C+ 2.3	Incomplete
C 2.0	
C- 1.7	

Homeschool Name and Address:

Teacher/Principal Signature:
_____Date:_____

Homeschool High School
OFFICIAL HIGH SCHOOL TRANSCRIPT

STUDENT INFORMATION	SCHOOL INFORMATION
FULL NAME: First and Last Name	**NAME:** Homeschool High School
ADDRESS: Street Address	**ADDRESS:** Street Address
My Town, My City, WA 98123	My Town, My City, WA 98123
PHONE NUMBER: 206-555-1212	**PHONE NUMBER:** 206-555-1212
EMAIL ADDRESS: myemail@gmail.com	**EMAIL ADDRESS:** ouremail@gmail.com
DATE OF BIRTH: 02/22/92	
PARENT/GUARDIAN: Mr. and Mrs. Last Name	

ACADEMIC RECORD

SCHOOL YEAR: 2002-2003   GRADE LEVEL: 9th

Course Title	Credit Attempted	Credit Earned	Final Grade
English 9	1.0	1.0	A
Algebra I	1.0	1.0	A
Biology with lab	1.0	1.0	B
Geography	1.0	1.0	C
Latin I	1.0	1.0	A
Logic	1.0	1.0	B
Piano	0.5	0.5	B
Theology	0.5	0.5	A

Total Credits: 7.0   GPA: 3.36   Cumulative GPA: 3.36

SCHOOL YEAR: 2003-2004   GRADE LEVEL: 10th

Course Title	Credit Attempted	Credit Earned	Final Grade
English 10	1.0	1.0	B
Geometry	1.0	1.0	B
Chemistry with lab	1.0	1.0	C
World History	1.0	1.0	A
Latin II	1.0	1.0	B
Rhetoric	1.0	1.0	A
Piano II	0.5	0.5	B
Old Testament Survey	0.5	0.5	B

Total Credits: 7.0   GPA: 3.14   Cumulative GPA: 3.25

SCHOOL YEAR: 2004-2005   GRADE LEVEL: 11TH

Course Title	Credit Attempted	Credit Earned	Final Grade
English 11	1.0	1.0	A
Algebra II	1.0	1.0	A
Physics	1.0	1.0	B
US History	1.0	1.0	A
Spanish I	1.0	1.0	B
Philosophy	1.0	1.0	B
Piano III	0.5	0.5	A
New Testament Survey	0.5	0.5	A

Total Credits: 7.0   GPA: 3.57   Cumulative GPA: 3.36

SCHOOL YEAR: 2005 - 2006   GRADE LEVEL: 12TH

Course Title	Credit Attempted	Credit Earned	Final Grade
English 12	1.0	1.0	A
Pre-Calculus	1.0	1.0	A
US Government	1.0	1.0	A
Economics *	1.0	1.0	B
Speech *	1.0	1.0	A
Spanish II	1.0	1.0	C
Drawing	0.5	0.5	B
Apologetics	0.5	0.5	B

Total Credits: 7.0   GPA: 3.43   Cumulative GPA: 3.38

ACADEMIC SUMMARY	GRADING SCALE	NOTES
Cumulative GPA: 3.38	90 – 100 = A	* Coursework taken at a Seattle community college. Official transcript will be sent separately
Credits Attempted: 28.0	80 – 89 = B	
Credits Earned: 28.0	70 – 79 = C	
	60 – 69 = D	
Diploma Earned: yes	59 – below = F	
Graduation Date: 6/15/2005		

I do hereby self-certify and affirm that this is the official transcript and record of Student Name in the academic studies of 2010-2014.

Signature: **Title: Principal   Date:**

Homeschool High School
OFFICIAL HIGH SCHOOL TRANSCRIPT

STUDENT INFORMATION	SCHOOL INFORMATION
FULL NAME: First and Last Name	**NAME:** Homeschool High School
ADDRESS: Street Address	**ADDRESS:** Street Address
My Town, My City, WA 98123	My Town, My City, WA 98123
PHONE NUMBER: 206-555-1212	**PHONE NUMBER:** 206-555-1212
EMAIL ADDRESS: myemail@gmail.com	**EMAIL ADDRESS:** ouremail@gmail.com
DATE OF BIRTH: 02/22/92	
PARENT/GUARDIAN: Mr. and Mrs. Last Name	

ACADEMIC RECORD

SCHOOL YEAR: GRADE LEVEL: 9th				SCHOOL YEAR: GRADE LEVEL: 10th			
Course Title	Credit Attempted	Credit Earned	Final Grade	Course Title	Credit Attempted	Credit Earned	Final Grade
Total Credits: GPA: Cumulative GPA:				Total Credits: GPA: Cumulative GPA:			

SCHOOL YEAR: GRADE LEVEL: 11TH				SCHOOL YEAR: GRADE LEVEL: 12TH			
Course Title	Credit Attempted	Credit Earned	Final Grade	Course Title	Credit Attempted	Credit Earned	Final Grade
Total Credits: GPA: Cumulative GPA:				Total Credits: GPA: Cumulative GPA:			

ACADEMIC SUMMARY	GRADING SCALE	NOTES
Cumulative GPA:	90 – 100 = A	
Credits Attempted:	80 – 89 = B	
	70 – 79 = C	
Credits Earned:	60 – 69 = D	
Diploma Earned: yes	59 – below = F	
Graduation Date:		

I do hereby self-certify and affirm that this is the official transcript and record of _____ in the academic studies of_____.

Signature: **Title: Principal** **Date:**

Appendix 3:
The HomeScholar Comprehensive Record

COMPREHENSIVE HIGH SCHOOL RECORD

FOR

FIRST MIDDLE LAST NAME
DOB 00/00/0000

Table of Contents

TRANSCRIPT HOMESCHOOL SENIOR HIGH 130
    Academic Record by Subject. *130*
    Academic Record by Year *131*
    Academic Record of Dual Enrollment. *132*
COURSE DESCRIPTIONS WITH TEXTS USED AND GRADING CRITERIA 133
    English 1: American Literature and Composition *133*
    English: Novel Writing *134*
    English 2: World Literature and Composition. *135*
    English 3: Honors Literature and Composition *136*
    Math: Algebra 1 . . . .*138*
    Math: Formal Geometry *139*
    Math: Algebra II *140*
    Math: Pre-Calculus *141*
    Math: Calculus *142*
    Science: Biology with Lab *143*
    Science: Chemistry with Lab *144*
    Science: Physics with Lab *145*
    Social Studies: American History *146*
    Social Studies: Ancient World History. *147*
    Social Studies: Washington State History *148*
    Social Studies: Modern World History. *149*
    Social Studies: American Government. *150*
    Foreign Language: Latin 1 . . . .*151*
    Foreign Language: Latin 2 . . . .*152*
    Foreign Language: Latin 3 . . . .*153*
    Foreign Language: French 1 . . . .*154*
    Foreign Language: French 2 . . . .*155*
    Foreign Language: French 3. . . . .*156*
    Music: Piano 2 with Performance *157*
    Music: Piano 3 with Performance *158*
    Music: Piano 4 with Performance *159*
    Fine Arts 1: American Art. *160*
    Fine Arts 2: History of Art *161*
    Fine Arts 3: Art and Music Appreciation. *162*
    Bible 1: Christian Manhood. *163*
    Bible 2: Apologetics. *164*

Bible 3: World View *165*
Elective: Critical Thinking in Chess *166*
Elective: Public Speaking *167*
Elective: Occupational Education *168*
Elective: Driver's Education *169*
Elective: Russian History. *170*
Elective: Formal Logic *171*
Physical Education 1. . . . . *172*
Physical Education 2. . . . . *173*
Physical Education 3. . . . . *174*

READING LISTS *175*
2002-2003 Reading List for Student Name. *175*
2003-2004 Reading List for Student Name. *178*
2004-2005 Reading List for Student Name. *181*

ACTIVITIES AND AWARDS LISTS *183*
2002-2003 Activities and Awards *183*
2003-2004 Activities and Awards *184*
2004-2005 Activities and Awards *185*

WORK SAMPLES *187*
The Common Monster. *187*
The Letter Y. *190*
A Virginian's Reflection. *191*
The Jungle. *194*

APPENDIX 3-A: COURSES COMPLETED OUTSIDE THE HOME. *195*
Music: Chorus I-II (Course from a public high school) *196*
Social Studies: World Geography (Includes Co-Op experiences) *197*
Math: Algebra 1 (Course taken with a private tutor) *198*

Homeschool Senior High
*Street Address Dr. SW * City Name, WA 98100*

Student: Last, First   **Gender**: Male   **Birth Date**: 00/00/00
Parents: M/M First, Last   **Address:** Street Address, City,   WA 98100

Academic Record by Subject

Course	Class Title	Completion Date	Credits	Grade
English	English 1: American Literature & Composition	06/03	1.0	4.0
	Novel Writing	06/04	1.0	4.0
	English 2: World Literature & Composition	06/04	1.0	4.0
	**English 3: Honors Literature & Composition	06/05	1.0	4.0
Math	Algebra 1	06/01	1.0	4.0
	Geometry	06/02	1.0	4.0
	Algebra 2	06/03	1.0	4.0
	Pre-Calculus	06/04	1.0	4.0
	Calculus	06/05	1.0	4.0
Science	Biology with Lab	06/03	1.0	4.0
	Chemistry with Lab	06/04	1.0	4.0
	Physics with Lab	06/05	1.0	4.0
Social Studies	**American History	06/03	1.0	4.0
	**Ancient World History	06/04	1.0	4.0
	Washington State History	06/04	0.5	4.0
	**Modern World History	06/05	1.0	4.0
	**American Government	06/05	1.0	4.0
Foreign Language	Latin 1	06/01	1.0	4.0
	Latin 2	06/02	1.0	4.0
	Latin 3	06/03	1.0	4.0
	French 1	11/02	1.0	4.0
	French 2	05/03	1.0	4.0
	French 3	06/04	1.0	4.0
Fine Arts	Music: Piano 2 with Performance	06/03	1.0	4.0
	Music: Piano 3 with Performance	06/04	1.0	4.0
	Music: Piano 4 with Performance	06/05	1.0	4.0
	Fine Arts 1: American Art	06/03	0.5	4.0
	Fine Arts 2: History of Art	06/04	0.5	4.0
	Fine Arts 3: Art and Music Appreciation	06/05	0.5	4.0
Bible	Bible: Christian Manhood	06/03	0.5	4.0
	Bible: Apologetics	06/04	0.5	4.0
	Bible: World View	06/05	0.5	4.0
Electives	Critical Thinking in Chess	06/03	1.0	4.0
	Public Speaking	06/03	1.0	4.0
	Occupational Education	06/04	0.5	4.0
	Driver's Education	07/04	0.5	Pass
	Russian History	06/04	0.5	4.0
	Formal Logic	06/04	0.5	4.0
Physical Education	PE 1	06/03	1.0	4.0
	PE 2	06/04	1.0	4.0
	PE 3	06/05	1.0	4.0
Activities:	Soccer Team 9, 10,11: Swim Team 9,10, 11 Coaches Award 10: Competitive Chess 9, 10, 11 Student Teacher 9,10, 11: Youth Mission Team 10: Youth Group 9, 10, 11: Worship 9,11			

SAT Results	Grade Point Equivalents		Summary
March 2005: Reading 740, Math 710, Writing 760, Total 2210	A =90-100% =4.0		**Summary**
June 2005: Reading 790, Math 770, Writing 690, Total 2250	B=80-89% = 3.0		Credits GPA
**Denotes Honors course, documented by passing CLEP exam	C=70-79% = 2.0		35.5 4.0
	D = 60-69% = 1.0		

OFFICIAL TRANSCRIPT
~Homeschool Senior High~

Homeschool Senior High
*Street Address Dr. SW * City Name, WA 98100*

Student: Last, First   **Gender**: Male   **Birth Date**: 00/00/00
Parents: M/M First, Last   **Address:** Street Address, City,   WA 98100

Academic Record by Year

Year	Class Title	Completion Date	Credits	Grade
Early High School	Algebra 1	06/01	1.0	4.0
Credits	Latin 1	06/01	1.0	4.0
	Geometry	06/02	1.0	4.0
	Latin 2	06/02	1.0	4.0
	French 1	11/02	1.0	4.0
2002-2003	English 1: American Literature & Composition	06/03	1.0	4.0
	Algebra 2	06/03	1.0	4.0
	Biology with Lab	06/03	1.0	4.0
	**American History	06/03	1.0	4.0
	Latin 3	06/03	1.0	4.0
	French 2	05/03	1.0	4.0
	Music: Piano 2 with Performance	06/03	1.0	4.0
	Fine Arts 1: American Art	06/03	0.5	4.0
	Bible: Christian Manhood	06/03	0.5	4.0
	Critical Thinking in Chess	06/03	1.0	4.0
	Public Speaking	06/03	1.0	4.0
	PE 1	06/03	1.0	4.0
2003-2004	English 2: World Literature & Composition	06/04	1.0	4.0
	Novel Writing	06/04	1.0	4.0
	Pre-Calculus	06/04	1.0	4.0
	Chemistry with Lab	06/04	1.0	4.0
	**Ancient World History	06/04	1.0	4.0
	Washington State History	06/04	0.5	4.0
	French 3	06/04	1.0	4.0
	Music: Piano 3 with Performance	06/04	1.0	4.0
	Fine Arts 2: History of Art	06/04	0.5	4.0
	Bible: Apologetics	06/04	0.5	4.0
	Occupational Education	06/04	0.5	4.0
	Russian History	06/04	0.5	4.0
	Formal Logic	06/04	0.5	4.0
	PE 2	06/04	1.0	4.0
	Driver's Education	07/04	0.5	4.0
2004-2005	**English 3: Honors Literature & Composition	06/05	1.0	4.0
	Calculus	06/05	1.0	4.0
	Physics with Lab	06/05	1.0	4.0
	**Modern World History	06/05	1.0	4.0
	**American Government	06/05	1.0	4.0
	Music: Piano 4 with Performance	06/05	1.0	4.0
	Fine Arts 3: Art and Music Appreciation	06/05	0.5	4.0
	Bible: World View	06/05	0.5	4.0
	PE 3	06/05	1.0	4.0

| Activities: | Soccer Team 9, 10,11: Swim Team 9,10, 11 Coaches Award 10: Competitive Chess 9, 10, 11 Student Teacher 9,10, 11: Youth Mission Team 10: Youth Group 9, 10, 11: Worship 9, 11 | | | |

SAT Results	Grade Point Equivalents	Summary
March 2005: Reading 740, Math 710, Writing 760, Total 2210 June 2005: Reading 790, Math 770, Writing 690, Total 2250	A =90-100% =4.0 B=80-89% = 3.0	Credits GPA
**Denotes Honors course, documented by passing CLEP exam	C=70-79% = 2.0 D = 60-69% = 1.0	35.5 4.0

OFFICIAL TRANSCRIPT
~Homeschool Senior High~

Homeschool Senior High
*Street Address Dr. SW * City Name, WA 98100*

Student: Last, First   **Gender**: Male   **Birth Date**: 00/00/00
Parents: M/M First, Last   **Address**: Street Address, City,   WA 98100

Academic Record of Dual Enrollment

Year	Class Title	Completion Date	Credits	Grade
Summer 2005	American Government**	7/13/05	TBD	52 Pass
CLEP exams	English Composition**	7/20/05	TBD	68 Pass
	Western Civilization I**	7/20/05	TBD	68 Pass
	History of the US II	8/03/05	TBD	55 Pass
	Western Civilization II**	8/03/05	TBD	63 Pass
	History of the US I**	8/17/05	TBD	64 Pass
2005-2006	Math 124: Calculus	12/08/05	5.0	4.0
Highline	Political Science 180	12/08/05	5.0	4.0
Community	Speech 100	12/08/05	5.0	4.0
College	Engineering 100	12/08/05	1.0	4.0
	Math 125: Calculus	03/15/06	5.0	3.8
	Physics 201: Mechanics	03/15/06	5.0	4.0
	Art 100: Intro to Art	03/15/06	5.0	4.0
	*Math 126: Calculus	Spring 06	5.0	TBD
	*Physics 202: Electricity/Magnetism	Spring 06	5.0	TBD
	*Math 220: Linear Algebra	Spring 06	5.0	TBD
	Cumulative GPA at Highline CC			**3.97**

Activities:	Soccer Team 9, 10,11: Swim Team 9,10, 11 Coaches Award 10: Competitive Chess 9, 10, 11 Student Teacher 9,10, 11: Youth Mission Team 10: Youth Group 9, 10, 11: Worship 9, 11
Awards:	National Merit Scholarship Program: Commended Student President's List: Highest Scholastic Achievement. Awarded by Highline Community College
*	Classes currently registered. Remaining Classes are projected.
**	High School Honors Course awarded by passing CLEP exam

Course Descriptions with Texts Used and Grading Criteria

Course Description
English 1: American Literature and Composition

In this American Literature course, the student will study the great American authors as they study history. Jack London and Mark Twain, and Edgar Allan Poe will be studied in depth, with an overview of eight American poets. Complete novels and short stories will be discussed, with an introduction to literary analysis. Composition skills will include essays, journal writing, and written reports. Daily work will include dictation, narration, analogies exercises, poetry appreciation, and SAT preparation. Reading for enjoyment is emphasized. Student will participate in writing across the curriculum. Written work available on request.

English usage: Spelling Power by Beverly L. Adams-Gordon
                         The Latin Road to English Grammar III by Barbara Beers
                         Analogies 2 by Arthur Liebman
                         Peterson's SAT Success 2001 by Kleinman and Steddin
                         Dictation exercises

Poetry books: Walt Whitman, Edgar Allan Poe, Ogden Nash, Carl Sandberg, Karen Hesse, Robert Service, Robert Frost, and Langston Hughes.

Short Stories: O.Henry, Edgar Allen Poe, Nathaniel Hawthorne, Jack London, Harper Lee, and Mark Twain.

Literature Analysis: Study Guide for The Adventures of Huckleberry Finn by Glencoe/McGraw-Hill
                         Study Guide for To Kill a Mockingbird by Glencoe/McGraw-Hill
                         Learn to Write the Novel Way by Carol Thaxton
                         Narration exercises

American Literature Analysis:
                         To Be a Slave by Julius Lester
                         Tom Sawyer by Mark Twain
                         Huckleberry Finn by Mark Twain
                         The Call of the Wild by Jack London
                         White Fang by Jack London
                         To Kill A Mockingbird by Harper Lee
                         Christy by Catherine Marshall

Reading List: Complete reading list is attached.

Composition: The student will complete 1-3 pages, typewritten reports on the topics of Walt Whitman, Edgar Allan Poe, O'Henry, and Ogden Nash. Compositions are available on request.

Course Grade
American Literature – Completed 06/03

Reading		Composition		Analysis	
------------1/3 grade------------		-------------1/3 grade------------		-----------1/3 grade---------	
Reading Grade	100%	Walt Whitman	100%	Analysis	100%
		Edgar Allen Poe	100%		
		O' Henry	100%		
		Ogden Nash	100%		
-------------- Final grade for American Literature = 100% = A ----------					
A =90-100% =4.0		*B=80-89% = 3.0*	*C=70-79% = 2.0*		*D = 60-69% = 1.0*

Course Description
English: Novel Writing

The student will learn, practice and apply the research and writing skills necessary to produce a novel. By the end of this course, the student will have written an entire novel with excellent style, vocabulary, grammar, and mechanics. Credit will be awarded based on a minimum of 150 hours of research and writing, as well as completion of a finished novel. Grades will be awarded based on language mechanics and completion of the project. The student workbook and completed novel are available on request. This is a 2-year course.

Composition Objectives:
- Overview of steps for writing fiction
- Evaluate personal preferences
- Pre-writing
- Character and scene description
- Appropriate use of person and tense
- Plot and sub-plot outline
- Sequencing
- Titling
- Paragraph division
- Computers in writing
- Writer's block
- Picture writing
- Detailing
- Dialog

- Communicating abstract concepts
- Simile and metaphor
- Word choice
- Concise language
- Active voice
- Positive form
- Connecting ideas
- Sentence variety
- Word variety
- Spotlighting
- Flashbacks
- Foreshadowing
- Openings and endings

Grammar and spelling objectives:
- Whole sentences
- Subject-verb agreement
- Parallelism
- Correct use of pronouns
- Correct use of verbs
- Correct use of modifiers
- Homonyms and common mix-ups

- Spelling rules
- Capitalization rules
- Common abbreviations
- Use of numbers in writing
- Punctuation rules
- Editor's marks

Publishing objectives: Publishing terms
- Book reviews
- Title page
- Copyright page
- Dedication page acknowledgements
- Table of contents

- Author description
- Layout
- Illustrations and book cover design
- Printing and binding
- Presentation

Texts: Learn to Write the Novel Way by Carol Thaxton. Published by Konos Connection 2001.

Course Grade
Novel Writing – Completed 06/04

Research -------------1/3 grade------------		Mechanics -------------1/3 grade-----------		Composition -----------1/3 grade---------	
Research	100%	Vocabulary	100%	Completed Novel	100%
Work text	100%	Comprehension	100%	Editing	100%
		Spelling	100%		
		Mechanics	100%		
		Expression	100%		

-------------- Final grade for Novel Writing = 100 % = A ----------

A =90-100% =4.0	B=80-89% = 3.0	C=70-79% = 2.0	D = 60-69% = 1.0

Course Description
English 2: World Literature and Composition

In this World Literature course, the student will study the great authors of the ancient world and medieval period as they study history. Homer, Sophocles, Sir Walter Scott, Alexandre Dumas, and William Shakespeare will be studied in depth, with an overview of other authors and poets. Composition skills will include essays, journal writing, written reports, and research papers. Daily work will include narration, poetry appreciation, and reading a wide variety of literature. Reading for enjoyment is encouraged, and the student will participate in reading and writing across the curriculum. Written work available on request.

Primary Texts:
Institute for Excellence in Writing Advanced Communication Series by Andrew Pudewa
Writing a Research Paper by Edward J. Shewan
How to Write a Term Paper by James and Barkin
Elements of Style by Strunk and White
Shakespeare – Yes You Can! By Scholastic Professional Books
Invitation to the Classics edited by Cowan and Guinness

Required Reading:
The Odyssey of Homer
Sophocles Trilogy
Ivanhoe,
Canterbury Tales
Three Musketeers
Gulliver's Travels
Robinson Crusoe

Reading Shakespeare plays accompanied by video, using "The Complete Dramatic Works of William Shakespeare" series, by BBC Television Service, Ambrose Video Publishing, 2000.
A Midsummer Night's Dream
As You Like It
Comedy of Errors
Much Ado About Nothing
Merry Wives of Windsor
The Taming of the Shrew
Two Gentlemen of Verona

Course Grade
World Literature and Composition – Completed 06/04

Research & Reading -------------1/3 grade-----------		Mechanics -------------1/3 grade-----------		Composition & Analysis -----------1/3 grade---------	
Research Completed Reading	100% 100%	Vocabulary	100%	Quick Essays	100%
		Comprehension	100%	Literature Analysis	100%
		Spelling	100%	Research Report	100%
		Mechanics	100%	Short Story	100%
		Expression	100%	Poetry	100%

---- Final grade for World Literature and Composition = 100% = A --------

A =90-100% =4.0	*B=80-89% = 3.0*	*C=70-79% = 2.0*	*D = 60-69% = 1.0*

Course Description
English 3: Honors Literature and Composition

In this Literature and Composition course, the student will study the great authors of the Western tradition from 1600 to the modern era. Composition skills will include short essays, journal writing, written reports, short stories, and poetry. Daily work will include reading, narration, poetry appreciation, and reading a wide variety of literature. Reading for enjoyment is encouraged, and the student will participate in reading and writing across the curriculum. Public Speaking and oral communication skills will be emphasized. A complete reading list is attached. Written work available on request. Honors credit will be awarded upon successful completion of CLEP exam with passing score of 50 or greater.

Primary Texts:
Secrets of the Great Communicators by Jeff Myers
Dynamic Writing and Study Skills Course by Global
    Learning Strategies
Rummy Roots and More Rummy Roots card game
Poetry Speaks edited by Elise Paschen, Rebekah Mosby, et al.
Invitation to the Classics by Louise Cowan and Os

Guinness
Literature: The American Experience by Prentice Hall
How to Write Poetry by Paul B. Janeczko
Elements of Style by Strunk and White
Eats, Shoots, and Leaves by Lynne Truss
Literature: A Crash Course by Cory Bell

Literature:
Frankenstein by Mary Shelley
Oliver Twist by Charles Dickens
Hard Times by Charles Dickens
Pickwick Papers by Charles Dickens
Common Sense by Thomas Paine
Poor Richard's Almanack by Benjamin Franklin
Dr. Jekyll and Mr. Hyde by Robert Louis Stevenson
Autobiography of Benjamin Franklin by Benjamin Franklin
The Deadliest Monster by J.F. Baldwin
Last of the Mohicans by James Fenimore Cooper
The Deerslayer by James Fenimore Cooper
Pride and Prejudice by Jane Austen
Walden: or Life in the Woods by Henry David Thoreau
On the Duty of Civil Disobedience by Henry David
    Thoreau
Little Regiment and other Civil War Stories by Stephen
    Crane
Autobiography of an Ex-Colored Man by James W.
    Johnson
Heart of Darkness by Joseph Conrad
The Secret Sharer by Joseph Conrad
Up From Slavery by Booker T. Washington
Life and Times of Frederick Douglass by Frederick

Douglass
Grapes of Wrath by John Steinbeck
The Pearl by John Steinbeck
Of Mice and Men by John Steinbeck
The Jungle by Upton Sinclair
The Metamorphosis by Franz Kafka
All Quiet on the Western Front by Erich Marla Remarque
War of the Worlds by H.G. Wells
Alas, Babylon by Pat Frank
The Great Gatsby by F. Scott Fitzgerald
A Separate Peace by John Knowles
Hiroshima by John Hershey
The Old Man and the Sea by Ernest Hemingway
Murder at the Vicarage by Agatha Christie
Lord of the Flies by William Golding
Animal Farm by George Orwell
The Chosen by Chaim Potok
Death Be Not Proud by John Gunther
Our Town by Thornton Wilder
The Crucible by Arthur Miller
Death of a Salesman by Arthur Miller
Brave New World by Aldous Huxley

Course Grade
English 3: Honors Literature and Composition – Completed 06/05

Research & Reading ----------1/3 grade----------		Mechanics -------------1/3 grade------------		Composition & Analysis -----------1/3 grade---------	
Reading Grade	100%	Vocabulary	100%	Quick Essays	90%
Research Skills	100%	Comprehension	100%	Essay Writing	96%
		Spelling	100%	Journal Writing	100%
		Mechanics	100%	Narration	100%
		Expression	100%	Poetry	100%

-------------- **Final grade for Honors Literature and Composition = 99% = A** ------------------
English Composition CLEP Exam Score = 68 (ACE passing score 50)

A =90-100% =4.0	*B=80-89% = 3.0*	*C=70-79% = 2.0*	*D = 60-69% = 1.0*

Writing and Quick Essay Grade for Honors Literature and Composition

Title of Essay	Writing Grade
USCF: Chess is My Mirror WINNER: US Chess Federation	100%
Guideposts: Love in Poverty	84% late
VFW Voice of Democracy: Humility WINNER: Federal Way Post	100%
Fleet Reserve: Right to be Wrong	100%
College Experience Means to Me	100%
Rebirth of Unity: American Dream	100%
Dangerous Protection: Free Speech	100%
The Tournament of Life	95%
Optimist: Renewer of Society WINNER: Vancouver Optimist's	100%
Cover Letter for Resume	100%
The Jungle	100%
Novel Outline: Ericsson's Secret	100%
A Virginian's Reflection WINNER Seattle Sons Amer. Rev.	100%
Dawn of Terrorism	85%
Poetry: The Pawn	88%
American Dream: Rebirth of unity	100%
MENSA: Golden Opportunity	100%
Battle Over the Board	100%
Defining Man	95%
3 short stories: The Letter Y WINNER: Half Price Books	100%
The Greek Vision	92%
The Dawn of Terrorism	95%
The Common Monster WINNER Holocaust Project	90%
Law of the Nazis	100%
Jane Austen Literature Analysis	100%
Patzers and Engineers	100%
Lessons Plans for chess lessons	100%
Total Grade for Writing	96%

Quick Essay	Writing Grade (1-12 scale)
Elderly Drivers	10
Life's Inconsistency	7
Certainty in Life	8
Existentialist Jean Paul Sartre	8
Adlai Stevenson	12
Terrorism	8
Courage: Heroic Firefighter	10
18th Century Europe	10
A Crisis	12
Firm Handshake	11
A Small Change	11
Ignorance of the Law	9
Fear of Punishment	8
Suffering Builds Character	6
Public School	11
Convictions	10
History	12
Test 8998 Princeton Review Online	8
Test 2/8 Princeton Review Online	12
Failure is Everywhere	11
Midlife Crisis and Adolescence	10
Chess	8
Technology	11
Political Involvement	10
Wardrobe Malfunction	12
Pursuit of Success	9
March SAT	9
June SAT	10
Total Grade for Reading	90%

Course Description
Math: Algebra 1

Primary Text: Algebra I by Paul A. Foerster, Scott Foresman Addison Wesley, 1999.
Supplemental Text: Elementary Algebra by Harold R. Jacobs

This course is the study of algebra with real-world problems and applications. Critical thinking is developed by a strong emphasis on graphing and creative problem solving. Applications problems challenge students to use many mathematical concepts to solve one problem. Course contents include:
➢ Expressions and equations
➢ Operations with negative numbers
➢ Distributing, axioms, and other properties
➢ Harder equations
➢ Some operations with polynomials and radicals
➢ Quadratic equations
➢ Expressions and equations containing two variables
➢ Linear functions, scattered data, and probability
➢ Properties of exponents
➢ More operations with polynomials
➢ Rational algebraic expressions
➢ Inequalities
➢ Functions and advanced topics
Tests in student handwriting available on request.

Course Grade
Algebra 1 –Completed 06/01

Tests ----------------1/3 grade-----------		Daily Work -------------1/3 grade-----------		Midterm and Final --------1/3 grade--------
Chapter 1	89%	Chapter 1	100%	
Chapter 2	82%	Chapter 2	100%	
Chapter 3	94%	Chapter 3	100%	
Chapter 4	91%	Chapter 4	100%	
Chapter 5	98%	Chapter 5	100%	
	-	Chapter 6	100%	
	-	Chapter 7	100%	
	-	Chapter 8	100%	
Chapter 9	94%	Chapter 9	100%	
Chapter 10	81%	Chapter 10	100%	
Chapter 11	93%	Chapter 11	100%	
Chapter 12	97%	Chapter 12	100%	
Chapter 13	85%	Chapter 13	100%	
Chapter 14	87%	Chapter 14	100%	Final Exam 98%
Tests average 90%		**Daily work average 100%**		**Exams 98%**

---------------------- **Final grade for Algebra 1 = 96% = A** ----------------------

A =90-100% =4.0	B=80-89% = 3.0	C=70-79% = 2.0	D = 60-69% = 1.0

The "Love Language" of Colleges

Course Description
Math: Formal Geometry

This course stresses logic, deductive reasoning, and formal proofs. The value of geometry is the development of logical thinking skills. This text spends the first 9 lessons on logic, to ensure logical thinking, before moving on to geometry topics. Given the foundation in logic, students immediately begin work with proofs. Work with circles follows introductory lessons on trigonometry. Construction activities are supplemented with an additional text.

Primary Text: <u>Geometry</u> by Harold R. Jacobs

Topics include:
➢ Deductive reasoning and logic
➢ Points, lines, and planes
➢ Rays and angles
➢ Congruent triangles
➢ Inequalitites
➢ Parallel lines
➢ Quadrilaterals
➢ Transformations
➢ Area
➢ Similarity
➢ Right Triangles
➢ Circles
➢ Concurrence Theorems
➢ Regular Polygons and the Circle
➢ Geometric Solids
➢ Non-Euclidean Geometries
➢ Coordinate Geometry

Supplements include:
Patty Paper Geometry by Michael Serra

Tests in student handwriting available on request.
\

Course Grade
Geometry – Completed 06/02

Tests		Daily Work		Midterm and Final
---------------1/3 grade----------		-------------1/3 grade----------		--------1/3 grade--------
Chapter 2	92%	Chapter 2	100%	
Chapter 3	87%	Chapter 3	100%	
Chapter 4	96%	Chapter 4	100%	
Chapter 5	88%	Chapter 5	100%	
Chapter 6	92%	Chapter 6	100%	
Chapter 7	100%	Chapter 7	100%	
Chapter 8	83%	Chapter 8	100%	Midterm Exam 90%
Chapter 9	95%	Chapter 9	100%	
Chapter 10	96%	Chapter 10	100%	
Chapter 11	93%	Chapter 11	100%	
Chapter 12	97%	Chapter 12	100%	
Chapter 13	98%	Chapter 13	100%	
Chapter 14	89%	Chapter 14	100%	
Chapter 15	95%	Chapter 15	100%	
Chapter 16	87%	Chapter 16	100%	Final Exam 94%
Tests average 93%		**Daily work average 100%**		**Exams 92%**
---------------------- **Final grade for Geometry = 95% = A** --------------------				
A =90-100% =4.0	*B=80-89% = 3.0*	*C=70-79% = 2.0*		*D = 60-69% = 1.0*

The "Love Language" of Colleges 139

Course Description
Math: Algebra II

Primary Text: <u>Algebra and Trigonometry,</u> by Paul A. Foerster, Scott Foresman – Addison Wesley, 1999.

This course is the study of algebra with real-world problems and applications. Critical thinking is developed by a strong emphasis on graphing and creative problem solving. Applications problems challenge students to use many mathematical concepts to solve one problem. Technology tools, including a graphing calculator, are used. Course contents include:
➢ Review of Algebra I and preliminary information
➢ Functions and relations
➢ Linear functions
➢ Systems of linear inequations and inequalities
➢ Quadratic functions and complex numbers
➢ Exponential and logarithmic functions
➢ Rational algebraic functions
➢ Irrational algebraic functions
➢ Quadratic relations and systems
➢ Higher degree functions and complex numbers
➢ Sequences and series
➢ Probability, data analysis, and functions of a random variable
➢ Trigonometric and circular functions
➢ Properties of trigonometric and circular functions
➢ Triangle problems
Tests in student handwriting available on request.

Course Grade
Algebra 2 –Completed 06/03

Tests		Daily Work		Midterm and Final
---------------1/3 grade-----------		-------------1/3 grade-----------		--------1/3 grade--------
Chapter 1	100%			
Chapter 2	97%	Chapter 2	100%	
Chapter 3	100%	Chapter 3	100%	
Chapter 4	97%	Chapter 4	100%	
Chapter 5	-	Chapter 5	100%	Midterm (1-5) 95%
Chapter 6	92%	Chapter 6	100%	
Chapter 7	94%	Chapter 7	100%	
Chapter 8	85%	Chapter 8	100%	Midterm (6-8) 90%
Chapter 9	95%	Chapter 9	100%	
Chapter 10	100%	Chapter 10	100%	
Chapter 11	98%	Chapter 11	100%	
Chapter 12	98%	Chapter 12	100%	
Tests average 97%		**Daily work average 100%**		**Exams 93%**
---------------------- **Final grade for Algebra 2 = 97 % = A** ----------------------				
A =90-100% =4.0	*B=80-89% = 3.0*		*C=70-79% = 2.0*	*D = 60-69% = 1.0*

The "Love Language" of Colleges

Course Description
Math: Pre-Calculus

This course contains an in-depth coverage of trigonometry, logarithms, analytical geometry with proofs, and upper-level algebraic concepts. It teaches the concepts and skills necessary for students to succeed in calculus, and disciplines that are mathematically based, such as chemistry and physics. The emphasis is on problem solving and the development of productive thought patterns. It contains instruction on functions, matrices, statistics and graphing calculators.

Primary Text:
Advanced Mathematics by Saxon, 2nd Edition.

Supplemental Text:
Digital Interactive Video Education: Advanced Mathematics computer tutorial by Dr. David Shormann. This is a video tutorial designed for Saxon Advanced Math, with a 20-30 minute lecture for each lesson.

Tests in student handwriting available on request.

Course Grade
Pre-Calculus – Completed 06/04

Tests		Daily Work		Final Exam	
---------------1/3 grade-----------		-------------1/3 grade-----------		--------1/3 grade--------	
Test 2	90%	Lessons 1 – 12	100%		
Test 4	92%	Lessons 13 – 20	100%		
Test 6	96%	Lessons 21 – 28	100%		
Test 8	100%	Lesson 29 – 36	100%		
Test 10	96%	Lesson 37 – 44	100%		
Test 12	96%	Lesson 45 – 52	100%		
Test 14	98%	Lesson 53 – 60	100%		
Test 16	95%	Lesson 61 – 68	100%		
Test 18	94%	Lesson 69 – 76	100%		
Test 20	100%	Lesson 77 – 84	100%		
Test 22	98%	Lesson 85 – 92	100%		
Test 24	88%	Lesson 93 – 100	100%		
Test 26	95%	Lesson 101 – 108	100%		
Test 28	85%	Lesson 109 – 116	100%		
Test 30	90%	Lesson 117 – 125	100%		
				Test 31: Final Exam	99%
Tests average 94%		**Daily work average 100%**		**Exams 99%**	

-------------------- **Final grade for Pre-Calculus = 98% = A** --------------------

A =90-100% =4.0	*B=80-89% = 3.0*	*C=70-79% = 2.0*	*D = 60-69% = 1.0*

Course Description
Math: Calculus

This integrated course covers calculus, trigonometry, and analytic geometry to develop a solid and rigorous foundation for college-level mathematics. It emphasizes application to complex problems in physics, chemistry, engineering, and business. The DIVE CDs provide video lectures that coordinate with each lesson of the textbook, with explanations and practice problems. The video series <u>Change and Motion</u> provides experience with the deeper theoretical concepts of calculus. Subjects include the fundamental theorem, the paradox of Zeno's arrow, the nature of motion, and calculus through history. This course explains key insights in calculus, using historical events and everyday examples from astronomy, cosmology, baseball, traffic, and money.

Primary Text:
<u>Calculus with Trigonometry and Analytic Geometry</u> by John Saxon

Supplemental Texts:
<u>DIVE Calculus 1ˢᵗ Edition Instructional CD</u> by Genesis Science, Inc.
<u>Change and Motion: Calculus Made Clear</u> by The Teaching Company

Tests in student handwriting available on request.

Course Grade
Calculus – Completed 06/05

Tests		Daily Work		Midterm and Final
--------------1/3 grade----------		-------------1/3 grade----------		-------1/3 grade------
Test 2	100%	Section Work	100%	
Test 6	90%	Section Work	90%	
Test 9	100%	Section Work	100%	
Test 13	91%	Section Work	100%	
Test 17	93%	Section Work	100%	
Test 19	87%	Section Work	100%	
Test 20	76%	Section Work	100%	
Test 21	83%	Section Work	100%	
Test 22	80%	Section Work	100%	
Test 24	100%	Section Work	100%	
Test 25	97%	Section Work	100%	
		Section Work	100%	Test 28 100%
Tests average 91%		**Daily work average 99%**		**Exams 100%**

---------------------- **Final grade for Calculus = 97% = A** --------------------

A =90-100% =4.0	*B=80-89% = 3.0*	*C=70-79% = 2.0*	*D = 60-69% = 1.0*

Course Description
Science: Biology with Lab

Text: <u>Exploring Creation with Biology</u>, by Dr. Jay Wile

Heavily emphasizing the vocabulary of biology, this course provides the student with a strong background in the scientific method, the five-kingdom classification scheme, microscopy, biochemistry, cellular biology, molecular and Mendelian genetics, evolution, dissection, and ecosystems. Course content includes: the study of Life, using a biological key, Kingdom Monera, Kingdom Protista, Kingdom Fungi, chemistry of life, cell structure, cellular reproduction, genetics, evolution, ecosystems, invertebrates of Kingdom Animalia, Phylum Arthropoda, Phylum Chordata, Kingdom Plantae anatomy and classification, Kingdom Plantae physiology and reproduction, reptiles, birds, and mammals. A microscopy lab will include 12 labs using self-prepared and prepared slides. These labs will include an introduction to microscopy and use of the microscope, observations of the Kingdom Monera, Kingdom Protista, Subkingdom Protozoa; Class Basidiomycetes, Yeasts, Molds, Imperfect Fungi, detailed cell structure, and mitosis. Dissection Labs include dissection and inspection of the following: worm, crayfish, perch, and frog. A registered nurse teaches dissection and Microscopy labs. Lab-work and tests available on request.

Course Grade
Biology – Completed 06/03

Tests		Lab Work	
----------------------1/2 grade--------------------		------------------------1/2 grade-------------------	
Chapter 1	100%	Lab 1.1	100%
		Lab 1.2 Microscopy	100%
Chapter 2	93%	Lab 2.1	100%
		Lab 2.1 Microscopy	80%
Chapter 3	100%	Lab 3.1 Microscopy	95%
		Lab 3.2 Microscopy	100%
		Lab 3.3 Microscopy	95%
Chapter 4	100%	Lab 4.1 Microscopy	95%
		Lab 4.2 Microscopy	100%
		Lab 4.3 Microscopy	100%
		Lab 4.4 Microscopy	100%
Chapter 5	93%	Lab 5.1	100%
		Lab 5.2	95%
Chapter 6	100%	Lab 6.1 Microscopy	100%
		Lab 6.2 Microscopy	100%
Chapter 7	98%	Lab 7.1	100%
		Lab 7.2 Microscopy	100%
Chapter 8	91%	Lab 8.1	100%
		Lab 8.2	100%
		Lab 8.3	100%
Chapter 9	100%	-	100%
Chapter 10	94%	Lab 10.1	100%
Chapter 11	90%	Lab 11.1 Microscopy	100%
		Lab 11.2 Microscopy	100%
		Lab 11.3 Microscopy	100%
		Lab 11.4 Dissection	90%
Chapter 12	94%	Lab 12.1 Dissection	90%
Chapter 13	91%	Lab 13.1 Dissection	100%
		Lab 13.2 Dissection	100%
Chapter 14	94%	Lab 14.1	100%
		Lab 14.2	100%
		Lab 14.3 Microscopy	100%
Chapter 15	98%	Lab 15.1 Microscopy	100%
		Lab 15.2	100%
Chapter 16	100%	Lab 16.1 Microscopy	90%
Tests Grade 96%		Lab Grade 98 %	

---------------------- **Final grade for Biology = 97% = A** ----------------------

A =90-100% =4.0   *B=80-89% = 3.0*   *C=70-79% = 2.0*   *D = 60-69% = 1.0*

Course Description
Science: Chemistry with Lab

Primary Texts:
1) Exploring Creation with Chemistry by Dr. Jay Wile, 2nd Edition
2) Exploring Creation with Chemistry Multimedia Companion CD by Dr. Jay Wile 2nd Edition. This is a video of additional experiments, animations, and practice problems, for use with the textbook.
3) Digital Interactive Video Education: Chemistry computer tutorial by Dr. David Shormann. This is a video tutorial designed for AP high school chemistry, with a 30-60 minute lecture for each module. Lab write-ups and tests available on request.

This course will contain learning modules and lab experiments on the following concepts:

Measurement and units
➤ Energy, heat and temperature
➤ Atoms and molecules
➤ Classifying matter and its changes
➤ Chemical equations
➤ Stoichiometry
➤ Atomic structure
➤ Molecular structure
➤ Polyatomic ions and molecular geometry

➤
➤ Acid/Base chemistry
➤ Chemistry of solutions
➤ Gas phases
➤ Thermodynamics
➤ Kinetics
➤ Chemical equilibrium
➤ Reduction/Oxidation reactions

Course Grade
Chemistry – Completed 06/04

Chapter Tests ----------1/3 grade----------		Lab Work ------------1/3 grade------------		Midterm & Final -----------1/3 grade----------	
Test 1	97%	Experiment 1.1	100%		
		Experiment 1.2	100%		
		Experiment 1.3	100%		
		Experiment 1.4	100%		
Test 2	98%	Experiment 2.1	95%		
		Experiment 2.2	100%		
Test 3	96%	Experiment 3.1	100%		
		Experiment 3.2	100%		
Test 4	100%	Experiment 4.1	100%		
		Experiment 4.2	100%		
		Experiment 4.3	100%		
Test 5	95%	Experiment 5.1	100%		
Test 6	93%	Experiment 6.1	100%		
Test 7	98%			Midterm Exam	92%
Test 8	94%				
Test 9	90%	Experiment 9.1	100%		
		Experiment 9.2	100%		
Test 10	87%	Experiment 10.1	90%		
		Experiment 10.2	100%		
Test 11	90%	Experiment 11.1	100%		
		Experiment 11.2	100%		
		Experiment 11.3	100%		
		Experiment 11.4	100%		
Test 12	90%	Experiment 12.1	100%		
Test 13	100%	Experiment 13.1	100%		
Test 14	91%	Experiment 14.1	90%		
		Experiment 14.2	90%		
Test 15	100%	Experiment 15.1	100%	Final Exam Part 1	93%
Test 16	97%			Final Exam Part 2	97%
Tests Grade 95%		**Lab Grade 99 %**		**Exam Grade 94 %**	
------------- **Final grade for Chemistry = 96% = A** -------------					
A =90-100% =4.0	*B=80-89% = 3.0*		*C=70-79% = 2.0*	*D = 60-69% = 1.0*	

Course Description
Science: Physics with Lab

This course provides a detailed introduction to the methods and concepts of general physics. Heavily emphasizing vector analysis, this class will prepare the student for a university-level physics course. It provides the student with a strong background in units, measurement, one-dimensional and two-dimensional motion, Newton's laws, and their application, gravity, work and energy, momentum, periodic motion, waves, optics, electrostatics, electrodynamics, electrical circuits, and magnetism. Laboratory exercises are included, and a lab notebook is required.   Daily work will include reading and analyzing the text, working though text questions, module review, and practice problems. Evaluations will include module tests, lab notebook experiment grades, midterm, and final exam. Lab write-ups and tests available on request.

Primary Text:
Exploring Creation with Physics by Dr. Jay Wile, 2nd Edition

Supplemental Text:
Einstein's Relativity and the Quantum Revolution: Modern Physics for Non-Scientists by Professor Richard Wolfson, The Teaching Company

Course Grade
Physics – Completed 06/05

Chapter Tests ------------1/3 grade------------		Lab Work -------------1/3 grade-------------		Midterm & Final -------------1/3 grade-------------	
Test 1	100%	Experiment 1.1	100%		
		Experiment 1.2	100%		
Test 2	91%	Experiment 2.1	100%		
		Experiment 2.2	100%		
		Experiment 2.3	100%		
Test 3	100%	Experiment 3.1	100%		
		Experiment 3.2	100%		
Test 4	86%	Experiment 4.1	100%		
		Experiment 4.2	100%		
Test 5	100%	Experiment 5.1	100%		
		Experiment 5.2	100%		
Test 6	96%	Experiment 6.3	100%	Midterm Part 1	88%
Test 7	83%	Experiment 7.1	100%	Midterm Part 2	100%
Test 8	96%	Experiment 8.1	100%		
		Experiment 8.2	100%		
Test 9	95%	Experiment 9.1	100%		
		Experiment 9.2	100%		
Test 10	100%	Experiment 10.1	100%		
		Experiment 10.2	100%		
Test 11	97%	Experiment 11.1	100%		
		Experiment 11.2	100%		
Test 12	100%	Experiment 12.1	100%		
		Experiment 12.2	100%		
		Experiment 12.3	100%		
Test 13	98%	Experiment 13.1	100%		
		Experiment 13.2	100%		
Test 14	100%	Experiment 14.1	100%		
Test 15	96%	Experiment 15.1	100%		
		Experiment 15.2	100%		
		Experiment 15.3	100%		
Test 16	100%	Experiment 16.1	100%	Final Exam Part 1	96%
		Experiment 16.2	100%	Final Exam Part 2	94%
Tests Grade 96%		**Lab Grade 100 %**		**Exam Grade 95%**	

----------------------- **Final grade for Physics = 97% = A** ---------------------

A =90-100% =4.0	B=80-89% = 3.0	C=70-79% = 2.0	D = 60-69% = 1.0

Course Description
Social Studies: American History

This course is a literature-based study of American history, culture, and geography. A wide selection of biographies, American literature, art, music, historical fiction and poetry provide an in-depth understanding of the primary text. The student will discuss the impact that history has on current events. Reading is accompanied by oral reports and class discussion. Daily work includes primary source reading, narration, mapping activities, timeline activities, current events study, and worldview evaluation. Honors credit will be awarded upon successful completion of CLEP exam with passing score of 50 or greater. Written work available on request.

Primary Text:
The History of US series by Joy Hakim
The First Americans by Joy Hakim
Making Thirteen Colonies by Joy Hakim
From Colonies to Country by Joy Hakim
The New Nation by Joy Hakim
Liberty for All? by Joy Hakim
War, Terrible War, by Joy Hakim
Reconstruction and Reform, by Joy Hakim
An Age of Extremes by Joy Hakim
War, Peace, and All That Jazz by Joy Hakim
All the People by Joy Hakim
"Our Sacred Honor" Audiotape series by William J. Bennett
Sonlight Curriculum American History in Depth: Curriculum Guide

Supplemental Texts: See reading list

Current Events: Daily newspaper reading
               Weekly "World Magazine" reading
               WorldView Academy "WorldView & Apologetics Lecture Series" audiotapes

Reports: The student will complete written reports throughout the course. The following reports are available on request: The Emancipation Proclamation, Dialog Interview with a Slave, The War in Iraq, The Vietnam War, Fidel Castro.

Course Grade
American History – Completed 06/03

Reading ------------1/3 grade------------		Daily Work ------------1/3 grade------------		Reports ------------1/3 grade------------	
Semester 1	100%	Semester 1	100%	Emancipation Proclamation	100%
				Dialog: Interview a Slave	100%
Semester 2	100%	Semester 2	100%	War in Iraq	100%
				Fidel Castro	100%
				Vietnam War	100%
Final Grade	100%	Final Grade	100%	Final Grade	100%

----------------- **Final grade for American History = 100% = A** -----------------
CLEP Exam Score = 64 (ACE passing score 50)

A =90-100% =4.0   *B=80-89% = 3.0*   *C=70-79% = 2.0*   *D = 60-69% = 1.0*

Course Description
Social Studies: Ancient World History

This course is a literature-based study of World history, culture, and geography from pre-history to the age of exploration. A wide selection of biographies, world literature, art, music, historical fiction and poetry provide an in-depth understanding of the primary texts. The student will discuss the impact that history has on current events. Reading is accompanied by oral reports and class discussion. Daily work includes primary source reading, narration, geography, current events study, and worldview evaluation. Honors credit will be awarded upon successful completion of CLEP exam with passing score of 50 or greater. Written work available on request.

Primary Texts:
World History for Christian Schools by Bob Jones University Press
History of the World by Dorling Kindersley
How Should We Then Live? By Francis A. Schaeffer
The High Middle Ages by The Teaching Company, 24 audiotape lectures
The Hundred Years' War: World History Series by William W. Lace

Course Grade
Ancient World History – Completed 06/04

Reading ------------1/3 grade------------		Tests ------------1/3 grade------------		Reports ------------1/3 grade------------	
Semester 1	100%	Test 1	80%	Current Events	100%
		Test 2	93%	Report	100%
		Test 3	96%	Essay Writing	100%
		Test 4	100%		
		Test 5	93%		
		Test 6	100%		
Semester 2	100%	Test 7	100%		
		Test 8	100%		
		Test 9	88%		
		Test 10	96%		
		Test 11	98%		
		Test 12	92%		
Final Grade	100%	Final Grade	95%	Final Grade	100%

----------------- **Final grade for Ancient World History = 98 % = A** -----------------
Western Civilization I CLEP Exam Score = 68 (ACE passing score 50)

A =90-100% =4.0	*B=80-89% = 3.0*	*C=70-79% = 2.0*	*D = 60-69% = 1.0*

Course Description
Social Studies: Washington State History

This course is a literature-based study of Washington State history, culture and geography. Beginning with the Native Americans, it will cover European exploration and settlement, early statehood, and present-day issues. The student will read about people of Washington's history, and historical novels set in Washington. Washington State Government, its Constitution, and local governments will be studied. Government studies will include elections and the political process. Students will be encouraged to develop critical thinking in evaluating the opinion column of the local paper. Political cartoons from Washington's past will also be explored.

Primary Texts:
It Happened in Washington by James A. Crutchfield
Historical Album of Washington by William Cooke
Beautiful Washington Volume II by Beautiful America Publishing Company
Our Evergreen State Government: State and Local Government in Washington by Richard Yates
Cartooning Washington by Glen Baron, edited by Maury Forman and Rick Marschall

Course Grade
Washington State History – Completed 06/04

Reading -------------1/2 grade-----------		Daily Work ----------1/2 grade-----------	
Semester 1	100%	Semester 1	100%
Semester 2	100%	Semester 2	100%
Final Grade	100%	Final Grade	100%
------- **Final grade for Washington State History = 100 % = A** ----------			
A =90-100% =4.0 *B=80-89% = 3.0* *C=70-79% = 2.0* *D = 60-69% = 1.0*			

Course Description
Social Studies: Modern World History

This course is a literature-based study of World history, culture, and geography from 1600 to the present. A wide selection of biographies, world literature, art, music, historical fiction, and poetry provide an in-depth understanding of the primary texts. The student will discuss the impact that history has on current events. Reading is accompanied by oral reports and class discussion. Daily work includes primary source reading, taking notes from lectures and textbook, narration, geography, current events study, and worldview evaluation. Honors credit will be awarded upon successful completion of CLEP exam with passing score of 50 or greater.

Primary Texts:
World History by Bob Jones University
History of US Sourcebook, Book 11, by Joy Hakim
European and Western Civilization in the Modern Age, by Professor Thomas Childers, University of Pennsylvania, a series of 48 audiotape lectures by The Teaching Company.

Supplemental Texts:
Poor Richard's Almanack by Benjamin Franklin
On Plymouth Rock by Samuel Drake
Common Sense by Thomas Paine
The Rights of Man by Thomas Paine
Autobiography of Benjamin Franklin by Benjamin Franklin
On the Duty of Civil Disobedience by Henry David Thoreau
Autobiography of an Ex-Colored Man by James Weldon Johnson
Up From Slavery by Booker T. Washington
The Life and Times of Frederick Douglass by Frederick Douglass
Flu: The Story of the Great Influenza Pandemic of 1918 by Gina Kolata
Our Century in Pictures For Young People edited by Richard B. Stolley
Hiroshima by John Hershey
We Interrupt This Broadcast by Joe Garner
A Nation Challenged: A Visual History of 9/11 and its Aftermath by The New York Times
What We Saw: The Events of September 11, 2001 – in Words, Pictures and Video by CBS News

Course Grade
Modern World History – Completed 06/05

Reading		Daily Work		Tests	
-------------1/3 grade-------------		-------------1/3 grade-------------		-------------1/3 grade-------------	
Semester 1	100%	Semester 1	100%	Test 13	93%
				Test 14	100%
Semester 2	100%	Semester 2	100%	Test 15	93%
				Test 16	87%
				Test 17	85%
				Test 18	87%
				Test 19	90%
				Test 20	95%
				Test 21	92%
				Test 22	95%
				Test 23	100%
Final Grade	100%	Final Grade	100%	Final Grade	92%

------------- **Final grade for Modern World History = 97% = A** ---------------
Western Civilization II CLEP Exam Score = 63 (ACE passing score 50)

A =90-100% =4.0	B=80-89% = 3.0	C=70-79% = 2.0	D = 60-69% = 1.0

Course Description
Social Studies: American Government

The student will experience democracy in action by participating in the Washington State YMCA Youth and Government, including the Youth Legislature. The student will learn how to research public policy issues, write legislation, practice public speaking and debating skills and cooperative working. Participants will develop critical thinking and analytical skills, learn the art of oral advocacy, and gain respect for the role of law and judiciary. The student will participate in the democratic process first hand. Assuming the roles of Senator, Representative, lobbyist, and press, the Youth Legislature meet in a four-day legislative session presided over by their statewide elected officials, including Governor, Secretary of State, Lieutenant Governor and Speaker of the House. This is a 32-week course with one week of internship at the Washington State Capitol. Honors credit will be awarded upon successful completion of CLEP exam with passing score of 50 or greater. Written work available on request.

Course Grade
American Government – Completed 06/05

Reading --------1/3 grade--------		Daily Work --------1/3 grade--------		Written Work --------1/3 grade--------	
Research Policy	100%	Classroom Discussion	100%	Bill Writing	100%
Current Events	100%	Oral Presentation	100%	Reports	100%
		Parliamentary Procedure	100%	Agenda Preparation	100%
		Debating Skills	100%		
		Participation in Olympia	100%		
Final Grade	100%	Final Grade	100%	Final Grade	100%

------------------ **Final grade for Civics = 100% = A** ------------------
American Government CLEP Exam Score = 52 (ACE passing score 50)

A =90-100% =4.0   *B=80-89% = 3.0*   *C=70-79% = 2.0*   *D = 60-69% = 1.0*

Course Description
Foreign Language: Latin 1

This course provides language study of Latin, as well as English grammar and vocabulary through the study of Latin. The student will make an English-Latin handbook of all information learned in the course. Students will translate from Latin to English and English to Latin, while clearly labeling parts of speech. Students will memorize reading passages presented. Student Notebook and tests are available on request.

Primary Text: The Latin Road to English Grammar Volume I, by Barbara Beers

Topics include:

➢ Review of English grammar
➢ Introduction to Latin grammar, pronunciation,
➢ Memorization of "The Lord's Prayer" in Latin
➢ Nouns: declensions, case, gender
➢ First declension
➢ Nominative case
➢ Memorization of "The Pledge of Allegiance"
➢ Verbs: mood, voice, tense, person, number, conjugations,
➢ Principle parts of a verb
➢ First conjugation
➢ Present tense
➢ Memorization of the song "America" sung in Latin
➢ The Verb "to be", uses of "sum"
➢ Interrogative sentences, prepositions
➢ Ablative of place where
➢ Memorization of the song "O Come All ye Faithful" sung in Latin
➢ Second declension masculine
➢ Possession, genitive case
➢ Second declension neuter
➢ Accusative place to which

➢ Ablative place from which, prefixes
➢ Adjectives: Imperfect tense
➢ Future tense
➢ The Roman calendar
➢ Adjectives ending in "-er"
➢ Indirect object, dative case
➢ Imperfect and future tenses of sum
➢ Ablative of means (Instrument)
➢ Ablative of accompaniment
➢ Vocabulary with military meanings
➢ Adverbs: interrogative particles
➢ Perfect tense: stems and personal endings
➢ Pluperfect tense
➢ Future perfect tense
➢ Synopsis
➢ Adjective prefixes, suffixes
➢ Imperative mood
➢ Noun of direct address
➢ Vocative case
➢ Ablative of manner
➢ Roman names

Course Grade
Latin I – Completed 06/01

Tests ------------1/3 grade------------		Daily Work ------------1/3 grade------------		Final ------------1/3 grade------------
Test 1	100%	Chapter 1	100%	
Test 2	94%	Chapter 2	100%	
Test 3	93%	Chapter 3	100%	
Test 4	90%	Chapter 4	100%	
Test 5	86%	Chapter 5	100%	
Test 6	86%	Chapter 6	100%	
		Chapter 7	100%	
		Chapter 8	100%	
		Chapter 9	100%	
		Chapter 10	100%	
		Chapter 11	100%	
		Chapter 12	100%	
		Chapter 13	100%	
		Chapter 14	100%	Final Exam 92%
Tests average 92%		Daily work average 100%		Final 92%
------------------------- Final grade for Latin 1 = 95% = A ------------------				
A =90-100% =4.0	*B=80-89% = 3.0*	*C=70-79% = 2.0*	*D = 60-69% = 1.0*	

Course Description
Foreign Language: Latin 2

This course provides language study of Latin, as well as English grammar and vocabulary through the study of Latin. The student will make an English-Latin handbook of all information learned in the course. Students will translate from Latin to English and English to Latin, while clearly labeling parts of speech. Student notebook and tests are available on request.

Primary Text: The Latin Road to English Grammar Volume II, by Barbara Beers

Topics include:

- Review of Latin I
- Second conjugation
- Coordinating conjunctions
- Idioms
- Third declension
- Third declension neuter
- Apposition
- Pronouns: antecedents, personal pronouns
- Third declension I-stems
- First conjugation passive voice
- Ablative of personal agent
- Third declension adjectives
- Predicate accusative
- Second conjugation passive voice
- Dative with adjectives

- Numerals: cardinal, ordinal, Roman numerals
- Ablative of time when
- Ablative of time within which
- Accusative of duration of time
- Third conjugation
- Developing word sense
- Third conjugation I-stems
- Objective genitive
- Partitive genitive
- Compound verbs
- Third conjugation passive voice
- Ablative of separation
- Demonstrative adjectives
- Demonstrative pronouns

Course Grade
Latin 2 – Completed 06/02

Tests ----------1/3 grade----------		Daily Work -----------1/3 grade-----------		Final -----------1/3 grade-----------
Test 1	92%	Chapter 1	100%	
Test 2	92%	Chapter 2	100%	
Test 3	94%	Chapter 3	100%	
Test 4	88%	Chapter 4	100%	
Test 5	88%	Chapter 5	100%	
Test 6	76%	Chapter 6	100%	
		Chapter 7	100%	
		Chapter 8	100%	
		Chapter 9	100%	
		Chapter 10	100%	
		Chapter 11	100%	
		Chapter 12	100%	
		Chapter 13	100%	
		Chapter 14	100%	Final Exam 91%
Tests average 88%		Daily work average 100%		Final 91%

-------------------- Final grade for Latin 2 = 93% = A --------------------------

A =90-100% =4.0	B=80-89% = 3.0	C=70-79% = 2.0	D = 60-69% = 1.0

The "Love Language" of Colleges

Course Description
Foreign Language: Latin 3

This course provides language study of Latin, as well as English grammar and vocabulary through the study of Latin. The student will make an English-Latin handbook of all information learned in the course. Students will translate from Latin to English and English to Latin, while clearly labeling parts of speech. Student notebook and tests are available on request.

Primary Text: The Latin Road to English Grammar Volume III, by Barbara Beers

Topics include:

➢ Review of Latin I and Latin II	➢ Ablative of respect
➢ Relative pronouns and clauses	➢ Subjective and objective infinitives
➢ Interrogative pronouns and adjectives	➢ Indirect statements
➢ Fourth conjugation	➢ Tenses of the infinitive
➢ Dative of possession	➢ Reflexives
➢ Accusative of extent of space	➢ Ablative of cause
➢ Fourth declension	➢ Dative of reference, double dative
➢ Fifth declension	➢ Participles, Ablative absolute
➢ Locative case	➢ Subjunctive mood: present and imperfect
➢ Verbals: introduction to infinitives	➢ Purpose clauses
➢ Compounds of "sum"	➢ Subjunctive mood: perfect and pluperfect
➢ Comparison of adjectives	➢ Sequence of tenses
➢ "Quam"	➢ Indirect questions
➢ Ablative of comparison	➢ Subordinate clauses in indirect discourse
➢ Irregular comparison of adjectives	➢ Result and "cum" clauses
➢ Ablative of degree of difference	➢ Irregular verbs: "eo, fero"
➢ Comparison of adverbs	➢ Indefinite pronouns and adjectives
➢ Ablative of degree of difference with adverbs	➢ Deponent verbs: "volo, nolo, malo, fio"
➢ "Quam" with superlative	➢ Gerund: gerundive
➢ "Idem" and "ipse"	➢ Impersonal verbs
➢ Irregular adjectives	➢ Relative clause of characteristic

Course Grade
Latin 3 – Completed 06/03

Tests		Daily Work	
----------------1/2 grade----------------		----------------1/2 grade----------------	
Test 1	82%	Chapter 1	100%
Test 2	94%	Chapter 2	100%
Test 3	82%	Chapter 3	100%
Test 4	87%	Chapter 4	100%
Test 5	88%	Chapter 5	100%
Test 6	89%	Chapter 6	100%
Test 7	86%	Chapter 7	100%
Test 8	81%	Chapter 8	100%
		Chapter 9	100%
		Chapter 10	100%
		Chapter 11	100%
		Chapter 12	100%
		Chapter 13	100%
		Chapter 14	100%
		Chapter 15	100%
		Chapter 16	100%
		Chapter 17	90%
Tests average 86%		**Daily work average 99%**	

-------------------- **Final grade for Latin 3 = 93% = A** -----------------------

A =90-100% =4.0	*B=80-89% = 3.0*	*C=70-79% = 2.0*	*D = 60-69% = 1.0*

Course Description
Foreign Language: French 1

This is a 2-semester course that combines kinesthetic, visual and auditory teaching modes. The program requires 20-40 minutes of French speaking daily, with regular quizzes and tests and reports. The course requires research papers (in English) on French history and culture. This course will cover an introduction to French music, art, and literature, and culture. Student notebook, writing, and tests, available on request.

Primary Text:
Power-Glide Foreign Language Course French Semester 1 and Semester 2

Music: Appreciation "Great French Classics" audio CD

Art: The Impressionists Art Book by Wenda O'Reilly
    "The Impressionists Art Game" by Birdcage Books

Literature:
    The Scarlet Pimpernel by Baroness Orczy
    The Little Prince by Antoine De Saint-Exupery
    Le Petit Prince by Antoine De Saint-Exupery (French Language version)
    Les Miserables by Victor Hugo

French Culture and Composition: Reports on Quebec, Luxembourg, and Morocco.

Course Grade
French 1 – Completed 11/02

Tests ----------1/3 grade--------		Daily Work -------------1/3 grade------------		Composition -----------1/3 grade---------	
Test 1	98%	Chapter 1	100%	Quebec	100%
Test 2	87%	Chapter 2	100%	Luxembourg	100%
Test 3	86%	Chapter 3	100%	Morocco	100%
Test 4	91%	Chapter 4	100%		
Test 5	89%	Chapter 5	100%		
Test 6	91%	Chapter 6	100%		
Tests average 90%		**Daily work average 100%**		**Composition Grade 100 %**	

---------------------- **Final grade for French 1 = 97% = A** ------------------

A =90-100% =4.0   *B=80-89% = 3.0*   *C=70-79% = 2.0*   *D = 60-69% = 1.0*

Course Description
Foreign Language: French 2

This is a 2-semester course that combines kinesthetic, visual and auditory teaching modes. The program requires 20-40 minutes of French speaking daily, with regular quizzes and tests and reports. The course requires research papers (in English) on French history and culture, and a written narrative in French, and creative project of the student's choice. This course will cover an introduction to French music, art, and literature, and culture. Student notebook, writing, and tests, available on request.

Primary Text: Power-Glide Foreign Language Course French Semester 3 and Semester 4

Music: Appreciation "Great French Classics" audio CD

Art: The Impressionists Art Book by Wenda O'Reilly
    "The Impressionists Art Game" by Birdcage Books

Literature:
    Le Petit Prince by Antoine De Saint-Exupery (French Language version)
    Les Miserables by Victor Hugo
    Easy French Reader by R. de Roussy de Sales (French Language)

French Culture and Composition: Reports on Switzerland, Federation Internationale d'Echecs, and Senegal.

French Composition: D'Echecs.

Course Grade
French 2 – Completed 05/03

Tests		Daily Work		Composition	
------------1/3 grade------------		------------1/3 grade------------		------------1/3 grade------------	
Test 7	92%	Chapter 1	100%	Switzerland	100%
Online 8	92%			Senegal	100%
Test 8	95%	Chapter 2	100%	FIDE	100%
Test 9	97%	Chapter 3	100%	D'Echecs	100%
Test 10	93%	Chapter 4	100%		
Online 11	98%				
Test 11	81%	Chapter 5	100%		
Online 12	97%				
Test 12	90%	Chapter 6	100%		
Tests average 93%		**Daily work average 100%**		**Composition Grade 100 %**	

---------------------- **Final grade for French 2 = 98% = A** ------------------

A =90-100% =4.0   *B=80-89% = 3.0*   *C=70-79% = 2.0*   *D = 60-69% = 1.0*

Course Description
Foreign Language: French 3

This course is designed to provide the student with an opportunity to read, write, speak, and listen in French, using a variety of materials and modalities. The French culture will be studied, with an emphasis on the literature of great French writers and the music of French Composers. Credit will be upon completion of 150 hours of work. Student writing available on request.

Primary Texts:
Learnables French Book 1by Harris Winitz
Learnables French Book 2 by Harris Winitz
Learnables French Book 3 by Harris Winitz
Learnables French Book 4 by Harris Winitz
Power-Glide French Ultimate Adventure by Dr. Robert Blair
Complete Idiot's Guide to Learning French by Gail Stein
Cracking the SAT II French by Princeton Review
How to Prepare for the SAT II French by Barron's

Supplemental Texts:
The Land and People of France by Jonathan Harris
Phantom of the Opera: The Original Novel by Gaston Leroux
Around the World in Eighty Days by Jules Verne
20,000 Leagues Under the Sea by Jules Verne
Journey to the Center of the Earth by Jules Verne
The Hunchback of Notre-Dame by Victor Hugo
Les Miserables by Victor Hugo
The Count of Monte Cristo by Alexandre Dumas
The Three Musketeers by Alexandre Dumas
The Man in the Iron Mask by Alexandre Dumas
Great French Short Stories by Germaine Bree
The Figaro Plays by Beaumarchais
Cyrano de Bergerac by Edmond Rostand

Course Grade
French 3 – Completed 06/04

Tests		Daily Work		Composition	
-----------1/3 grade-----------		-----------1/3 grade-----------		-----------1/3 grade-----------	
SAT II French	470	Learnables	100%	Composition	100%
		Power-Glide	100%		
		Read Aloud	100%		
		Literature	100%		
Tests average A		**Daily work grade 100%**		**Composition Grade 100 %**	
-------------------- Final grade for French 3 = 100 % = A -----------------					
A =90-100% =4.0		*B=80-89% = 3.0*	*C=70-79% = 2.0*	*D = 60-69% = 1.0*	

Course Description
Music: Piano 2 with Performance

The student will attend private professional piano lessons twice monthly throughout the year, and will practice lessons 30 minutes daily. Students will learn practical aspects of playing the piano as well as the technical aspects such as scales and chording. Different piano playing styles, such as jazz and   classical music will be explored. Sight reading and music theory will be studied. The student will study a variety of composers and musical styles. Performances are required.

Texts:
Alfred's Basic Piano Library: Chord Approach, Solo Book Level 2 by Palmer, Manus, and Lethco.
Alfred's Basic Piano Library: Chord Approach, Theory Book Level 2 by Palmer, Manus, and Lethco.
Alfred's Basic Piano Library: Chord Approach, Lesson Book Level 2 by Palmer, Manus, and Lethco.
Alfred's Basic Piano Library: Sight Reading Complete Levels 2 & 3 by Kowalchyk and Lancaster.
Alfred's Basic Piano Library: Intermediate Musicianship Book 2 by Palmer, Manus and Lethco.
Finger Builders by Robert Pace.
Piano Solo: The World's Favorite Classical Themes by Hal Leonard
Christmas Carols: Piano Arrangements by Golden Books
Patriotic Melodies: An American Songbook for Piano, Vocal and Guitar by Jonathon Robbins

Music history and appreciation resources:
> "Great French Classics" audio CD
> "Great Choral Classics" audio CD
> "In The Christmas Mood II" The Glenn Miller Orchestra audio CD
> "The Christmas Song" Nat King Cole audio CD
> "Highlights from the Messiah" by Handel, audio CD
> "Great Brass Classics" audio CD
> "Great Opera Classics" audio CD
> "Kind of Blue" Miles Davis audio CD
> "Great American Classics" audio CD
> "Silhouette" by Kenny G. audio CD
> "Play" by Bobby McFerrin and Chick Corea audio CD
> "Medicine Man" by Bobby McFerrin

Performances:
1) Christmas Piano Recital, December 10, 2002.   "Fur Elise" and "O Come all Ye Faithful."
2) Weekly keyboard performance with church Worship Ensemble: Normandy Church.
3) Spring Piano Recital, June 17, 2003. "Jesu, Joy of Man's Desiring" and "Minuet in G."

Course Grade
Piano Level 2 – Completed 06/03

Daily Work		Performance	
------------------1/2 grade------------------		------------------1/2 grade------------------	
Piano Practice	100%	Performance	100%
--------------- **Final grade for Piano Level 2 = 100% = A** ---------------			
A =90-100% =4.0	B=80-89% = 3.0	C=70-79% = 2.0	D = 60-69% = 1.0

Course Description
Music: Piano 3 with Performance

The student will attend private professional piano lessons weekly throughout the year, and will practice lessons 45 minutes daily. Students will learn practical aspects of playing the piano and the technical aspects such as scales and chording. Different piano playing styles, such as jazz and   classical music will be explored. Sight reading and music theory will be studied. The student will study a variety of composers and musical styles. The student will develop musicianship and performance skills. Performances are required.

Primary Texts:
Piano Adventures: A Basic Piano Method Lesson Book Level 3A by Faber and Faber
Alfred's Basic Piano Library: Lesson Book Level 3 Piano by Palmer, Manus and Lethco
Alfred's Basic Piano Library: Theory Book Level 3 Piano by Palmer, Manus and Lethco
Alfred's Basic Piano Library: Ear Training Book Level 3 Piano by Kowalchyk and Lancaster
Alfred's Basic Piano Library: Sight Reading Book Level 3 Piano by Kowalchyk and Lancaster
Alfred's Basic Piano Library: Classical Themes Book Level 3 Piano by Allan Small
Scales and Chords are Fun: Book 1 by David Hirschberg
Alfred's Basic Piano Library: Technic Book Level 4 Piano by Palmer, Manus and Lethco
Finger Builders 2 by Robert Pace, Hal Leonard Corporation
Hanon: The Virtuoso Pianist in Sixty Exercises for the Piano by Schirmer's Library of Classical Music

Supplemental Texts:
Piano Solo: The World's Favorite Classical Themes by Hal Leonard
At the Piano With Scott Joplin by Maurice Hinson
Christmas Carols: Piano Arrangements by Golden Books
Top 10 Classical Favorites by Sharon Aaronson

Performances:
1. National Federation of Music Clubs Junior Festival: Rated Excellent
2. Spring Recital
3. Performance at Church Mission Trip Fundraiser

Course Grade
Piano Level 3 – Completed 06/04

Daily Work		Performance	
-------------------1/2 grade-------------------		-------------------1/2 grade-------------------	
Piano Practice	100%	Performance	100%
		Competition	100%
--------------- Final grade for Piano Level 3 = 100% = A ---------------			
A =90-100% =4.0	*B=80-89% = 3.0*	*C=70-79% = 2.0*	*D = 60-69% = 1.0*

The "Love Language" of Colleges

Course Description
Music: Piano 4 with Performance

The student will attend private professional piano lessons weekly throughout the year, and will practice lessons 45 minutes daily. Students will learn practical aspects of playing the piano as well as the technical aspects such as scales and chording. Different piano playing styles, such as jazz and   classical music will be explored. Sight reading and music theory will be studied. The student will study a variety of composers and musical styles. The student will develop musicianship and performance skills. Performances are required. Performance awards available on request.

Primary Texts:
Hanon: The Virtuoso Pianist in Sixty Exercises for the Piano by Schirmer's Library of Classical Music
The Kits Music Theory Course, Step 2 Keynote Independent Theory Service

Supplemental Texts:
Piano Solo: The World's Favorite Classical Themes by Hal Leonard
Moonlight Sonata by Beethoven, G. Schirmer, Inc.
Snowbird's Journey by Kathleen Massoud, Alfred Signature Series.
Full Moon Serenade by Carol Matz, Spotlight solo Sheets.
Daydreams by Randall Hartsell, Alfred Signature Series.
Summer's Nocturne by Catherine Rollin, Alfred Signature Series.
Elegy by George Peter Tingley, Alfred Signature Series.
Poetry at the Piano by Martha Sherrill Kelsey, Keyboard Gallery.
The Classical Period: An Anthology of Piano Music Volume 2, edited by Denes Agay.
The Romantic Period: An Anthology of Piano Music Volume 3, edited by Denes Agay.

Performances:
Winter Recital
National Federation of Music Clubs Junior Festival: Rated Excellent
Spring Recital
Church Offertory music
Vacation Bible School Worship Keyboardist

Course Grade
Piano Level 4 – Completed 06/05

Daily Work ----------------1/2 grade----------------		Performance ----------------1/2 grade----------------	
Piano Practice	100%	Performance	100%
Completed	100%	Competition	100%
Assignments		Worship	100%
--------------- Final grade for Piano Level 4 = 100% = A --------------			
A =90-100% =4.0	B=80-89% = 3.0	C=70-79% = 2.0	D = 60-69% = 1.0

Course Description
Fine Arts 1: American Art

This course provides an overview of the fine arts in American History, including the artists, composers, and musical styles unique to America. Art classes provide a hands-on experience with pottery wheel technique. Field trips provide exposure to other art forms. Written work available on request.

Art History and Appreciation:
The Impressionist Art Book by Wenda O'Reilly, Ph.D.
"The Impressionists Art Game" by Birdcage Books
Norman Rockwell's American Memories Published by MJF Books
Georgia O'Keeffe by Britta Benke
Famous Artists: Miro by Nicholas Ross
Sister Wendy's American Masterpieces by Sister Wendy Beckett
M.C. Escher: The Graphic Work Published by Barnes and Noble
"Where Art Thou?" American Paintings Art Game

Music History and Appreciation:
"Great French Classics" audio CD
"Great Choral Classics" audio CD
"In The Christmas Mood II" The Glenn Miller Orchestra audio CD
"The Christmas Song" Nat King Cole audio CD
"Highlights from the Messiah" by Handel, audio CD
"Great Brass Classics" audio CD
"Great Opera Classics" audio CD
"Kind of Blue" Miles Davis audio CD
"Great American Classics" audio CD
"Silhouette" by Kenny G. audio CD
"Play" by Bobby McFerrin and Chick Corea audio CD
Amadeus motion picture on DVD

Studio Art: Teen Pottery Wheel Class, Moshier Arts Center in Burien. Students experience working on a pottery wheel. Fundamentals of centering, throwing, trimming, and glazing will be covered.

Field Trips:
1. Glass Blowing Field Trip at M&M Glass Studio in Covington.
2. Burien Glass Studio: Glass bead-making demonstrated

Analysis: The student will complete 5 written essays on the Fine Arts.

Course Grade
Fine Arts 1 – Completed 06/03

Reading		Participation		Analysis	
-------------1/3 grade------------		-------------1/3 grade------------		-------------1/3 grade------------	
Reading	100%	Discussion	100%	Handel	100%
		Pottery Class	100%	Norman Rockwell	100%
				MC Escher	100%
				Georgia O'Keefe	100%
				Modern Art	100%

--------------- **Final grade for Fine Arts 1 = 100% = A** ---------------

A =90-100% =4.0	*B=80-89% = 3.0*	*C=70-79% = 2.0*	*D = 60-69% = 1.0*

Course Description
Fine Arts 2: History of Art

This course provides an overview of the fine arts in Ancient and Medieval Art. It covers the art, artists, composers, and musical styles of each period. French composers will be emphasized. For studio art, the student will participate in classes that provide a hands-on experience creating original art. Student charcoal drawings available on request. Written work available on request.

Art History and Appreciation:
Essential Art History by Parragon Publishing
Fandex Family Field Guides: Masters of Western Art Painters by Workman Publishing
Leonardo and His Times by Andrew Langley
Michelangelo and Raphael in the Vatican published Special Edition for the Museums and Papal Galleries
100 of the World's Most Beautiful Paintings by Shorewood Reproductions
Art and History of Washington D.C. by Bruce R. Smith, Bonechi
National Art Museum, Washington DC

Studio Art:
Draw Today Complete with Video by Steven Golden
Charcoal Drawing Class

Stage Presentations:
Les Miserable: School Edition musical presentation by the Hi-Liners, Burien, Washington.
The Nutcracker by Pacific Northwest Ballet at McCaw Hall
Paradiso a Inferno by Auburn Symphony Orchestra, Auburn Performing Arts

Music History and Appreciation:
Masters of Music: Their Works, Their Lives, Their Times by Dorothy and Joseph Samachson
Spiritual Lives of the Great Composers by Patrick Kavanaugh
Lives of the Great Composers by Harold C. Schonberg

Course Grade
Fine Arts 2: History of Art – Completed 06/04

Reading ---------1/3 grade---------		Participation ---------1/3 grade---------		Analysis ---------1/3 grade---------	
Reading	100%	Discussion	100%	Composition	100%
		Studio Art	100%	Oral Report	100%
----- **Final grade for Fine Arts 2: History of Art = 100 % = A** ----------					
A =90-100% =4.0	*B=80-89% = 3.0*		*C=70-79% = 2.0*		*D = 60-69% = 1.0*

Course Description
Fine Arts 3: Art and Music Appreciation

This course provides a survey of fine arts that emphasizes Classical music, Impressionism, and Poetry as a literary art form, in the time of the Renaissance to Modern History. It includes the art, artists, poets, composers and musical styles of the period. Field trips provide exposure to these and other art forms. Written work available on request.

Primary Texts:
How to Listen to and Understand Great Music by Professor Robert Greenberg, San Francisco Conservatory of Music, a series of 48 audiotape lectures by The Teaching Company.

From Monet to Van Gogh: A History of Impressionism by Professor Richard Brettell, University of Texas at Dallas, a series of 12 videotape lectures by The Teaching Company.

How to Read and Understand Poetry by Professor Williard Spiegelman, Southern Methodist University, a series of 24 videotape lectures by The Teaching Company.

Masters of Western Art: Painters Fandex Family Field Guide by Workman Publishing

Field Trips:
Seattle Art Museum: From Van Gogh to Modrian
Hi-Liners Stage Production, "42nd Street"
Hi-Liners Stage Production, "Beauty and the Beast"
Seattle Orchestra and Seattle Chamber Singers, June 4, 2005

Course Grade
Fine Arts 3 – Completed 06/05

Reading ------------1/3 grade------------		Participation ------------1/3 grade------------		Analysis ------------1/3 grade------------	
Impressionism	100%	Discussion	100%	Narration	100%
Music	100%	Note Taking	100%	Poetry Writing	100%
Poetry	100%	Attend Performance	100%		

--------------- **Final grade for Fine Arts 3 = 100% = A** --------------

A =90-100% =4.0	B=80-89% = 3.0	C=70-79% = 2.0	D = 60-69% = 1.0

Course Description
Bible 1: Christian Manhood

This course will focus on becoming Christian men in the modern world. Communicating the Christian faith is emphasized. This course requires personal devotions, Bible reading, and applying the Bible to daily life. Written work available on request.

Primary Texts:
The Bible, various versions
Christian Manhood by Gary Maldaner
Becoming a Contagious Christian by Mittelberg, Strobel and Hybels.
WorldView & Apologetics Lecture Series audiotape series by WorldView Academy
"The Duties of a Good Soldier" by Bill Jack
"Introduction to Worldviews" by Randy Sims
"Blind Faith" by Jeff Baldwin
"Critical Thinking" by Bill Jack
"The Roots of Order" by Todd Kent
"Creation vs. Evolution" by Bill Jack
"Servant Leadership" by Randy Sims

Analysis: The student will write two reports on applying the Christian Faith to daily life.

Course Grade
Bible 1: Christian Manhood – Completed 06/03

Reading ------------1/3 grade------------		Daily Work ------------1/3 grade------------		Analysis ------------ 1/3 grade ------------	
Reading	100%	Participation	100%	Communion Message	100%
Narration	100%	Discussion	100%	Alcohol Report	100%

---------- **Final grade for Bible 1: Christian Manhood = 100% = A** ----------

A =90-100% =4.0	*B=80-89% = 3.0*	*C=70-79% = 2.0*	*D = 60-69% = 1.0*

Course Description
Bible 2: Apologetics

This is a self-directed course in which the student will explore issues of Christian Apologetics in Literature. The student is required to write four essays and one report on the books read for this course. The student will develop a habit of independent Bible reading. The student will attend church regularly and participate in Youth Group. Written work available on request.

Primary Text: The One Year Bible: NIV Version for personal devotions

Supplemental Texts:
1. Boy Meets Girl Audiotape by Josh Harris
2. Good Dads & Bad Dads by Gregg Harris, 3 audiotape series
3. Christianity in Crisis by Hank Hannegraaff
4. The Face: That Demonstrates the Farce of Evolution by Hank Hanegraaff
5. In Six Days: Why 50 Scientists Choose to Believe in Creation by John Ashton
6. What is Creation Science by Henry Morris and Gary Parker
7. The Case for a Creator by Lee Strobel
8. The Case for Christ by Lee Strobel
9. The Case for Faith by Lee Strobel
10. The Case for Easter by Lee Strobel
11. The Jesus I never Knew by Philip Yancey.
12. Disappointment with God by Philip Yancey.
13. What's So Amazing About Grace? by Philip Yancey.
14. Mere Christianity by C.S. Lewis
15. The Screwtape Letters by C.S. Lewis
16. More Than a Carpenter by Josh McDowell
17. Don't Check Your Brains at the Door by Josh McDowell and Bob Hostetler
18. Luther's Catechism by Martin Luther
19. No Compromise by Melody Green
20. Shine: Make Them Wonder What You've Got by the Newsboys
21. Jesus Freaks by DC Talk and the Voice of the Martyrs
22. The Narrow Road by Brother Andrew with Jars of Clay
23. The Calling by Brother Andrew
24. Loving God by Charles Colson
25. How Now Shall We Live? By Charles Colson
26. How Then Shall We Live? By Francis Schaeffer
27. A Modest Proposal By Francis Schaeffer
28. The Book of God: The Bible as a Novel by Walter Wangerin, Jr.
29. Three From Galilee by Marjorie Holmes
30. Jesus Among Other Gods by Ravi Zacharias
31. The God Chasers by Tommy Tenney
32. He Chose The Nails by Max Lucado
33. 7 Men Who Rule the World From the Grave by Dave Breese

Course Grade
Bible 2 – Completed 06/04

Reading		Participation		Analysis	
-------------1/3 grade-------------		-------------1/3 grade-------------		-------------1/3 grade-------------	
Reading	100%	Discussion	100%	Composition	100%
Narration	100%		100%	Essay Writing	100%
-------------- **Final grade for Bible 2 = 100% = A** --------------					
A =90-100% =4.0	*B=80-89% = 3.0*		*C=70-79% = 2.0*		*D = 60-69% = 1.0*

Course Description
Bible 3: World View

This is the study of the fundamental worldviews of Western civilization: Biblical Christianity, Marxism/Leninism, Secular Humanism, and Eastern New Age. The student will study the major ideas, issues and personalities of the twentieth century, and compare that to Biblical Christianity. The text is designed to help the student appreciate God's truth, grow in their ability to speak confidently from Scripture on current issues, and increase their knowledge and understanding about viewpoints that oppose Christianity. The student will develop a habit of independent Bible reading. The student will attend church regularly and participate in Youth Group. Written work available on request.

Primary Text:
Understanding the Times by David A. Noebel, 1997, Harvest House.

Supplemental Texts:
Boy Meets Girl by Josh Harris
Life Lessons with Max Lucado: Book of Romans by Max Lucado
The New Tolerance by Josh McDowell and Bob Hostetler
Alpha for Youth by David C. Cook
Icons of Evolution by Jonathan Wells
The Privileged Planet: How Our Place in the Cosmos is Designed for Discovery by Guillermo Gonzalez and Jay Richards.

Field Trips:
1. Discovery Institute Event: Case for the Creator Seminar, presented by Lee Strobel
2. Discovery Institute Event: Human Cloning and Embryonic Stem Cell Research, presented by Wesley J. Smith
3. Discovery Institute Event: Unintelligent Evolution: The Key Problem for Darwin's Theory, presented by William Dembski

Course Grade
Bible 3 – Completed 06/05

Reading		Participation		Analysis	
----------1/3 grade----------		----------1/3 grade----------		----------1/3 grade----------	
Textbook Reading	100%	Discussion	100%	Composition	100%
Supplemental	100%	Current Events	100%		

----------------Final grade for Bible 3 = 100% = A --------------

A =90-100% =4.0	B=80-89% = 3.0	C=70-79% = 2.0	D = 60-69% = 1.0

Course Description
Elective: Critical Thinking in Chess

This is a self-directed course. Studying a variety of books, the student will independently investigate logic and critical thinking through the study of chess. The student will participate in competitive chess. Credit will be determined by time spent in tournament play. Grades will be awarded based on student's understanding of chess, and teaching that understanding to others.

Texts used:
200 Perplexing Chess Puzzles by Martin Greif
The Art of Attack in Chess by Vladimir Vukovic
Best Lessons of a Chess Coach by Weeramantry and Eusebi
Bobby Fischer Teaches Chess by Bobby Fischer
Chess Openings: Traps and Zaps by Bruce Pandolfini
Chess: 5334 Problems, Combinations, and Games by Laszlo Polgar
How to Reassess Your Chess by Jeremy Silman
How to Reassess Your Chess Workbook by Jeremy Silman
How to Think in Chess by Przewoznik and Soszynski
Multiple Choice Chess by Graeme Buckley
My System: 21st Century Edition by Aron Nimzowitsch
Pandolfini's Chess Complete by Bruce Pandolfini
Play Winning Chess by Yasser Seirawan
Secrets of the King's Indian by Gufeld & Schiller
The Amateur's Mind by Jeremy Silman
The Art of Chess Analysis by Jan Timman
The Best of Chess Life and Review Volume 2 edited by Bruce Pandolfini
The Complete Chess Addict by Fox and James
The Seven Deadly Chess Sins by Jonathan Rowson
The Seven Deadly Chess Sins by Jonathan Rowson
Understanding Chess Move by Move by John Nunn
Winning Chess Brilliancies by Yasser Seirawan
Winning Chess Openings by Yasser Seirawan
Winning Chess Strategies by Yasser Seirawan
Winning Chess Tactics by Yasser Seirawan
World Champion Combinations by Keene and Schiller

Analysis:
The student will teach chess in a classroom environment, and teach individual tutorial students. The student will compete in rated chess tournaments. The student will regularly analyze chess games for training purposes. The student will practice "Blindfold Chess" regularly.

Awards:
The student has participated in numerous Scholastic and Adult rated chess competitions. During the 2002-2003 school year, he was rated 13th in Washington State for High School students, and first in State for 9th graders.

Course Grade
Critical Thinking in Chess – Completed 06/03

Reading		Participation		Analysis	
-----------1/3 grade-----------		-----------1/3 grade-----------		-----------1/3 grade-----------	
Reading	100%	Tournaments	100%	Teaching others	100%
------- Final grade for Critical Thinking in Chess = 100% = A ----------					
A =90-100% =4.0		*B=80-89% = 3.0*	*C=70-79% = 2.0*	*D = 60-69% = 1.0*	

Course Description
Elective: Public Speaking

Communication theory is applied to on-the-job speaking, audience analysis, and listening skills. This course will lay the foundation for strong oral communication in a variety of settings, with emphasis on teaching skills. Written work available on request.

Learning Activities:
1) Teacher
    The student will teach a chess class to homeschool students at the Manhattan Home School Center. The class will consist of more than 20 students, between the ages of 6 to 18. He will plan the lessons, schedule his time, give his lesson with demonstration, and provide individual help and encouragement as necessary. The class was held on Wednesdays, 2:30-3:30 from September 2002 until May 2003. Sample lesson plans and the school calendar are enclosed.

2) Scripture Reading at Church
    The student will read the Scriptures Church sermons on Sunday, once a month, as requested by the Pastor of Normandy Christian Church.

3) Communion Message
    The student will provide the Communion Message for Youth Sunday, March 2003 at Normandy Christian Church.

4) Youth Program Teacher
    The student will teach beginning chess during the youth program of the WATCH Conference, April 11-12, 2003. Basic moves and strategies of chess will be taught, gradually building up to more advanced concepts in chess. The "Washington Association of Teaching Christian Homes" conference brochure available on request.

Course Grade
Public Speaking – Completed 06/03

Preparation ----------1/3 grade----------		Speaking ----------1/3 grade----------		Analysis ----------1/3 grade----------	
Lesson Preparation	100%	Speaking	100%	Speech Evaluation	100%

----------- Final grade for Public Speaking = 100% = A ------------

$A =90-100\% =4.0$	$B=80-89\% = 3.0$	$C=70-79\% = 2.0$	$D = 60-69\% = 1.0$

Course Description
Elective: Occupational Education

This is a self-directed course. The student will work to pursue their area of interest, seeking work and volunteer opportunities in that area. Within his area of interest, the student will demonstrate initiative, responsibility, reliability, and enthusiasm in the workplace. The student will demonstrate basic computer and word processing skills. Written work available on request.

Skills and Opportunities include:
- Teaching chess at Manhattan Homeschool Center
- Teaching chess at Marvista Elementary School, Normandy park
- Teaching chess with individual tutorial students
- Teaching chess at Stella Schola Middle School, Redmond
- Substitute chess teacher at Issaquah Chinese Academy
- Experience in interviewing
- Experience in making resume, cover letter, and obtaining letter of recommendation
- Experience with handling regular pay

Course Grade
Occupational Education – Completed 06/04

Daily Work -----------1/2 grade-----------		Preparation -----------1/2 grade-----------	
Teacher: Manhattan Homeschool Center – Volunteer Position	100%	Preparation for Class	100%
Teacher: Marvista Elementary School – Paid Position	100%	Preparation for Class	100%
Teacher: Stella Schola Middle School – Paid Position	100%	Preparation for Class	100%
Substitute Teacher: Issaquah Chinese School – Paid position	100%	Preparation for Class	100%
Private Tutor with individual students	100%	Preparation for Students	100%
Yard Maintenance –Paid Position	100%		
Basic Computer and Typing Skills	100%		

------------ **Final grade for Occupational Education = 100% = A** ------------

A =90-100% =4.0	*B=80-89% = 3.0*	*C=70-79% = 2.0*	*D = 60-69% = 1.0*

Course Description
Elective: Driver's Education

Credit awarded based on successful achievement of Driver's License. It includes all activities required to obtain a license, by Washington State Law. The student will spend a minimum of 50 hours driving with a parent, in addition to class time. Course grade is not included in GPA.

Primary Texts:
Washington Driver Guide by the Washington State Department of Licensing
Responsible Driving by the American Automobile Association, published by Glencoe
Steer Clear Driver's Program by State Farm Mutual Automobile Insurance Company

Driver's Education Class:
Diamond Driving School, Burien Washington.

Course Grade
Driver's Education - Completed 07/04

Preparation		Participation		Exam	
------------1/3 grade------------		------------1/3 grade------------		------------1/3 grade------------	
Reading	100%	Narration and Discussion	100%	Classroom grades	Pass
		Daily Work	100%	Department of Licensing	Pass

----------- **Final grade for Driver's Education = 100% = A** ------------

A =90-100% =4.0	*B=80-89% = 3.0*	*C=70-79% = 2.0*	*D = 60-69% = 1.0*

Course Description
Elective: Russian History

This is a self-directed course. Studying a variety of books, college lecture material, and other resources, the student will independently investigate Russian History from the ancient to the modern era. The student will discuss his findings, write one or more research papers on the topic of his choosing, within that subject. Credit will be awarded based on 150 hours of study and research, and successful completion of a written report. Written work available on request.

Primary Text:
 A History of Russia: From Peter the Great to Gorbachev by Professor Mark Steinberg, University of Illinois at Urbana-Champaign, The Teaching Company. This course is a series of 36 half-hour audio lectures examining key individuals, groups, the contexts in which they thought and acted, and their driving ideas.

Supplemental Texts:
Waterloo: Day of Battle by David Howarth, Unabridged on Cassette.
At Napoleon's Side in Russia by Armand De Caulaincourt
Great Russian Short Novels translated by Andrew R. MacAndrew
Anna Karenina by Leo Tolstoy
War and Peace by Leo Tolstoy
Napoleon Bonaparte by Alan Schom
1812: Napoleon's Russian Campaign by Richard K. Riehn
The Age of Napoleon: World History Series by Harry Henderson
Russia of the Tsars: World History Series by James E. Strickler
The War of the Roses World History Series by William W. Lace
The Crimean War: World History Series by Deborah Bachrach

Course Grade
Russian History – Completed 06/04

Reading		Daily Work		Reports	
------------1/3 grade------------		------------1/3 grade------------		------------1/3 grade------------	
Semester 1	100%	Semester 1	100%	Research Report	100%
Semester 2	100%	Semester 2	100%		
Final Grade	100%	Final Grade	100%	Final Grade	100%

---------- **Final grade for Russian History = 100 % = A** ----------------

A =90-100% =4.0   *B=80-89% = 3.0*   *C=70-79% = 2.0*   *D = 60-69% = 1.0*

Course Description
Elective: Formal Logic

This course covers informal and formal logic. The objectives include development of discernment in reading and listening, and clarity of thought in speaking and writing. Through video lectures, reading and class discussions, students consider and analyze a variety of realistic situations. Exercises are drawn from newspapers, newscasts, advertisements, conversations, political speeches, and government regulations. Topics include: use and misuse of words, logic without quantified statements, common errors in reasoning, techniques of propaganda and argument, probabilities of truth and falsity, logic with quantified statements, characteristics of arguments, supporting arguments, solving problems. Critical thinking will also be developed while studying for college placement tests.

Primary Texts:
Introductory Logic by Douglas Wilson and James Nance, Mars Hill Textbook Series
Introductory Logic Video Series by Douglas Wilson and James Nance
Critical Thinking Book 2 by Anita Harnadek, Critical Thinking Books and Software.
10 Real SATs by The College Board
The Princeton Review: Cracking the SAT 1997 edition

Supplements:
SAT Test: Practice exam given by the Princeton Review
PSAT Test: given at Highline High School October 21, 2003

Course Grade
Formal Logic - Completed 06/04

Logic ----------1/3 grade----------		Participation -----------1/3 grade-----------		SAT Review -----------1/3 grade-----------	
Reading	100%	Narration and Discussion	100%	SAT Preparation	100%
View Video	100%	Daily Work	100%	SAT Testing	100%
---------- Final grade for Logic = 100% = A ------------					
A =90-100% =4.0	B=80-89% = 3.0	C=70-79% = 2.0		D = 60-69% = 1.0	

Course Description
Physical Education 1

This physical education course will include a variety of team and individual sports, human anatomy and health. Credit will be given when 150 hours of physical activity is achieved. Grades are based on participation.

Swimming: Normandy Park Sharks Swim Team 2002
Description: Student will participate in daily workout with the team. Student will compete twice weekly in swim meets. Skills include: butterfly, breaststroke, backstroke, freestyle, flip-turns, racing starts and sportsmanship.

Soccer: West Highline Soccer Club 2002
Description: Student will participate in twice weekly workout with the team. Student will participate in soccer competition once weekly. Skills include: ball handling, shooting, passing, teamwork and sportsmanship.

Skiing Instruction 2003
Description: The student will receive 3 hours of professional snow skiing instruction and demonstrate proficiency in beginning downhill skiing.

Strength Training 2003
Description: The student will perform strength training exercised at home.

Health 1
Description: This health section includes an overview of the human body. It covers the general structure, cells, genes, tissues, organs, and organ systems. Eleven organ systems are studied in detail: skeletal, muscular, nervous, sensory, reproductive, digestive, excretory, circulatory, immune and lymphatic, respiratory, and endocrine. Branches of medicine are introduced. The student will describe each organ system in essay form. Food allergies and anaphylaxis are studied in depth, including a field trip to the local emergency room, and the role of the Food and Drug Administration in food ingredient labeling.

Primary Texts:
Lyrical Life Sciences Volume 3: The Human Body
The Human Body Reproducibles by Vriesenga
8 Minutes in the Morning by Jorge Cruise.
Human Eye Kit model
The Visible Man Kit
Food Allergy News newsletter

Course Grade
Physical Education 1 – Completed 06/03

Health		Individual Sports		Team Sports	
-------------1/3 grade-------------		-------------1/3 grade-------------		-------------1/3 grade-------------	
Health 1	100%	Swimming	100%	Soccer	100%
		Skiing	100%		
		Strength Training	100%		

------------- Final grade for Physical Education 1 = 100% = A ------------
A =90-100% =4.0   *B=80-89% = 3.0*   *C=70-79% = 2.0*   *D = 60-69% = 1.0*

The "Love Language" of Colleges

Course Description
Physical Education 2

This physical education course will include a variety of team and individual sports, human anatomy and health. Credit will be given when 150 hours of physical activity is achieved. Grades are based on participation.

Swimming: Normandy Park Sharks Swim Team 2003
Description: Student will participate in daily workout with the team. Student will compete twice weekly in swim meets. Skills include: butterfly, breaststroke, backstroke, freestyle, flip-turns, racing starts and sportsmanship.
➢ Award: Coaches Award given for sportsmanship Normandy Park Swim Club 2003 18U Division

Soccer: West Highline Soccer Club 2003
Description: Student will participate in twice weekly workout with the team. Student will participate in soccer competition once weekly. Skills include: ball handling, shooting, passing, teamwork and sportsmanship.

Skiing: Intermediate Lessons
The student will participate in intermediate skiing lessons at Snoqualmie Summit. The student will spend a minimum of 5 hours practice time skiing.

Health 2
Description: Student will read and discuss the text Total Health: Choices for a Winning Lifestyle by Susan Boe. Student will demonstrate healthy lifestyle habits.

CPR Certification
The student will participate in a Cardiopulmonary Resuscitation Course taught according to the American Heart Association 2000 Guidelines presented by Medic One, Fire Department of Burien and Normandy Park. Course provided by Manhattan Homeschool.

Course Grade
Physical Education 2 – Completed 06/04

Health		Individual Sports		Team Sports	
-------------1/3 grade-------------		-------------1/3 grade-------------		-------------1/3 grade-------------	
Health 2	100%	Swimming	100%	Soccer	100%
CPR	100%	Skiing	100%	Sportsmanship	100%
------------ Final grade for Physical Education 2 = 100% = A ------------					
A =90-100% =4.0 *B=80-89% = 3.0* *C=70-79% = 2.0* *D = 60-69% = 1.0*					

Course Description
Physical Education 3

This physical education course will include a variety of team and individual sports. Long-term personal health and hygiene will be stressed. Credit will be given when 150 hours of physical activity has been achieved. Grades are based on participation.

Swimming: Normandy Park Sharks Swim Team 2004
Description: Student will participate in daily workout with the team. Student will compete twice weekly in swim meets. Skills include: butterfly, breaststroke, backstroke, freestyle, flip-turns, racing starts and sportsmanship.

Soccer: West Highline Soccer Club 2004
Description: Student will participate in twice weekly workout with the team. Student will participate in soccer competition once weekly. Skills include: ball handling, shooting, passing, teamwork and sportsmanship.

Swimming: Normandy Park Sharks Swim Team 2005
Description: Student will participate in daily workout with the team. Student will compete twice weekly in swim meets. Skills include: butterfly, breaststroke, backstroke, freestyle, flip-turns, racing starts and sportsmanship.

Course Grade
Physical Education 3 – Completed 06/05

Health ------------1/3 grade------------		Individual Sports ------------1/3 grade------------		Team Sports ------------1/3 grade------------	
Strength Training	100%	Swimming	100%	Soccer	100%
				Sportsmanship	100%

------------ **Final grade for Physical Education 3 = 100% = A** ------------

A =90-100% =4.0	*B=80-89% = 3.0*	*C=70-79% = 2.0*	*D = 60-69% = 1.0*

The "Love Language" of Colleges

Reading Lists

2002-2003 Reading List for Student Name

<u>1984</u> by George Orwell
<u>200 Perplexing Chess Puzzles</u> by Martin Greif
<u>A Day No Pigs Would Die</u> by Robert Newton Peck
<u>A Jar of Dreams</u> by Yoshiko Uchida
<u>After the Dancing Days</u> by Margaret I. Rostkowski
<u>All the People</u> by Joy Hakim
<u>All-of-a-Kind Family</u> by Sydney Taylor
<u>An Age of Extremes</u> by Joy Hakim
<u>Best Lessons of a Chess Coach</u> by Weeramantry and Eusebi
<u>Blue Willow</u> by Doris Gates
<u>Bobby Fischer Teaches Chess</u> by Bobby Fischer
<u>Bonanza Girl</u> by Patricia Beatty
<u>Calico Captive</u> by Elizabeth George Speare
<u>Chess Openings: Traps and Zaps</u> by Bruce Pandolfini
<u>Chess: 5334 Problems, Combinations, and Games</u> by Laszlo Polgar
<u>Christy</u> by Catherine Marshall
<u>Cornerstones of Freedom: The Story of the Panama</u> Canal by R. Conrad Stein
<u>Dear Mr. Henshaw</u> by Beverly Cleary
<u>Dragon's Gate</u> by Laurence Yep
<u>Dragonwings</u> by Laurence Yep
<u>Duel of the Ironclads</u> by Fred Freeman
<u>Earthquake at Dawn</u> by Kristiana Gregory
<u>Famous Artists: Miro</u> by Nicholas Ross
<u>Farewell to Manzanar</u> by Houston and Houston
<u>From Colonies to Country</u> by Joy Hakim
<u>From the Mixed-Up Files of Mrs. Basil E. Frankweiler</u> by E. L. Konigsburg
<u>Georgia O'Keeffe</u> by Britta Benke
<u>Gone-Away Lake</u> by Elizabeth Enright
<u>Haunting Tales</u> by Nathaniel Hawthorne
<u>Helen Keller: The Story of My Life</u> by Helen Keller
<u>How to Reassess Your Chess</u> by Jeremy Silman
<u>How to Reassess Your Chess Workbook</u> by Jeremy Silman
<u>How to Think in Chess</u> by Przewoznik and Soszynski
<u>Huckleberry Finn</u> by Mark Twain
<u>I Am an American</u> by Jerry Stanley
<u>I Kissed Dating Goodbye</u> by Joshua Harris
<u>In Search of the Source</u> by Anderson and Moore
<u>Les Miserable</u> by Victor Hugo
<u>Liberty for All?</u> by Joy Hakim
<u>M.C. Escher: The Graphic Work</u> Published by Barnes and Noble
<u>M.C. Escher: The Graphic Work</u> Published by Barnes and Noble
<u>Making Thirteen Colonies</u> by Joy Hakim

Man of the Family by Ralph Moody
Maniac MaGee by Jerry Spinelli
Moonshiner's Son by Carolyn Reeder
Multiple Choice Chess by Graeme Buckley
My Side of the Mountain by Jean Craighead George
My System: 21st Century Edition by Aron Nimzowitsch
Norman Rockwell's American Memories, Published by MJF Books
Nothing to Fear by Jackie French Koller
Of Mice and Men by John Steinbeck
Out of the Dust by Karen Hesse
Pandolfini's Chess Complete by Bruce Pandolfini
Play Winning Chess by Yasser Seirawan
Poetry for Young People: Carl Sandburg Edited by Frances Schoonmaker Bolin
Poetry for Young People: Edgar Allan Poe Edited by Brod Bagert
Poetry for Young People: Walt Whitman Edited by Jonathan Levin
Reasoning and Argument by John L. Schneider
Reconstruction and Reform by Joy Hakim
Rosa Parks: My Story by Rosa Parks
Secrets of the King's Indian by Gufeld & Schiller
Sister Wendy's American Masterpieces by Sister Wendy Beckett
Smoky the Cowhorse by Will James
Sounder by William H. Armstrong
The Amateur's Mind by Jeremy Silman
The Art of Attack in Chess by Vladimir Vukovic
The Art of Chess Analysis by Jan Timman
The Best of Chess Life and Review Volume 2 edited by Bruce Pandolfini
The Best of Robert Service by Robert Service
The Call of the Wild by Jack London
The Celebrated Jumping Frog and Other Stories by Mark Twain
The Complete Chess Addict by Fox and James
The Cross and the Switchblade by David Wilkerson
The Day Pearl Harbor Was Bombed by George Sullivan
The DreamKeeper and Other Poems by Langston Hughes
The First Americans by Joy Hakim
The Gift of the Magi and Other Stories by O.Henry
The Girl Who Owned a City by O.T. Nelson
The Gold-Bug and Other Tales by Edgar Allan Poe
The Hiding Place by Corrie Ten Boom
The Impressionist Art Book by Wenda O'Reilly, Ph.D.
The Life and Times of Frederick Douglass by Frederick Douglass
The Little Prince by Antoine De Saint-Exupery
Le Petit Prince by Antoine De Saint-Exupery - French Language Version
The New Nation by Joy Hakim
The Pocket Book of Ogden Nash with an Introduction by Louis Untermeyer (excerpts)
The Prophet by Frank E. Peretti
The Scarlet Letter by Nathaniel Hawthorne
The Scarlet Pimpernel by Baroness Orczy
The Seven Deadly Chess Sins by Jonathan Rowson

The Seven Deadly Chess Sins by Jonathan Rowson
The Slopes of War: A Novel of Gettysburg by N. A. Perez
The Terrible Wave by Marden Dahlstedt
To Be a Slave by Julius Lester
To Kill A Mockingbird by Harper Lee
Tom Sawyer by Mark Twain
Tramp for the Lord by Corrie ten Boom
Understanding Chess Move by Move by John Nunn
War, Peace, and All That Jazz by Joy Hakim
War, Terrible War by Joy Hakim
White Fang by Jack London
Winning Chess Brilliancies by Yasser Seirawan
Winning Chess Openings by Yasser Seirawan
Winning Chess Strategies by Yasser Seirawan
Winning Chess Tactics by Yasser Seirawan
World Champion Combinations by Keene and Schiller
You Come Too: Favorite Poems for Young Readers by Robert Frost

2003-2004 Reading List for Student Name

20,000 Leagues Under the Sea by Jules Verne
7 Habits of Highly Effective Teens by Sean Covey
7 Men Who Rule the World From the Grave by Dave Breese
A Midsummer Night's Dream by William Shakespeare
A Modest Proposal by Francis Schaeffer
A Walk in the Woods by Bill Bryson
Adventures of Robin Hood by Roger Lancelyn Green
Ancient Rome: How it Affects You by Richard J. Maybury
Animal Farm by George Orwell
Antigone by Sophocles
Around the World in Eighty Days by Jules Verne
Art and History of Washington D.C. by Bruce R. Smith, Bonechi
As You Like It by William Shakespeare
Billy Budd by Herman Melville
Boy Meets Girl Audiotape by Josh Harris
Canterbury Tales by Chaucer
Capitalism for Kids: Growing Up to be Your Own Boss by Karl Hess
Christianity in Crisis by Hank Hannegraaff
Columbus Was Last by Patrick Huyghe
Comedy of Errors by William Shakespeare
Connecticut Yankee in King Arthur's Court by Mark Twain
Cyrano de Bergerac by Edmond Rostand
Deadline by Randy Alcorn
Disappointment With God by Philip Yancey.
Dominion by Randy Alcorn
Don Quixote by Miguel De Cervantes
Don't Check Your Brains at the Door by Josh McDowell and Bob Hostetler
Dr. Jekyll and Mr. Hyde by Robert Louis Stevenson
Essential Art History by Parragon Publishing
Fandex Family Field Guides: Masters of Western Art Painters by Workman Publishing
Gilgamesh Epic by Bernarda Bryson
Great French Short Stories by Germaine Bree
Great Russian Short Novels by Andrew R. MacAndrew
Gulliver's Travels by Jonathan Swift
He Chose The Nails by Max Lucado
How Now Shall We Live? By Charles Colson
How Then Shall We Live? By Francis Schaeffer
How to Win Friends and Influence People by Dale Carnegie
I'm a Stranger Here Myself by Bill Bryson
In His Steps by Sheldon
Ivanhoe by Sir Walter Scott
Jane Eyre by Charlotte Bronte
Jesus Among Other Gods by Ravi Zacharias
Jesus Freaks by DC Talk and the Voice of the Martyrs
Journey to the Center of the Earth by Jules Verne
Kidnapped by Robert Louis Stevenson

Leonardo and His Times by Andrew Langley
Les Miserables by Victor Hugo
Lives of the Great Composers by Harold C. Schonberg
Loving God by Charles Colson
Luther's Catechism by Martin Luther
Magna Charta by James Daugherty
Masters of Music: Their Works, Their Lives, Their Times by Dorothy and Joseph Samachson
Mere Christianity by C.S. Lewis
Merry Wives of Windsor by William Shakespeare
Michelangelo and Raphael in the Vatican published Special Edition for the Museums and Papal Galleries
More Than a Carpenter by Josh McDowell
Much Ado About Nothing by William Shakespeare
Mythology by Edith Hamilton
No Compromise by Melody Green
Oedipus Rex by Sophocles
Phantom of the Opera: The Original Novel by Gaston Leroux
Pharaohs of Ancient Egypt by Elizabeth Payne
Prince and the Pauper by Mark Twain
Roanoke: Solving the Mystery of the Lost Colony by Lee Miller
Robinson Crusoe by Daniel Defoe
Seven Daughters and Seven Sons
Shine: Make Them Wonder What You've Got by the Newsboys
Slander by Ann Coulter
Son of Charlemagne by Barbara Willard
Spiritual Lives of the Great Composers by Patrick Kavanaugh
Tales of Shakespeare by Charles and Martha Lamb
Taming of the Shrew by William Shakespeare
The Book of God: The Bible as a Novel by Walter Wangerin, Jr.
The Calling by Brother Andrew
The Case for a Creator by Lee Strobel
The Case for Christ by Lee Strobel
The Case for Faith by Lee Strobel
The Count of Monte Cristo by Alexandre Dumas
The Extraordinary Cases of Sherlock Holmes by Sir Arthur Conan Doyle
The Face: That Demonstrates the Farce of Evolution by Hank Hanegraaff
The God Chasers by Tommy Tenney
The Hunchback of Notre-Dame by Victor Hugo
The Hundred Years' War: World History Series by William W. Lace
The Jesus I Never Knew by Philip Yancey.
The Land and People of France by Jonathan Harris
The Making of Modern Economics: The Lives and Ideas of the Great Thinkers by Mark Skousen
The Man in the Iron Mask by Alexandre Dumas
The Narrow Road by Brother Andrew with Jars of Clay
The Odyssey by Homer
The Screwtape Letters by C.S. Lewis

The Taming of the Shrew by William Shakespeare
Three From Galilee by Marjorie Holmes
Three Musketeers by Alexandre Dumas
Treasure Island by Robert Louis Stevenson
Trumpeter of Krakow
What's So Amazing About Grace? by Philip Yancey.
Whatever Happened to Penny Candy? by Richard Maybury
Secrets of Modern Chess Strategy: Advances since Nimzowitsch by John Watson
New Ideas in the Nimzo-Indian Defence by Tony Kosten
Think Like a Grandmaster by Alexander Kotov
The Inner Game of Chess: How to Calculate and Win by Andrew Soltis
The Road to Chess Improvement by Alex Yermolinsky
Chess Strategy in Action by John Watson

Audiotapes:
The High Middle Ages by The Teaching Company, 24 audiotape lectures
Thomas Jefferson: American Visionary by The Teaching Company, 12 lectures
A History of Russia: From Peter the Great to Gorbachev by The Teaching Company, Part I
A History of Russia: From Peter the Great to Gorbachev by The Teaching Company, Part II
Good Dads & Bad Dads by Gregg Harris, 3 audiotape series

2004-2005 Reading List for Student Name

A Nation Challenged: A Visual History of 9/11 and its Aftermath by The New York Times

A Separate Peace by John Knowles

Alas, Babylon by Pat Frank

All Quiet on the Western Front by Erich Marla Remarque

Alpha for Youth by David C. Cook

Animal Farm by George Orwell

Autobiography of an Ex-Colored Man by James Weldon Johnson

Autobiography of Benjamin Franklin by Benjamin Franklin

Boy Meets Girl by Josh Harris

Brave New World by Aldous Huxley

Common Sense by Thomas Paine

Death Be Not Proud by John Gunther

Death of a Salesman by Arthur Miller

Dr. Jekyll and Mr. Hyde by Robert Louis Stevenson

Eats, Shoots, and Leaves by Lynne Truss

Elements of Style by Strunk and White

Flu: The Story of the Great Influenza Pandemic of 1918 by Gina Kolata

Frankenstein by Mary Shelley

Grapes of Wrath by John Steinbeck

Hard Times by Charles Dickens

Heart of Darkness by Joseph Conrad

Hiroshima by John Hershey

How to Write Poetry by Paul B. Janeczko

Icons of Evolution by Jonathan Wells

Invitation to the Classics by Louise Cowan and Os Guinness

Last of the Mohicans by James Fenimore Cooper

Life and Times of Frederick Douglass by Frederick Douglass

Life Lessons with Max Lucado: Book of Romans by Max Lucado

Literature: A Crash Course by Cory Bell

Literature: The American Experience by Prentice Hall

Lord of the Flies by William Golding

Murder at the Vicarage by Agatha Christie

Of Mice and Men by John Steinbeck

Oliver Twist by Charles Dickens

On Plymouth Rock by Samuel Drake

On the Duty of Civil Disobedience by Henry David Thoreau

Our Century in Pictures For Young People edited by Richard B. Stolley

Our Town by Thornton Wilder

Pickwick Papers by Charles Dickens

Poetry Speaks edited by Elise Paschen, Rebekah Mosby, et al.

Poor Richard's Almanack by Benjamin Franklin

Pride and Prejudice by Jane Austen

The Chosen by Chaim Potok

The Crucible by Arthur Miller

The Deadliest Monster by J.F. Baldwin

. . . .

The Deerslayer by James Fenimore Cooper
The Great Gatsby by F. Scott Fitzgerald
The Jungle by Upton Sinclair
The Life and Times of Frederick Douglass by Frederick Douglass
The Little Regiment and other Civil War Stories by Stephen Crane
The Metamorphosis by Franz Kafka
The New Tolerance by Josh McDowell and Bob Hostetler
The Old Man and the Sea by Ernest Hemingway
The Pearl by John Steinbeck
The Privileged Planet by Guillermo Gonzalez and Jay Richards.
The Rights of Man by Thomas Paine
The Secret Sharer by Joseph Conrad
Up From Slavery by Booker T. Washington
Walden: or Life in the Woods by Henry David Thoreau
War of the Worlds by H.G.Wells
We Interrupt This Broadcast by Joe Garner
What We Saw: The Events of September 11, 2001 – in Words, Pictures and Video by CBS News

Audiotapes:
Change and Motion: Calculus Made Clear by The Teaching Company
Einstein's Relativity and the Quantum Revolution The Teaching Company
European and Western Civilization in the Modern Age The Teaching Company
How to Listen to and Understand Great Music The Teaching Company.
From Monet to Van Gogh: A History of Impressionism The Teaching Company.
How to Read and Understand Poetry The Teaching Company.
Economics The Teaching Company.

Activities and Awards Lists

2002-2003 Activities and Awards

Competitive Chess Tournaments
Tacoma Chess Club: August 15, 2002
Seattle Chess Club: various tournaments
Master's Academy Chess Tournament: September 21, 2002, First place overall K-12 Division
Thanksgiving Scholastic, First place for Grades 7 - 12
Washington High School Championship, Rated first for 9th Grade, Rated 13th overall in Washington State
Washington Junior High Championship, Rated first for 9th Grade, Rated 13th overall in Washington State
Junior Reserve Chess Grade 7-9 Division: 2003, tied for first place
Washington Open Quads: May 31, 2003, tied for first place, U1600 division

Chess Instructor
Manhattan Homeschool Center Chess Class, Volunteer Instructor
Washington Association of Teaching Christian Homes (WATCH) annual homeschool convention,   Volunteer Chess Instructor, April 11-12, 2003
Chess Tutor: private chess tutor for individual students

Soccer
West Highline Soccer Club 2002: Second place team in the division.

Swimming
Swimming: Normandy Park Sharks Swim Team 2002, Boys 14 and Under
  1st place 50 Yard Breaststroke 7/18/2002, time 43.56 seconds
  1st place 200 Yard Freestyle Relay 7/16/2002
  1st place 200 Yard Medley Relay 7/16/2002

Church Activities
Youth Worship Band: Normandy Christian Church youth group, keyboard and piano
Active Youth Group Member, Normandy Christian Church
Scripture Reader, Normandy Christian Church
Communion Message for Youth Service, Normandy Christian Church

2003-2004 Activities and Awards

Competitive Chess Tournaments
Candidates Intermat, October 2003, First Place for grade
Thanksgiving Scholastic, First place for Grades 7 - 12
2003 Intermat: International Chess Competition with British Columbia
      Represented Washington State as a Sophomore.
Washington High School Individual tournament 1-23-04, 7th in State
Washington Junior Open 3-27-04, 8th overall
Seattle Chess Club: various tournaments

Chess Instructor
Manhattan Homeschool Center Chess Class, Volunteer Instructor
Normandy Park Community Club Chess Class, Volunteer Instructor
Stella Schola Middle School Chess Class
West Seattle Christian School Chess Class
Sammamish Christian Academy
Sammamish Chess Camps Tactics Coach
Calvary Chapel South Chess Club
Chess Tutor: private chess tutor for individual students

Soccer
West Highline Soccer Club 2003

Swimming
Swimming: Normandy Park Sharks Swim Team 2003, 18 and Under
➢ Coaches Award 18U boys
➢ 1st place SSSL Southern Division B Champs 50 yard backstroke 7/24/2003, time 34:50 seconds

Church Activity
Youth Mission team member: Midway Community Covenant Church mission trip to Harambee, California,   July 3-13, 2004
Youth Worship: Midway Community Covenant Church, keyboard and piano
Active Youth Group Member, Midway Community Covenant Church

Piano
National Federation of Music, Junior Festival 2004, rating excellent

2004-2005 Activities and Awards

Competitive Chess Tournaments
Candidates Intermat, October 2004, First Place for grade
Thanksgiving Scholastic, First place for Grades 7 - 12
2004 Intermat: International Chess Competition with British Columbia,
      Represented Washington State as a Junior
Washington High School Individual tournament, January 2005, 9th in State for High School
Washington Junior Open 3-27-04, 8th overall
2005 Action Championship, 5th overall
2005 Washington Premier- Washington Open, 1st place tie overall, Premier division (U2000)

Chess Instructor
Manhattan Homeschool Center Chess Class
Issaquah Chinese School Chess Class
Bryant Elementary School Chess Class
Stella Schola Middle School Chess Class
West Seattle Christian School Chess Class
Sammamish Christian Academy
Lowell Elementary School
Sammamish Chess Camps Tactics Coach
Bryant Chess Camps, Tactics Coach
Chess Tutor: private chess tutor for individual students

Soccer
West Highline Soccer Club 2004

Swimming
Swimming: Normandy Park Sharks Swim Team 2005, boys 18 and under
Qualified for Boys Prelims, Southern Division 2005
1st place 200 yard Freestyle Relay team B 6/30/2005
2nd place 200 Yard Medley Relay team B 6/15/2005
2nd place 200 yard Freestyle Relay team A 6/15/2005
2nd place 200 yard Medley Relay team A 6/15/2005
2nd place 200-yard Free Relay 1/6/23/2005
3rd place 50 Yard Freestyle 7/12/2005, time 26.06
3rd place 50 Yard Butterfly 7/12/2005, time 29.84
3rd place 50 Yard Backstroke 6/15/2005, time 32.58
Swimming: Normandy Park Sharks Swim Team 2004, boys 18 and under
1st place 100 yard Freestyle 6/24/2004, time 1:00:57
1st place Medley Relay 6/29/2004

Church Activity
Youth Mission team member: Midway Community Covenant Church mission trip to Harambee,
California, July 3-13, 2004
Youth Worship: Midway Community Covenant Church, keyboard and piano
Active Youth Group Member, Midway Community Covenant Church
Pastoral Search Committee, Midway Community Covenant Church

YMCA Youth and Government
Chairman of Highline Delegation
Lobbyist in Olympia

Piano
National Federation of Music, Junior Festival 2005, rating superior minus
Midway Covenant Church offertory piano music
Christmas Recital, December 3, 2004

Awards
US Chess Federation Scholar Chessplayer Outstanding Achievement Award
      Award published in Chess Life Magazine, June 2005
VFW Voice of Democracy Essay Competition, Post 2886
Holland and Knight 2005 Holocaust Remembrance Project second place winner
Half Price Books *Say Good Night to Illiteracy* Bedtime Story Contest, winner for "The Letter Y"
poem. Publication date, November 2005
Sons of the American Revolution Bronze Good Citizenship Award
Sons of the American Revolution, George and Stella M. Knight Essay Contest, Chapter Level
Winner

Work Samples

The Common Monster
The American fascination with the Holocaust threatens to relegate this extraordinary historical occurrence into a mere cultural cliché. The torrent of analytical works published on the Holocaust in the last sixty years would seem to render original interpretations of this event increasingly rare. But the Holocaust retains its vital relevance to modern society because of its multi-faceted complexity. In particular, it forms an ideal platform for an analysis of human nature. Acknowledging humanity's susceptibility to evil behavior remains an essential component to an accurate conception of our world. Only when the next generation accepts this fundamental truth can we hope to prevent similar atrocities in our era.

Human Nature
An appreciation of the Holocaust should yield much more than simply a rejection of fascism. The Holocaust remains controversial because it offers an unvarnished glimpse of true human nature. How could millions of Germans tolerate and condone such barbarism? What causes such evil to develop in the first place? Paradoxically, the Holocaust maintains its significance because it was *not* unique. History is littered with comparable examples of heartless slaughter. This well-documented reality leads to the unsettling conclusion that something is not quite right with the human race. Moral responsibility cannot be solely pinned to one's environment. Humans must ultimately hold themselves accountable for the evil that festers in this world.

This moral principle is so disconcerting that there have been repeated attempts to undermine its validity. This can be witnessed in the popular notion that Nazi guards were nothing more than sadistic monsters. Holocaust survivors themselves rebut this assumption. As Auschwitz survivor Benedikt Kautsky points out, "Nothing could be more mistaken than to see the SS as a sadistic horde driven to abuse and torture…by instinct, passion, or some thirst for pleasure. Those who acted in this way were [in the] minority." (Todorov, pg. 122) As Kautsky makes clear, normal human beings, not perverted monsters, perpetuated the atrocities of the concentration camps. Observations such as these validate Primo Levi's assertion that: "Monsters exist, but they are too few in number to be truly dangerous. More dangerous [is] the common man." (Todorov, pg. 123)

The philosophy of Humanism offers a more sophisticated, and yet ultimately flawed explanation of the Holocaust. Adhering to their faith in man's inherent goodness, humanists blame the environment and culture for the sins of the individual. This reluctance to assign moral responsibility can be witnessed in the denunciation of the Treaty of Versailles. Humanists, averse to consigning blame, like to "explain" Nazism because of the sense of desperation that this treaty inspired. Richard J. Maybury suggests that the Treaty of Versailles was so harsh that, "[Germany was] ready to fly into the arms of anyone who would promise to make them strong and prosperous again." (Maybury, pg. 190) This sort of reasoning seems, at some level, to excuse Germany from responsibility for the perpetuation of the Holocaust. Mr. Maybury ignores the fact that external factors can never fully override human free will. World War Two was not inevitable after the signing of the Treaty of Versailles. A combination of human failings, on both sides, was responsible for the rise of Nazism and all that followed.

The Holocaust did not open a new chapter in human history. It merely represents a particularly brutal demonstration of human depravity. Despite idealistic arguments that insist upon our inherent goodness, the Holocaust demands a very different explanation. Without minimizing man's potential for good deeds, history demands that we acknowledge the individual's vulnerability to evil. This lesson simply must be learned by each new generation. Armed with this rudimentary understanding of human nature, we can begin to apply it in modern society.

Prevention of the Holocaust

A very natural question arises out of our examination of the Holocaust: "How can we hope to prevent a recurrence of such evil?" Lamentably, on the individual level, we cannot. Human nature ensures that prejudice, discrimination, and violence will always exist in society. However, the Holocaust was maintained on a societal, not an individual, level. It is our duty to prevent a repetition of the conditions that led to the universal abandonment of justice and social harmony. If we glean lessons from our failure, we can hope to avert its recurrence. Our government must retain its system of checks and balances, uphold fundamental human rights, and advocate tolerance. Only with a recommitment to these principles can America hope to suppress humanity's natural inclination toward evil.

Our forefathers recognized the dangers of unrestrained government. James Madison presented democracy this way: "If angels were to govern men... controls on government would [not] be necessary. In framing a government, which is to be administered by men over men, the great difficulty lies in this: You must ... oblige [the government] to control itself." (Noebel, pg. 624) Because, as Madison argues, men are not angels, controls must be placed on elected officials to avoid any imprudent concentration of power. Should these controls not be firmly established, it is only a matter of time before another Hitler assumes and abuses authority. It is the next generation's responsibility to understand and maintain the great American commitment to checks and balances.

But we must do far more than merely limiting the government's ability to persecute the minority. We must utterly reject the mindset that led to this tragedy. The Holocaust was characterized by an absolute denial of human dignity. Despite its realistic appraisal of human nature, our democracy also stipulates fundamental human rights, among which are "life, liberty, and the pursuit of happiness." As these rights are inalienable, they may never be altered. Nor are these protections limited by race or ethnic background – they are universal, regardless of whether a government acknowledges them. America must stand as a beacon of liberty and protection, not allowing totalitarianism philosophy to soil her shores.

America has sustained its great interest in the Holocaust because it has begun to comprehend its fearful and terrible lesson about humanity. This event stands as the supreme example of man's natural impulse towards evil. Yet there is hope. State-sponsored terrorism, as witnessed in the German concentration camps, only exists with the consent of the populace. America must reestablish the two bedrock constitutional principles: checks and balances, and inalienable rights. It is the duty of my generation to preserve, protect and defend these pillars of civilization.

Works Cited

Bauer, Yehuda. <u>Rethinking the Holocaust</u>. New Haven, CN: Yale University Press, 2001

Langer, Lawrence L. <u>Admitting the Holocaust</u>. New York, NY: Oxford University Press, 1995

Maybury, Richard J. <u>World War One</u>. Placerville, CA: Bluestocking Press, 2002

Noebel, David A. <u>Understanding the Times</u>. Manitou Springs, CO: Harvest House Publishers, 1991

Todorov, Tzvetan. <u>Facing the Extreme</u>. New York, NY: Henry Holt and Company, Inc., 1996

. . . .

Appendix   189

The Letter Y

Lowly and unwanted Y,
Living in the town of Letter.
With 25 other residents,
Each one of them his better.

Lonely and unwanted Y,
Harassed and teased unto the end.
Because he's only a part-time vowel,
No one wants to be his friend.

Nameless and unwanted Y,
Simply a quadratic function.
While X is presented with flourish,
Y has no introduction.

Annoyed and unwanted Y,
Has chosen a new profession.
For now he moonlights overtime,
As a Frequently Asked Question.

Joyful and contented Y,
Surrounded by the very young.
If you listen you will hear his voice,
On every small child's tongue.

A Virginian's Reflection

Fully two hundred years after his death, debate continues to swirl around Thomas Jefferson's views on slavery and race. Some claim that he was an enlightened reformer, vehemently opposed to slavery. Others claim that he was a run-of-the-mill 18th century racist who ardently believed that whites were born superior to blacks. Surprisingly, they are both correct. In fact, this extraordinary paradox helps us understand not only Thomas Jefferson's, but America's dilemma during and after the Revolutionary War.

To many, Thomas Jefferson's assessment of slavery seems witheringly accurate and years ahead of his contemporaries. He openly acknowledged many inherent evils in the institution. "The [relations] between master and slave," he lamented, "is a perpetual exercise of the most boisterous passions, the most unremitting despotism on the one hand, and degrading submissions on the other[1]." Jefferson condemned slaveholders as "despots[2]" for trampling on their slaves' God-given liberty. He recognized the terrible wrongs suffered by the blacks, and expressed his belief that God would avenge them. In one passage, Jefferson pleads with masters to not expose their children to "the intemperance of passion towards his slave[3]." His heartfelt plea to preserve childhood innocence hints at how deeply he despised slavery.

From his devastating critique of slavery, one might expect Jefferson to be an early abolitionist. Nothing could be further from the truth! To his death, Thomas Jefferson remained a wealthy aristocrat, with over a hundred slaves at his command. Despite personal convictions, he could never bring himself to emancipate even a single one of his slaves. He depended on slave labor to support his fragile financial condition. This dependency drove Jefferson to ignore his personal loathing of slavery. His tortured hypocrisy made it extremely difficult for Jefferson to objectively examine the issue of race. "...It is impossible to be temperate and to pursue this subject through the various considerations of policy, of morals, of history[4]...."

Like so many of his contemporaries, Thomas Jefferson was an adamant racist. It is indeed remarkable that the one who coined "all men are created equal" did not fully believe in the ideal he professed. Yet from his copious writings on the subject, Jefferson made it very clear that he believed the Negro to be inferior physically, mentally and emotionally. He claimed that the blacks suffered from a "want of forethought," were less steady under danger, and that their love was lustful and animal-like (compared to white affections, which he deemed "tender and delicate[5].") He unequivocally classified their race as subhuman, and ideally suited for servitude. "In general," he observed, "their existence appears to participate more of sensation than reflection[6]." Jefferson was, tragically, a product of his time. This type of blatant, revolting racism was commonplace in the Revolutionary War era.

Some revisionists have tried to argue that Jefferson was only saying black men were inferior due to their unfortunate environment. Yet Jefferson goes out of his way to

---

[1] Peterson, <u>Political Writings of Thomas Jefferson</u>, pg. 60
[2] <u>Ibid.</u>
[3] <u>Ibid.</u>

[4] Jefferson, <u>Thomas Jefferson on Slavery</u>, pg. 171
[5] Jefferson, <u>Notes on the State of Virginia</u>, pg. 51
[6] <u>Ibid.</u>

refute this argument. In a lengthy section of his *Notes on the State of Virginia*, devoted to demonstrating the black man's natural inferiority, he compared the current system to that of the Romans. "The condition of their [Roman] slaves was much more deplorable than that of the blacks on the continent in America.... Yet notwithstanding these and other discouraging circumstances among the Romans, their slaves were often their rarer artists. They excelled too in science..." Why? Because "they were a race of whites[7]."

Thomas Jefferson and his contemporaries faced an apparently insurmountable dilemma. While their consciences dictated that slavery was morally reprehensible, they were unwilling to do anything about it due to a combination of practical and racial reasons. They consoled themselves with the ungrounded fantasy that slavery would eventually die out. From this a new problem arose: what to eventually do with all the free, unemployed, supposedly lazy blacks?

What then, was Thomas Jefferson's long-term vision for the "Negro problem?" His proposed solution grew to be a very popular idea in the 18th century – colonization. Believing that slavery would ultimately decline, he supported the transport of free blacks back to Africa. But why take such extraordinary measures to remove the black's from America? Once again Jefferson is very clear about his reasoning: "Why not retain and incorporate the blacks into the state...? Deep rooted prejudices entertained by the whites; ten thousand recollections, by the blacks, of the injuries they have sustained; new provocations; the real distinctions which nature has made...will divide us into parties, and produce convulsions, which will probably never end but in the extermination of the one or the other race[8]." In short, Jefferson feared a race war and believed that blacks and whites could never live together peacefully.

Just as the Declaration of Independence expound on the American dilemma in the 18th century, Thomas Jefferson's writings on slavery presage the great American dilemma of the 19th century. Hundreds of thousands of young soldiers gave their lives in a desperate struggle to resolve the issue of race. We should be thankful that Jefferson turned out to be wrong about a race war. Despite deep prejudices and in some cases new provocations, our nation has proven that it is possible for blacks and whites to peacefully live side by side. Though it is easy to condemn Jefferson on the basis of historical hindsight, we must appreciate how accurately Jefferson reflected the inner struggles of his countrymen. As he demonstrated in the Declaration of Independence and his writings on slavery, this one Virginian gentleman has captured the essence of the 18th century American.

Bibliography

Jefferson, Thomas. <u>Notes on the State of Virginia</u>. Chapel Hill: Omohundro Institute, 1995

---

[7] <u>Ibid.</u>, p. 56

[8] <u>Ibid.</u>, p. 49

Jefferson, Thomas. <u>Thomas Jefferson on Slavery</u>. Gronigen, Netherlands: University of Gronigen, Department of Alfa-Information, 2001

Bernstein, R.B. <u>Thomas Jefferson</u>. New York: Oxford University Press, 2003

Edited by Peterson, Merrill D. <u>The Political Writings of Thomas Jefferson.</u> Annapolis Junction, MD: GraphTec, 1993

Staloff, Darren M. <u>Thomas Jefferson.</u> Springfield, VA: Teaching Co., 1999

Hakim, Joy. <u>The New Nation.</u> New York NY: Oxford University Press, 1993

The Jungle

"We didn't know we were poor," my grandmother reflected as she relived her childhood memories of the Great Depression. I almost laughed. *Not know they were poor?* This statement sounded absurd to my modern ears. I suspect that if I were put in her position, I would have griped about the poverty, hunger, and long food lines. It dawned on me how much America had changed in her lifetime. It is no longer a lack of money that presents a challenge to today's youth. It is America's prosperity and obsession with material possessions that most threatens the new generation.

America emerged from the 20th century as history's most prosperous nation. Unfortunately, somewhere along the way we have fallen prey to the demonic influence of materialism. Our children are growing up in a culture where selfishness and irresponsibility are often celebrated. Indeed, many have eagerly embraced the principle of entitlement; believing they *deserve* whatever strikes their fancy. Their concept of ideal government has evolved to serve this egotistical worldview. Far from Thomas Paine's "necessary evil," the federal government is now viewed as a paternalistic figure that lovingly supplies all our wants. This sense of entitlement is also demonstrated in our growing dependence on credit cards. Our young men and women have become addicted to credit because it represents the American Nirvana: money without consequences.

The vortex of debt is disturbingly easy to fall into. Many of today's youth look at life through a magnifying glass when they should be using binoculars. Their short-term focus blinds them to the long-term consequences of fiscal irresponsibility. Once in debt, it is very difficult to recover. Debtors watch as their creditors mercilessly extract every dime owed. And high interest rates ensure that the young consumer will continue in this wretched condition for a long time.

Americans living through World War Two – dubbed "The Greatest Generation" by Tom Brokaw – are in some ways similar to the new generation. They, too, were unexpectedly assailed in a surprise attack that launched a generational war. The difference between our two generations is that the America of the 1940's was slowly recovering from a severe Depression, while we are "recovering" from the prosperity of the 1980's and 90's. From these different environments evolved radically different ways of looking at money. The Great Depression taught America about the importance, value, and consequences of monetary decisions. Debt and fiscal irresponsibility were not a cultural norm; they were practically unthinkable. The Greatest Generation looked at their government and vividly understood the consequences of a short-term financial focus.

The story of the Greatest Generation offers hope to our imperiled generation. We must look past our egotism and examine consequences. There is no such thing as instant credit and free money. What we truly own, we must earn from the fruits of our labor. Fiscal irresponsibility and naïveté, like dangerous beasts, are silently waiting for us to let down our guard. Only by following the path laid out for us by those who came before, can we escape this jungle unharmed.

Appendix 3-a:
Courses Completed Outside the Home

Course Description
Music: Chorus I-II (Course from a public high school)

During the 2006-2007 school year, the student attended Seattle High School for music instruction. She completed Chorus I-II with instructor Mrs. Block, Director of City High School Choirs. She earned 0.5 credits per semester, earning a grade of "A" from the instructor during every grading quarter. The student was a member of the "City Chorus." The chorus is a non-auditioned choir for girls only. The choir grade included a solo/ensemble performance, and the student performed a duet. At the end of the year, she was granted 1.0 credit in Chorus I-II.

The school district website contains the following details of this course. All students are expected to work on improving their vocal and music reading skills and to grow in their understanding of basic music theory and history. In the process of developing these skills and knowledge, the group will participate in a variety of learning activating that include performing, listening, reading, writing, and participating in class discussions. The grading scale indicated that 93-100% would earn a letter grade of "A." The school provides an "employability" grade, which is a measurement of the student's citizenship, dependability, work ethic and commitment. The student received an employability grade of A during each semester.

Grading is based on the following assumptions:
1. Singing with a proper tone, reading music, and knowledge of music theory are skills that can be taught, learned, and evaluated.
2. As in any subject area, each individual brings to the choral experience knowledge and skills based on ability, previous learning, and effort.
3. It is reasonable then that a student's grade reflect the acquisition of such knowledge and skills the instructor feels is appropriate for each level.
4. It is understood that some students will be able to achieve a higher level more easily than others.
5. Being a member of choir is being a member of a team, and as such students are obligated to their team members to exhibit behaviors and attitudes that contribute to the success of the choir as a whole.

Grading Procedures:
1. Five points a day for attendance, being prepared, and being on task
2. Attendance at all scheduled performances and contests is required, worth 20 points each.
3. Music assignments will be given for theory, vocabulary, sight singing, small group singing and listening assignments, with various point weights.
4. Choice points may be earned outside of class time for vocal practice, 1 point per hour, attendance at concerts 5 points each, listening to CDs with listening form 5 points, volunteering for concert and music events, with points based on time spent.

Course Grade
Chorus I-II– Completed 06/07

Semester 1		Semester 2	
--------------------1/2 grade--------------------		-----------------------1/2 grade----------------------	
Quarter 1	A	Quarter 1	A
Quarter 2	A	Quarter 2	A
Employability	A	Employability	A
Semester 1 Grade A		**Semester 2 Grade A**	
----------------------- **Final grade for Chorus I-II = A** ----------------------			
93-100% A, 90-92.9 A-, 88-89.9 B+, 82-87.9 B, 80-81.9 B-, 78-79.9 C+, 72-77.9 C, 70-71.9 C-, 68-69.9 D+, 60-67.9 D, 0-59.9 F			

Course Description
Social Studies: World Geography (Includes Co-Op experiences)

This course will have two components. First, the student will participate in the City Home Education Co-op, Inc course of World Geography, with instructor Mrs. Adkins. Secondly, the student will complete a homeschool course utilizing the book "Mapping the World by Heart" by David J. Smith. In the co-op class, the student will participate in weekly hands-on activities designed to encourage understanding of other cultures around the world. Students will study the location, movement, culture, environment, history, and regional economy of worldwide cultures. At home, the student will utilize the book, worksheets, and activities to locate and identify places, learn geographical knowledge about map directions and symbols, understand topographical maps and map projections, and study earth's rotation and seasons. The student will learn to draw a map of the entire world in free hand, including latitude and longitude markings without copying. This course will require a minimum of 5 hours per week for 32 weeks.

Primary Text:
Mapping the World by Heart by David J. Smith

Supplemental Texts:
Museum Masterpieces: The Louvre by Richard Brettell, The Teaching Company. This college level lecture series has 12 lectures, approximately 30 minutes each.
Rick Steves' Italy 2007 DVD by Rick Steves
Rick Steves' Europe DVD: France and Benelux DVD by Rick Steves
Red Sails to Capri by Ann Weil

Field Trips:
Two field trips to Europe are included in this study of World Geography. The student will study the geography, geology, history, society, and economics of each region visited. The student will prepare for and experience one trip to Italy. The student will prepare for and experience a second field trip to Europe, spending two weeks in France. While in Paris the student will visit The Louvre and include the history of art in the study of World geography.

Course Grade
World Geography – Completed 06/07

Cooperative Class		Daily Work		Mapping the World	
---------1/3 grade---------		----------1/3 grade-----------		--------1/3 grade--------	
Semester 1	100%	Semester 1	100%	Semester 1	100%
Semester 2	100%	Semester 2	100%	Semester 2	100%
		Field Trip Preparation	100%	Field trips	100%
Final Grade	100%	Final Grade	100%	Final Grade	100%
-------------- Final grade for World Geography = 100% = A ---------------					
A =90-100% =4.0	B=80-89% = 3.0	C=70-79% = 2.0	D = 60-69% = 1.0		

Course Description
Math: Algebra 1 (Course taken with a private tutor)

This complete mathematics course will be provided by private tutor and certified teacher Mr. Jeff Johnson. This course is the study of algebra with real-world problems and applications. Critical thinking is developed by a strong emphasis on graphing and creative problem solving. Applications problems challenge students to use many mathematical concepts to solve one problem. The student will complete each chapter as directed by the tutor. Each chapter will involve discussion, demonstration, two quizzes, and one or more tests to assess student learning.

- Uses of variables
- Multiplication in algebra
- Addition in algebra
- Subtraction in algebra
- Linear sentences
- Division in algebra
- Slopes and lines
- Exponents and powers
- Quadratic equations and square roots
- Polynomials
- Linear systems
- Factoring
- Functions

Tests in student handwriting are available on request.

Primary Text: <u>University of Chicago School Mathematics Project Algebra: Integrated Mathematics</u> by Prentice Hall. 1999.

Course Grade
Algebra 1 – Completed 06/07

Daily Work		Work with Tutor		Tests	
------------1/3 grade----------		------------1/3 grade----------		--------1/3 grade--------	
Chapter 1	100%	Chapter 1	100%	Chapter test	96%
Chapter 2	100%	Chapter 2	100%	Chapter test	89%
				Cumulative test	90%
Chapter 3	100%	Chapter 3	100%	Chapter test	88%
				Cumulative test	90%
Chapter 4	100%	Chapter 4	100%	Chapter test	90%
				Cumulative test	90%
Chapter 5	100%	Chapter 5	100%	Chapter test	88%
				Cumulative test	80%
Chapter 6	100%	Chapter 6	100%	Chapter test	86%
				Cumulative test	90%
Chapter 7	100%	Chapter 7	100%	Chapter test	89%
Chapter 8	100%	Chapter 8	100%	Chapter test	88%
Chapter 9	100%	Chapter 9	100%	Chapter test	____
Chapter 10	100%	Chapter 10	100%	Chapter test	____
Chapter 11	100%	Chapter 11	100%	Chapter test	____
Chapter 12	100%	Chapter 12	100%	Chapter test	____
Chapter 13	100%	Chapter 13	100%	Chapter test	____
Chapter 14	100%	Chapter 14	100%	Chapter test	____
Chapter 15	100%	Chapter 15	100%	Chapter test	____
Chapter 16	100%	Chapter 16	100%	Chapter test	____
Daily Work Grade 100%		**Tutor Lesson 100%**		**Tests Grade**	**%**

-------------------- **Final grade for Algebra 1 = 100% = A** --------------------

A =90-100% =4.0	B=80-89% = 3.0	C=70-79% = 2.0	D = 60-69% = 1.0

Appendix 4: Ann's Example

Ann has been homeschooling independently for the last 19 years. She has graduated three of her 7 children already. Her three graduates have been admitted to colleges of their choice - and her family has been awarded over $300,000 in scholarships thus far. Her two oldest have graduated with Highest Honors, Suma Cum Laud, from the University.

Ann is an international minister, motivational speaker and the author of five books. She speaks at homeschool conventions, and helps her friends homeschool high school. You can contact Ann Dunagan at Harvest Ministry, Harvestministry. org, and read her book, "The Mission-Minded Family."

Ann created her homeschool records with the title "The Grand Plan." She made the document in a Pagemaker file, but you can use any program you have at home. She provided a transcript on one page. Her Grand Plan provided the details of her homeschool, including course descriptions.

HARVEST ACRES

SCHOOL ADDRESS • CITY, STATE • ZIP
PHONE & FAX • Email

(A PRIVATE HOME SCHOOL – SAT SCHOOL CODE # 003899)

LAST NAME, FIRST NAME, MIDDLE INITIAL
DATE OF BIRTH:
SOCIAL SECURITY NUMBER: #

STANDARDIZED TEST SCORES:
CAT TEST DATE - MAY 2005 TOP 97% NATIONAL PERCENTILE
SAT TEST DATES - OCT 2004 VERBAL 540 MATH 660 TOTAL SAT: 1200

COURSE NUMBER		COURSE TITLE	GRADE EARNED	COURSE CREDIT	QUALITY POINTS
		CREDIT FOR THIS HIGH SCHOOL WAS GIVEN FOR THE FOLLOWING HIGH SCHOOL COURSES COMPLETED IN EARLIER YEARS:			
SS	101	HS WORLD GEOGRAPHY (BJU)	A	1.0	4.0
SS	110	INTL FIELD STUDY: EUROPE & AFRICA	A	1.0	4.0
SCI	101	WORLD HISTORY (BJU)	A	1.0	4.0
MAT	101	SCIENCE - BIOLOGY W/DISSECTION LAB - (BJU)	A	1.0	4.0
OCC	101	HS ALGEBRA I (SAXON)	A	0.5	2.0
		HOME BUILDING & CONSTRUCTION		ERN	GPTS	GPA
		HS CUMULATIVE		4.5	18.0	4.0
			ATT 4.5		
		FRESHMAN YEAR 2002-2003			
ELE	101	BIBLE: CHRISTIAN DISCIPLESHIP & MISSIONS	A	0.5	2.0
ENG	101	ENGLISH: CLASSICAL LITERATURE I	A	1.0	4.0
		VOCAB, GRAMMAR & COMPOSITION I			
COM	101	SPEECH & LEADERSHIP SKILLS I	A	0.5	2.0
MAT	201	MATH: GEOMETRY (CHALKDUST-VIDEO)	A	1.0	4.0
SS	201	UNITED STATES HISTORY (BJU)	A	1.0	4.0
SCI	201	SCIENCE - ANATOMY/HEALTH & LAB (BJU)	A	1.0	4.0
LAN	101	LANGUAGE: SPANISH I (POWER GLIDE)	A	1.0	4.0
ARTS	101	MUSIC: GUITAR & PIANO STUDY	A	0.25	1.0
OCC	110	CRITICAL THINKING, LOGIC & CHESS	A	0.25	1.0
OCC	120	MONEY MANAGEMENT & ECONOMICS	A	0.25	1.0
PE	101	PE - SOCCER, RUNNING, SWIMMING, WEIGHTS	A	0.25	1.0
				ERN	GPTS	GPA
		HS CUMULATIVE		11.5	46.0	4.0
			ATT 11.5		
		SOPHOMORE YEAR 2003-2004			
ELE	201	BIBLE: CHRISTIAN DISCIPLESHIP & MISSIONS	A	0.5	2.0
ELE	210	INTERNATIONAL STUDY: SINGAPORE/MALAYSIA	A	0.5	2.0
ENG	201	ENGLISH: CLASSICAL LIT II, SHAKESPEARE	A	1.0	4.0
		VOCAB, GRAMMAR & COMPOSITION II			
COM	201	SPEECH & LEADERSHIP (INCLUDING VFWS	A+	1.0	4.0
		VOICE OF DEMOCRACY STATE COMPETITION)			
MAT	301	MATH: ALGEBRA II/SAT PREP MATH	A	1.0	4.0
LAN	201	LANGUAGE: SPANISH II (POWER GLIDE)	P	1.0	4.0
ARTS	201	FINE ARTS & CLASSICAL COMPOSERS	A	0.25	1.0
ARTS	210	MUSIC: GUITAR/PIANO STUDY /WORSHIP TEAM)	A	0.25	1.0
PE	201	PE - SOCCER, RUNNING, SWIMMING, WEIGHTS	A	0.25	1.0
OCC	201	OFFICE TYPING/COMPUTER SKILLS	A	0.25	1.0
ELE	210	DRIVERS EDUCATION	A		
				ERN	GPTS	GPA
		HS CUMULATIVE		17.5	70.0	4.0
			ATT 17.5		

COURSE NUMBER		COURSE TITLE	GRADE EARNED	COURSE CREDIT	QUALITY POINTS
		JUNIOR YEAR 2004-2005			
ELE	301	BIBLE/CHRISTIAN DISCIPLESHIP & MISSIONS	A	0.5	2.0
ENG	301	VOCAB, GRAMMAR & COMPOSITION III	A	1.0	4.0
ENG	310	FRESHMAN COLLEGE COMP (CLEP)	A	1.0	4.0
COM	310	ORAL COMMUNICATIONS (COLLEGE)	A	1.0	4.0
		AMERICAN LEGION ORATORICAL COMPETITION	A+	1.0	4.0
		(STATE WINNER/NATIONAL PARTICIPANT)			
SS	401	US GOVT & CONSTITUTION STUDY	A	1.0	4.0
SCI	301	OCEANOGRAPHY WITH LAB (COLLEGE)	A	1.0	4.0
SCI	310	GEOLOGY WITH LAB (COLLEGE)	A	1.0	4.0
MAT	401	MATH: COLLEGE ALGEBRA (CLEP EXAM)	A	1.0	4.0
LAN	301	LANGUAGE: CONVERSATIONAL SPANISH	A	1.0	4.0
		HISPANIC MENS SOCCER LEAGUE			
ELE	310	DOMINICAN REPUBLIC/COSTA RICA MISSIONS	P	0.25	1.0
OCC	301	HOME CONSTRUCTION: LIFE SKILLS	A	0.25	1.0
ARTS	301	MUSIC - GUITAR & WORSHIP TEAM	A	0.25	1.0
PE	301	PE - SOCCER, X/C/RUNNING, TENNIS, WEIGHTS	A	0.25	1.0
				ERN	GPTS	GPA
		HS CUMULATIVE		29.0	116.0	4.0
			ATT 29.0		
		SENIOR YEAR 2005-2006			
ELE	401	BIBLE/CHRISTIAN DISCIPLESHIP & MISSIONS	A	0.5	2.0
COM	401	SPEECH & LEADERSHIP (VFW COMPETITION)	A+	1.0	4.0
SCI	401	METEOROLOGY WITH LAB (COLLEGE)	A	1.0	4.0
SS	510	ACCOUNTING I & II (COLLEGE)	A	1.0	4.0
ENG	401	SOCIOLOGY/WORLDVIEW (CLEP EXAM)	A	1.0	4.0
OCC	403	ENGLISH COMPOSITION (COLLEGE)	P	1.0	4.0
		ACCOUNTING III (COLLEGE)	A	2.0	8.0
SS	501	US HISTORY & US GOVT (2 CLEP EXAMS)	P	1.0	1.0
ARTS	401	MUSIC: GUITAR & WORSHIP TEAM	A	0.25	1.0
PE	401	PE - SOCCER, X/C/RUNNING, TENNIS, WEIGHTS	A	0.25	1.0
				ERN	GPTS	GPA
		HS CUMULATIVE		38.0	150.0	4.0

TOTAL HIGH SCHOOL CREDITS: 38.0

ENGLISH (4.0)   SCIENCE (5.0)
SOCIAL STUDIES (5.5)   MATH (4.0)
OCCUPATIONAL (10.0) 4.5   PHYSICAL ED (PE) 1.3
FINE ARTS (1.0)   FOREIGN LANG (3.0) 3
COMMUNICATIONS 4.5   ELECTIVE (3.5)

(***NOTE: 34 college semester credits were completed in simultaneous enrollment)

FULL NAME
HOME ADDRESS
CITY, STATE, ZIP, USA

GRADUATION DATE: JUNE, 2006
OFFICIAL TRANSCRIPT ISSUED: JULY 17, 2006

SIGNATURE

High School Course List

(Harvest Acres High School - City, State, USA)

Approved Graduation Plan for "Student Name"

THE GRAND PLAN

English Requirements:	Video?	Primary Text:	Credit:
*English Composition & Grammar	yes - 2	*Various writing materials*	1
*Shakespeare Study	yes - 3	S. D. Shakespeare Videos 1	
		Shakespeare Books	
*Classical Literature		Invitation to the Classics	1
		Various Classic Books	
*Public Speaking & Intro. to Debate		VFW Audio Competition 1	
		(Teen Pact Intro. to Debate & Speech)	
*C.L.A.S.S. Destiny: Christian Leadership And Speaking Skills		*CLASS Destiny Materials*	
*Oral Communications		*(at C.G. Community College)*	
*English Vocabulary		WordSmart/BJU Vocab	1
		Latin & Greek Root Study	
*SAT Verbal Review	yes - 1	SAT Workbook/Tests	

Foreign Language:		Primary Text?	Credit:
*SPANISH I		PowerGlide Spanish	1
*SPANISH II		PowerGlide Spanish	1
(Practical Spanish & Foreign Study)			

Math Requirements:	Video?	Primary Text:	Credit:
*Algebra I		SAXON ALGEBRA I	1
*Geometry	yes - 12	CHALKDUST Course	1
*College Algebra & Trig.	yes - 4	S.D. College Algebra &	
*SAT Math Review	yes - 1	S.D. Videos & Test forms	
		SAT Math Workbook/Tests	

Science:	Video?	Primary Text:	Credit:
*Health/Nutrition		BJU Health	1
*Biology & Biology Lab		ABEKA Biology Text/Tests 1	
	yes - 1	BJU Disection Lab Course	
*Creation/Evolutions Study		*Answers in Genesis* Materials	
*Science with LABS (Biology & Chemistry)		*(at C.G. Community College)*	3

Social Studies Requirements:	Video?	Primary Text?	Credit:
*Geography		BJU Text/Tests	1
*World History		BJU Text/Tests	2
*US History I & II (& CLEP exams)		BJU Text/Tests	2
*US Goverment & Economics	(yes - 2)	S.D. Videos & Texts	1
*Oregon State History & Government		US Constitution Study	
*Christian Worldview & Sociology		Understanding THE TIMES 1	
		Evidence/Answers/Religions	

Social Studies Travel Study:		Primary Text?	Credit:
*Travel Study - (Varies each year)			

(The Grand Plan - page 2)

Bible Requirements:	Video?	Primary Text:	Credit:
*Bible & Christian Discipleship		The Holy Bible	1
		Discipleship Manuals	
*World Missions Emphasis		Missions Books/Biographies	

Fine Arts Requirements:		Primary Text?	Credit:
*PIANO and GUITAR/music theory		Private Lessons	1
*Fine Arts Study		Famous Artists & Composers	
		Drama & Mime Class	

Home & Occupational Education:	Video?	Primary Text?	Credit:
* Building/Construction/Drafting		A Blueprint for Geometry	1
* Home Economics/Life Skills		Life Skills/Practical Instruction	
* Money Management & Economics		Larry Burkett Materials	
* Critical Thinking/Logic/Chess Training		Critical Thinking	
• Driver's Education	yes - 12	Driver's Ed in a Box	

P.E. Requirements:		Primary Text:	Credit:
*P.E. (Soccer, Swimming & Weight Training, Cross Country)			1

Total High School Credits

English:	5
Foreign Langauge:	2
Math:	3
Science/Health:	3
Social Studies:	8
Occupational:	1
P.E.:	1
Bible:	1
Fine Arts:	1
TOTAL CREDITS:	25

*A Christ Centered Academy
Emphasizing Excellence in Education
for Fulfilling God's Destiny*

A Private Home School

Official Transcripts & Records Compiled for
Student Name

HARVEST ACRES
H I G H   S C H O O L

A Private Home School • Address • City, State, Zip USA • Phone & Fax # • Email

OUR SCHOOL PROFILE:

HARVEST ACRES HIGH SCHOOL (& ACADEMY) is a private home school, with "student enrollment" which has consisted of the seven children in the FAMILY NAME (currently ages 6, 9, 11, 14, 16, 18 and 20). We have chosen this education to ensure academic excellence in our children's education; to allow for family-schedule-flexibility (which has enabled us to provide a broad range of world experiences); to encourage leadership participation in local and international community service activities; as well as for reasons of personal and religious conviction.

The educational curriculum of **HARVEST ACRES HIGH SCHOOL** is carefully hand-selected for each student, to ensure admission eligibility at the specific college or university of each student's choice, to meet specific career-preparation goals for each student, and to encourage the unique development of each student's unique gifts and talents. Our philosophy of education includes a combination of traditional textbooks, classical education, on-line computer courses, CD, DVD and video courses, cooperative homeschool classes and simultaneous high school/college course enrollment through the local community college "NAME" in "City, State." For "student" FAMILY NAME these joint-enrollment courses are scheduled to include: Writing 122, Oral Communications 101 and selected Art & Photography classes in preparation for admission to the Graphic Arts & World Missions Department of UNIVERSITY NAME, CITY, STATE. All high school grades and credits have been carefully calculated on a 4.0 GPA scale utilizing test scores, homework assignments, participation and consistent effort in leadership and self-motivation.

Along with these joint-enrollment college classes, our "Honors" courses include private study and preparation for a selection of CLEP (College Level Entrance Preparation) courses. For "student" FAMILY NAME, this has already included successful completion of Freshman College Composition and College Sociology. Currently "student" FAMILY NAME is studying to test-out of college-level Analyzing and Interpreting Literature, American History I, Psychology, Western Civilization I, and Human Growth & Development. This student is scheduled to take these CLEP exams in the Spring of "date."

As teenagers, our children are encouraged to participate in many extracurricular activities, including varsity sports through a local public high school, local and national competitions (which for "student" FAMILY NAME included competing at the state level of "Miss Oregon's Outstanding Teenager" program), church/youth group/missions/community service involvement, and activities related to our nation's government and current international affairs.

And you can't argue with success. Our first students have received high academic scholarships including a Presidential Scholarship to an excellent private university, strong SAT scores, a national "Coca-Cola Scholar" award, national speech awards, and admission into the university honors program at Oxford (in England). "Student" FAMILY NAME's academic program is following in this same proven direction, with unique emphasis toward a chosen field of International Mission Work focussing specifically on the needs of African AIDS Orphans and specific talents of Art, Photography and Graphic Design.

Enclosed is "student" FAMILY NAME's current high school transcript.

"For the harvest truly is plenteous, but the laborers are few." Matthew 9:37

Classical Literature & Shakespeare

Required Texts:
- •William Shakespeare, *The Complete Works*
- •*Lambs Tales from Shakespeare*
- •Shakespeare - Library Materials
  - Videos: *Macbeth, Hamlet, Julius Caesar, Romeo & Juliet*
  - Books: *Shakespeare: Bard of Avalon, Poetry from Shakespeare,*
    Famous Plays of Shakespeare,
- •Standard Deviants Video: *Shakespeare - Style & Language*
- •*Invitation to the Classics*
- •Unabridged Classics
  - Homer, *The Iliad & The Oddesy*
  - Nathaniel Hawthorn, *The Scarlet Letter*
  - C.S. Lewis, *The Screwtape Letters*
  - Charles Dickens, *A Tale of Two Cities*
  - Five other classics referred to in *"Invitation to the Classics"* - your choice

Class Requirements:

__ 1. Read all of *"Lambs Tales from Shakespeare"* and selected Shakespeare library books

__ 2. Orally describe ten Shakespeare plays including all main characters and story lines.

__ 3. Memorize famous Shakespeare selections - total of 50 lines

__ 4. Watch three complete Shakespeare plays. Read also in *"The Complete Works"*

__ 5. Watch the Standard Deviant Shakespeare Video - several times (at least 3x)

__ 6. Highlight famous Shakespeare lines in *"The Complete Works"*

__ 7. Read *"Invitation to the Classics"* -
   __ Be familiar with all mentioned authors and classics

__ 8. Reading/Writing Assignment 1: Read the five unabridged classics referred to,
   __   and five others. Type a complete list of classical books & authors read.

__ 9. Written Assignment 2: Essay - Shakespeare Character Study
   Write a two-page typewritten essay to compare or contrast a specific
   Shakespeare character to a modern-day person. Or use 1-3 specific
       Shakespeare characters to describe an admirable or non-admirable trait.
   Use specific examples.

__10. Written Assignment 3: Essay - Classical Literature Review
   Write a two-page classical literature review geared for high school students:
   Recommend four famous authors and a few of their specific works, then
contrast with two specific authors or works you personally do not enjoy.
   Use specific examples, quotes, and reasons to support your opinion.

__ 11. Attend two live Shakespeare performances:
   __ *Romeo and Juliet* and
       Twelfth Night

FINAL EXAM: CLEP (College Level Entrance Preparation) TEST -
                           "Understanding & Analyzing Literature"

Christianity & Modern Worldviews

Required Texts:
- *The Holy Bible*
- *Understanding THE TIMES*
- *Answers to Tough Questions*
- *So What's the Difference?*
- Creation Magazine
- *Darwin's Black Box*
- *Teaching with God's Heart for the World -*
    Volume II - Section on World Religions

Class Requirements:
- Read and understand the selected texts
- Orally explain the major belief systems of the following worldviews:
    Christianity - including Protestantism & Roman Catholicism
    Judaism
    Islam
    Secular Humanism
    Marxist/Lenonism
    The New Age Movement
    Buddhism
    Hinduism
    Mormonism
    Jehovah's Witnesses
- Be able to answer each of the "Tough Questions"
- Re-read ten complete *Creation* Magazines
- Final Written Assignment - 3 typewritten pages
    What will you do when confronted with other worldviews?
        cults knocking at your door?
        evolutionary views in books or college?
        other political worldviews in the news?
        other religions overseas?
    How do you know Christianity is true, and what makes it different?

NOTE to other homeschoolers:

Our family created course descriptions for most (but not all) of our high school courses; however, these descriptions were used only for our personal educational goals. We did not send course descriptions to the universities our children applied for. Instead, we included a letter of explanation to explain the vision (and strengths) of our homeschool, along with official SAT and CLEP exam scores, and our GRAND PLAN sheet (individually made for each student with only the major text/ curriculum utilized).

We also included a full-color suppliment attachment of approximately 10-15 pages (complete with color photographs, scanned newspaper articles, pictures from various schoalrship competitions (even at local and introductory levels), highlights from extra-curricular activities, a page of brief several-sentence recommendations, an example of a top-notch essay, and highlighting the unique strengths of each student. We saw this as a way to provide strategic "MARKETING" for each student, to highlight each one's individual strengths.

Examples of individual focus themes included:

"U.S. Citizenship & Patriotism,"
"Christian Leadership & Service,"
"International Compassion & Art,"
"All-Around Character & Critical Thinking."

A verse that really encouraged us in our parenting and homeschooling:

"Train up a child in the way he should go [and in keeping with his individual gift of bent], and when he is old he will not depart from it." --Proverbs 22:6 (AMPLIFIED)

On a personal note, our family has chosen to emphasize to our children a deep passion and love for God's Great Commission and reaching people throughout the world with the Good News of Jesus Christ (See Matthew 26:19, Mark 16:15). A missionary to China, Hudson Taylor, often said, "The Great Commission is not an option to consider, but a command to obey." We say, "Missions is not just for missionaries, God's call is for ALL!" Every Christian family, both as corporate units and as individual members -- including every mom, every dad, and every child of every age -- is called to be an ambassador for Christ and a strategic part of advancing God's kingdom in our specific sphere of inclucence. We're all to SHINE the light of Jesus to a dark and needy world.

Appendix 5: Christina's Example

Christina was very successful with the college admission process, and her homeschool records look very different than mine. This really emphasizes the point that there are many "right ways" to make your homeschool records. Christina was willing to share her homeschool records, to provide encouragement to others. Here are her notes and her homeschool records so that you have another option to consider as you prepare your own records for college. I retained her original font and layout exactly as it was submitted to the colleges.

A Note from Christina

We submitted a cover letter which introduced our son and explained our homeschooling philosophy. Not knowing whether the colleges would have had experience with unschoolers before, I thought I should talk about how our son went about becoming an educated individual. I also highlighted a few reasons why I thought our son would be an asset to their college. Our letter turned out to be 2 pages long. I did not include this here because it is very personal.

The actual transcript itself was 14 pages. I have included the first 9 pages here, which was the main part of the transcript. We chose to set up the transcript by subject, rather than by year. My son started doing high-school level work when he was about 10, so it just made more sense for us to do it that way. Also, he didn't do each subject every year, and I didn't necessarily want to draw attention to this fact. I think I would have set it up by subject anyway, because it's easier to see what he covered for each subject, since we don't have the standard curriculum of English 9, 10, 11, 12, etc. We put the subjects that he liked, and therefore did more work in, first. You can order yours however you like, or list courses by year if that's your preference.

Our son did quite a few organized classes, even though we believe in unschooling. You don't need to do any organized classes to use this type of transcript. Just figure out what you want to call each subject that your child studied and talk about the resources used, topics covered, projects or papers done, etc. It would probably be best to break things down into smaller units; for instance, don't just list 4 years of English-type stuff in one paragraph. Under English, come up with some "unit studies" that you can list individually, for example, British Literature, American Literature, Poetry, The Novel, Short Stories, Public Speaking,

Drama, Shakespeare, etc. It doesn't matter if the student didn't do all of the work you lump together in one unit in the same year.

You will notice some repetition between the academic portion of his transcript and his extracurricular activities. It was often hard to decide where to draw the line, when it hasn't been predetermined for you by the school.

I have not attached the lists of books and plays that were read, which I refer to in the transcript. In addition to those 2 lists, at the end we attached a list of books he had read in the last year, for "school" and for pleasure. We chose to do this because this is an area in which he really shines. The list was very impressive, in terms of quantity and variety, and showed the level of his reading comprehension. One of the colleges asked for the list, so we decided to send it to all since reading is one of my son's favorite activities.

I included the paragraph about his passion for Japanese in the transcript because I thought it captured both an important facet of my son's personality and demonstrated how he learned by immersing himself in a subject. You might be able to find a passion of your child's to focus on as well.

There is one other thing I thought I would mention that isn't part of the transcript. Colleges usually have a form for the student's school counselor to fill out. I wrote this recommendation myself since there was no other person who had the knowledge about my son to do this. I don't know if they read this once they realized it was from "mommy," and I'm sure they took it with a grain of salt if they did actually read it. However, I think it's hard to completely forget something you've read, so I was happy to have the opportunity to plant some seeds in their minds; and I assume that the other recommenders and his test scores backed up what I had to say anyway.

I hope the following example of a narrative transcript is helpful and will inspire you to write one if you think this type of transcript would work best for your homeschooler. This is just one of many ways you could organize your transcript. Put the information in a form and order that makes sense for your situation.

Good luck!
Christina

Student Name
Homeschool Transcript & Permanent Record
Date transcript was prepared
Social Security Number

NOTES: As a homeschooler, (Student) chose what, when, and how to learn—this applies to subjects he pursued for his own interests as well as subjects he needed to learn to be a well-rounded individual and to fulfill the requirements commonly considered "college prep." Besides learning on his own, he also took courses at the following places:

Harvard University Extension School, Cambridge, MA—college credit courses—*an official transcript has been ordered which will be mailed to you directly from the University*

Middlesex Community College, Bedford, MA—noncredit, un-graded, <u>high-school level</u> courses that the college developed for us

The Japan Society of Boston, Boston, MA—this non-profit organization dedicated to promoting relations between Japan and MA offers noncredit, un-graded, Japanese language classes for adults

Voyagers, Inc., Acton, MA—a non-profit homeschool cooperative and resource center; participation is based on ability and interest rather than age. Classes meet weekly. Most classes are taught by parents; occasionally, certified teachers and professors have been enlisted as instructors. Classes are typically an hour long, but some are 1-1/2 or 2 hours. No grades or credits are awarded.

The listing of courses below emphasizes the organized courses (Student) has taken at the above-listed institutions, and as such it misses much of the learning (Student) has done. For example, he has made minor studies of several mathematical topics: probability and statistics, inductive and deductive logic, and Gödel's theorem. In the course of his novel writing, he has researched the role of angels and demons in various religions, studied biblical apocrypha, linguistics and the history of sword craft. He has read books on punctuation and grammar, as well as numerous books on the craft and business of writing. He has the ability to learn what he needs to know about any specific topic.

ACADEMICS

ENGLISH:

Literature: (Voyagers) For 6 semesters, (Student) participated in a high-school level literature discussion group. He has studied important works by American, British, and European authors from the 19th and 20th centuries; he has also studied epics from many cultures and time periods. Discussions were centered on the books' themes; however we also discussed plot elements, setting, characterization, point of view, tone, irony, figurative language, symbolism, allusion, etc. For each book, one student was assigned to give a brief oral presentation about the author's life, and another student would talk about the relevant literary movement or some other pertinent topic. A list of the books read is attached.

Poetry: (Student) is currently studying Poetry on his own. Textbooks he is using include: *Painless Poetry* (Elizabeth, Barron's Educational Series, Inc., 2001) and various anthologies. He will be writing some poetry and studying at least one poet in depth.

Play-Reading: (Voyagers) (Student) also participated in Play-Reading group for 4 years. The class read classic plays aloud, assigning the roles to different class members. The class has covered a variety of styles and themes in the past four years. A small sample of plays read includes *Arsenic and Old Lace, Mousetrap, The Crucible, The Laramie Project, Twelve Angry Men,* and *Our Town.* A list of the plays read is attached.

Shakespeare's Big 4: (Voyagers) The class read and discussed *Hamlet, Macbeth, Othello,* and *King Lear.* Selected scenes were staged in class. (Student) has been to Stratford-on-Avon, England, where he toured many of Shakespeare's homes (including his birthplace), as well as the cottage of Anne Hathaway (his wife) and the church where he is buried.

Expository Writing Workshop AND Academic Writing and Critical Reading: (Harvard Extension) In the Spring 2005 Term, (Student) was enrolled in a noncredit writing workshop, Intro. to Expository Writing (EXPO E-1). No grades were awarded, but he attended all the classes and completed all assignments. Textbook: The Writer's Options: Lessons in Style and Arrangement (Morenberg et al., Longman, 2002, 7th Ed.). (Student) then passed Harvard's writing placement test, which allowed him to skip 3 writing courses and enroll directly in Academic Writing and Critical Reading (EXPO E-25). He took this course Spring 2006 Term. Textbooks used: Writing Worth Reading: The Critical Process (Packer and Timpane, Bedford/St. Martin's, 1997) and Fields of Reading: Motives for Writing (Comley et al., Bedford/St. Martin's, 2003, 7th Ed.). Course descriptions have been attached. He earned an _.

Writing: (Student) took a 12-week on-line course, Mastering Essay-Writing. The course focused on mastering the five paragraph thesis-essay, including writing critiques, persuasive essays, literary and historical analyses, and SAT essays. The course used the Write Well process, with emphasis on developing topic and concluding sentences, introductions and conclusions, thesis statements, and logical arguments supported by appropriate evidence.

. . . .

Creative Writing: (Student) has been working on several novels for about 3 years. He works on them almost daily—when he is not actually writing, he does research, fleshes out characters, and discusses his ideas with whomever will listen. He uses several online resources for writing tips, individual critique, and information on the publishing process.

Speaking Skills: (Voyagers) (Student) has had plenty of opportunities to hone his speaking skills, including presenting oral reports in his history classes, participating in Mock Trial and Model UN, and his theatre roles. The Mock Trial Team holds workshops in public speaking skills.

Theater: (Voyagers) (Student) acts with the Voyagers Shakespeare Company, which we count as an extracurricular. However, each year before auditions and rehearsals start, the chosen play is studied in depth for a number of weeks. The cast traveled to Connecticut to see a production of *A Winter's Tale*, and several cast members, including (Student), were lucky enough to see *Much Ado About Nothing* at Shakespeare's Globe Theatre in London. He usually watches film versions of the plays to prepare for his roles, and enjoys watching films of plays by other playwrights as well. (Student) saw *Cats* in London and *Les Miserables* in Boston. He also enjoys attending local high-school, community theatre, and regional theatre productions. These have included various Shakespeare plays, *Jesus Christ Superstar*, *Arsenic and Old Lace*, and some Gilbert & Sullivan shows, among others.

FOREIGN LANGUAGES:

Japanese: (Student) was tutored for 4 years by a native speaker. His weekly, semi-private lessons were 1-1/2 hours long. He finished the three books in the series *Japanese for Young People* (Kodansha, Intl., 1999), and got about half-way through *Minna no Nihongo* (3A Corp., 1998), which is entirely in Japanese. In the summer of 2005, he was accepted to Concordia College's Japan Credit Abroad Program (1 year high school credit). A group of 24 students and 4 teachers spent one month traveling and studying in Japan, including a 10-day homestay with a Japanese family. Places traveled to include Tokyo, Kyoto, Fukuoka (homestay), Hiroshima, Nagoya (for the World Expo), Nara, Kobe, and Mt. Fuji. The equivalent of 2 years of high school Japanese was required for acceptance to the program, which was assessed by writing a letter of introduction to the family in Japanese, and by a telephone interview with the Program Dean. Once accepted, the students were divided into 3 groups based on their proficiency. (Student) was placed in the highest level, and earned an A in the program. Last year he took Japanese language classes at the Japan Society of Boston with adult learners. He took a placement test to determine the appropriate level, and he was placed in Advanced A. The 9 Beginner and Intermediate levels finish the three books in the series *Japanese for Busy People*, a popular series for adults. Although he did not use these texts, the placement test showed that he had almost the equivalent knowledge. He was a little behind in his Kanji compared to someone who completed this series. A course description is attached. This year, he has chosen to study on his own, focusing on kanji, idiom, and honorific and informal speech. He is using the following textbooks: *Genki: An Integrated Course in Elementary Japanese, Vol. II* (Banno, Ohno, Sakane, Shinagawa, and Tokashiki, The Japan Times, Ltd., 1999) and *Essential Kanji* (O'Neill, Weatherhill, 1973). *Genki* is the book they used on the Credit Abroad Program, and the Japan Society used handouts from this book for his class there.

Latin: (Voyagers) (Student) took Latin for 2-1/2 years, completing the third unit of Book II of the *Ecce Romani* (Longman, 1995, 2nd Ed.) series. He took the National Latin Examination twice, finishing Summa Cum Laude his first year, and Magna Cum Laude his second year.

Ancient Greek: (Voyagers) One year of Ancient Greek, completing half of *Athenaze: An Introduction to Ancient Greek, Book I* (Balme & Lawall, Oxford Univ. Press, 2003, 2nd Ed.).

Spanish: (Student) used the Power-glide Spanish materials (Adult version) for about 6 months when he was 11, but then he decided he wanted to learn Japanese instead.

SOCIAL SCIENCES:

Introduction to Psychology: (Harvard Extension PSYC E-15)—earned a grade of _.
One semester course; description attached. Texts used: *Fundamentals of Psychology: The Brain, The Person, The World* (Kosslyn and Rosenberg, Allyn & Bacon, 2004, 2nd Ed.), *Dibs in Search of Self* (Axline, Ballantine Books, 1986), and *The Question of Lay Analysis* (Freud, W.W. Norton & Co., 1978).

Principles of Economics: (Harvard Extension ECON E-10a)—earned a grade of _.
One semester course; description attached. Texts used: *Principles of Economics* (Mankiw, Thomson South-Western, 2004, 3rd Ed.).

History: (Voyagers) Over a period of 4 years, (Student) has studied World History from the Ancient Civilizations to WWII. He has studied American History from the pre-colonial era through the 19th century. Textbooks used were *World History to 1800* and *Modern World History* (Spielvogel, West Educational Publishing, 1999); and two books from the HarperCollins College Outline series, *United States History to 1877* and *United States History from 1865* (HarperResource, 1991, 20th Ed.). Course work included writing reports, giving oral presentations, and participating in some simulations. (Student) was a prosecuting attorney in Martin Luther's Trial, a Cardinal in a Medieval Life sim, an African tribal chief in a debate about the *Amistad* controversy, and took the part of Italy in negotiations attempting to prevent the outbreak of WWI. It is important to note that these sims were not scripted—the students had to do a lot of research to write their position papers, successfully argue their position in class debates, and act out their role in the specific society. Our family has also been involved with Revolutionary War re-enactments with our town's Colonial Minute Men. In addition to recreating battles, this group does living history, such as cooking period recipes over open fires or in fireplaces; practicing crafts such as candle-making, broom-making, and casting pewter buttons; and explaining to the public about daily life in the colonial era as well as specific historical events. Living near Boston, we have taken many field trips to all types of important Revolutionary War and early American sites. We have also visited Valley Forge, Colonial Williamsburg, and two important Civil War battlefields, Gettysburg and Yorktown. We live 2 miles out of Lowell, MA, which was the seat of the Industrial Revolution in America, with its textile mills. We have availed ourselves of all the wonderful resources for field trips it provides. We have seen Roman ruins in Italy (including Pompeii), England, and Wales (we even stumbled upon a camp of Roman Centurion re-enactors at a museum there!). We have seen many other sites of historical importance from many eras in our trips to Europe and Mexico.

Philosophy: (Voyagers) Two semesters, Introduction to Epistemology AND Introduction to Ethics. In Epistemology, the teacher assigned reading selections from philosophers such as Plato, Descartes, and Russell. The teacher gave short lectures on the subject, which were followed by class discussion. The Ethics teacher handled the class similarly, except that the reading included works by Immanuel Kant, Thomas Hobbes, and John Stuart Mill. This class emphasized discussion of ethics itself, using the reading assignments to provide touchstones and common concepts, which students could draw on in formulating and communicating their own ideas.

American Government: (Student) will be studying American Government next semester. We have not worked out the curriculum yet. He has read The Declaration of Independence, Constitution of the United States, and Bill of Rights and Later Amendments before, and he has also read books about government such as Take Back Your Government (Heinlein) and Playing Politics (Michael Laver).

Mock Trial AND **Model UN:** These subjects are described under the activities section; we count them primarily as extracurricular, but they were also academic experiences. For instance, for Model UN, besides studying and learning about the specific countries, issues, and specific UN bodies that the team would need to know about to participate in the conference, they spent a semester just studying about the UN—its charter and history, and organs and agencies.

SCIENCES:

AP Physics: This class is taught by MIT students on the MIT campus. It meets weekly for 3.5 hours, from September to May, when the AP exams are given. Textbook: *Physics: Principles With Applications* (Giancoli, Pearson Prentice Hall, 2005, 6th Ed.). They are starting with calculus-based Newtonian mechanics and electro-magnetism.

Chemistry with Lab: (Middlesex CC) (Student) took 3 semesters of a high-school level chemistry course with lab at a local community college; this noncredit class was developed by the college for homeschoolers. Textbook: *Heath Chemistry*.

Cell Biology with Lab: (Middlesex CC) (Student) took 2 semesters of a high-school level cell biology course with lab at a local community college; this noncredit class was developed by the college for homeschoolers. Instructor provided handouts.
Biology: (Student) has completed the Biology textbook, *Biology—The World of Life* (Wallace, Benjamin/Cummings, 1997, 7th Ed.). He also took a one-day lab, "In Search of the Body's Antibodies," at BU City Labs (Boston University program for high school students).

High-School Science Lecture Series: For the second year, (Student) is attending some of the lectures from this series at the Museum of Science in Boston. Each lecture features a prominent scientist who talks about their research. Some topics he has learned about include Green Chemistry, Robotics, and various NASA programs.

There are often experiments or exhibits that tie into the lecture which the students can participate in after the lecture.

MATHEMATICS:

Algebra I: (Student) used *Key to Algebra* (King and Rasmussen, Key Curriculum Project, Inc., 1990) and *Algebra* (Jacobs, W.H. Freeman and Co.).

Algebra II AND Geometry: Last October, (Student) starting using an Internet program called ALEKS, which was developed by the University of California. He has since finished both their Algebra II and Geometry courses. ALEKS is perfect for someone such as (Student), who had gaps in his knowledge of particular topics. ALEKS assessed what he already knew, so that he just had to learn the topics that he lacked. (Student) had started studying Algebra II and Geometry a few years ago, but Math got put on hold as he pursued his passions in humanities. He used a variety of resources, including a class at Voyagers, learning on his own, and discussions with his father (a chemical engineer who teaches at the college level). Textbooks he has used include *Key to Geometry* (King and Rasmussen, Key Curriculum Project, Inc., 1980), *Geometry* (Jacobs, W.H. Freeman and Co., 1987, 2nd Ed.) and *Algebra* (Jacobs, W.H. Freeman and Co.).

Trigonometry: (Student) is currently learning trigonometry using ALEKS.

Calculus: He is also learning calculus on an as-needed basis in his AP Physics class.

FINE ARTS:

Art: (Voyagers) (Student) took an Introduction to Drawing course. The course covered basic elements and principles of composition, such as line, shape, texture, color, form, space, and movement. A wide variety of media were used: pencil, charcoal, oil pastel, dry pastel, eraser drawing. (Student) has seen many masterpieces and artworks of all types and from many different cultures and historical eras when he has visited Boston's Museum of Fine Arts; the Uffizi Gallery in Florence, and the Capitoline Museum and the Borghese Gallery in Rome, Italy; and the British Museum, the Dali Museum, and works of art in Buckingham Palace, Windsor Castle, and Hampton Court Palace in England.

Music: Although (Student) took violin from ages 6-8, he now only engages in music appreciation. He is currently watching the Young People's Concerts lecture series presented by Leonard Bernstein. When he has completed those lectures, he will use a college textbook, *The Enjoyment of Music* (Machlis, W.W. Norton & Co., 1977, 4th Ed.), which requires the student to listen to select pieces by great composers. Our music collection includes artists from all genres, and from all over the world. (Student)'s favorites used to be musicals, but he has started listening to rock music and more contemporary music this past year. (Student) also did take dance lessons (jazz, tap, Irish step) for seven years, from ages 4-10, before he switched over to martial arts at age 11.

PHYSICAL EDUCATION:

(Student) takes American Kenpo Karate, and has earned his 1st Degree Black Belt; he has a one-hour class twice a week. He also assists in the kids' classes and performs in demonstrations as part of the Leadership Team. In the winter, (Student) participates in a homeschool ski program; in the summer, he plays volleyball with a group of homeschoolers. He took swim lessons for many summers—he has currently passed American Red Cross Level 6. Hiking and biking are other activities he enjoys.

OTHER:

International Travel with Educational Groups: (Student) took a 12-day trip to Italy with EF Tours during the 2005/2006 winter break. Our small group of 7 homeschoolers was combined with high-school groups from California and Virginia; our bus of 50 people traveled to Venice, Florence, Assisi, Pompeii, and Rome, visiting many historical and cultural museums and sites. (Student) opted to complete an accredited course (1 high school elective credit) in conjunction with this tour. Course requirements of 100 hours included reading in advance of the tour (4 books from the Natl. Council on Social Studies list of books for Global Connections learning standards and 2 non-fiction books about the places he would be traveling to), keeping a travel journal during the tour, and completing a photoessay and writing 7 essays upon his return (five 1000-word and two 1500-word). He earned an _. (Student) spent a month in Japan in an academic program during the summer of 2005—this was detailed in the paragraph about his Japanese studies.

Other International Travel: (Student) spent two weeks in London the summer of 2004, with a group of 19 homeschoolers, on a trip which was organized and led by his mother. The group took day trips to Bath, Cambridge, and Salisbury and Stonehenge. (Student) traveled to Mexico four years ago with his family, spending a week in the Copper Canyon region, which is still home to the Tarahumara Indians. We were able to see a modern-day cave dwelling, watch the women doing handcrafts, and observe them walking with bundles on their heads and babies on their backs. The year before, (Student) and his family spent 12 days in Wales, traveling all over the country visiting castles and other historical sites, as well as a coal mine, a slate quarry, and a cheddar cheese factory; on a previous 12-day trip, (Student) and his family went to London, Canterbury, and Stratford-on-Avon.

Volunteer Service: Assists with teaching classes as part of the Karate Leadership Team; taught Japanese for 2 years to homeschool students at Voyagers; taught Dungeons & Dragons 1 year at Voyagers; volunteered at a *Beyond IQ* conference held at Voyagers, helping with set-up, food service and co-teaching a games class; volunteered at the library one summer; currently interning with a local podcaster.

Paid Work Experience: Assisting with birthday parties at the Karate School; assistant Strategy Games instructor at Summer Voyage; babysitting and pet sitting.

AWARDS: Johns Hopkins University Mathematics & Verbal Talent Search (7th & 8th Grades)—2003 and 2004 State Award for being among the highest scoring participants from Massachusetts, and also 2003 National Verbal Talent Search Award for scoring above 700 SAT Verbal before Age 13; National Latin Examination (twice)—Summa Cum Laude and Magna Cum Laude; National Merit Scholarship Program Commended Student; College Board National Hispanic Recognition Program Scholar.

TEST SCORES: SAT I   Critical Reading: ___   SAT II Literature: ___
    Math: ___   World History: ___
    Writing: ___   Japanese: ___

(Student) has been interested in Japanese culture since he was 6 or 7. It started with an interest in the Samurai and their weapons and way of life. He has read books about Japan—its history, people, culture, mythology, etc. He has also read Miyamoto Musashi's medieval text, *The Book of Five Rings*, and parts of *The Tale of the Genji*; and he has read books about Japanese business practices such as *Alchemy of a Leader* (Rehfeld) and *Made in Japan* (Morita, Reingold, and Shimomura). He loves to eat Japanese food, especially sushi, whenever he can. He has even made sushi from scratch with raw salmon at home. When he was 10 or 11 he attended Japan Camp, a one-week day camp at a Boston-area Japanese intercultural college. He interacted with the Japanese students while exploring their culture through games, crafts (reading and writing haiku, doing calligraphy and origami, singing), observing a tea ceremony and cooking food. They also had language classes a couple of times daily. At age 12, (Student) started studying the Japanese language with a tutor. (Student) enjoys watching anime, eating with chopsticks, and learning martial arts. He likes to talk to Japanese tourists. He makes occasional excursions to a Japanese mini-mall near Boston, which has all types of Japanese eateries, a grocery, clothing stores, and gift stores. As previously mentioned, he has taught Japanese, and he has achieved his life-long dream of actually traveling to Japan, where he participated in an academic program. This passion for Japan is completely self-motivated; (Student) does not have any Japanese heritage and he was not required to study Japan as part of his homeschooling.

HIGH SCHOOL ACTIVITIES

Theatre Student Assistant Director: This year (Student) won the role of Romeo in Voyagers Shakespeare Company's *Romeo & Juliet;* he also has a minor role in the second cast. Last year he was both Count Orsino and Antonio (it had also been double cast) in Shakespeare's *Twelfth Night.* (Student) performed as Benedick, one of the leads, in the production of Shakespeare's *Much Ado About Nothing* the year before last, and he had two major roles, Camillo (Act I only) and Florizell, in Shakespeare's *A Winter's Tale,* the Company's first-ever production. He only had a month to learn the role of Camillo, because the original actor had to resign from the play suddenly. The cast traveled to Connecticut to see a production of *A Winter's Tale*, and (Student) was lucky enough to see *Much Ado About Nothing* at Shakespeare's Globe Theatre in London. (Student) has been a Student Assistant Director for 2 years, and he has also been in charge of choreographing fight scenes. This year he is helping to write the lighting script.

Mock Trial Team Captain: (Student) is in his fifth year of participating in Mock Trial. He has had defense attorney and plaintiff attorney roles. The Mock Trial teams that our homeschool team competes against are composed of mostly high-school juniors and seniors. (Student) was 13 when he first competed. For the last two years, his team won all of their preliminary round trials; however, they lost their tie-breaker against another undefeated team, so they did not advance to the next round. To prepare for the trials, the class studied civil law and trial procedure; read actual case decisions, statutes, and the rules of criminal procedure; wrote legal briefs; had a presentation skills workshop; and visited a courtroom with trials in session to view the proceedings. (Student) has been appointed "Designated Objector" and he also frequently gives the closing argument. These roles are difficult because they require quick thinking, and the closing argument for the case changes based on the progress of the trial in a specific competition. This year he is Team Captain, a position that is new for the team. The lawyer who had coached the team for 4 years was unable to continue this year, so (Student) decided to try to put together a team anyway. He found a parent willing to be the Teacher-Coach (the Mock Trial organization requires that an adult register the team), he advertised in homeschooling venues for participants and made many calls to personally invite homeschool teens, and put together a series of training sessions, some taught by him, and some taught by lawyers and other adults with public speaking skills, to prepare the team; luckily, he eventually found a lawyer who is willing to commit for the whole season. Since this lawyer is new to Mock Trial, (Student) is still very involved with the running of the team. He advises the lawyer on what he should teach the team, and (Student) teaches when the lawyer has to miss a class. He also had input on assigning the roles in the case.

Teaching: (Student) has volunteered as a Japanese instructor at Voyagers for 2 years, and was also paid to work as an Assistant Instructor of Strategy Games at the summer camp program hosted by Voyagers. He also volunteered to run the Dungeon & Dragons activity at Voyagers for one year.

Karate Leadership Team: (Student) has taken American Kenpo Karate for 6 years, and is a 1st degree Black Belt. He is on the Leadership team, which assists in teaching the classes and performs special demonstrations.

Podcasting: (Student) recently began interning with a local podcaster, whose podcasts feature a 15-minute interview with primarily local grassroots progressives, political and sports commentary, and music. He has learned to edit the podcasts using Audacity. (Student) requested permission to conduct an interview of two students involved with the homeschool UN Club, and submitted a list of questions he would ask. He has since conducted the interview with assistance from his mentor; the interview can be found at Episode 48 at saintkermit.com/joom. (Student) also edited Episodes 26, 28, and 34. Episode 23 contains an interview with (Student) as part of the Voyagers Shakespeare Company.

Voyagers Student Forum AND Voyagers Teen Committee: (Student) was a Student Reporter for the Voyagers Student Council (for one term), later renamed Student Forum. This entailed taking minutes and reporting on the events of the meetings. He also helped to write agendas and develop procedures for the meetings. (Student) is also a member of the Teen Committee, which plans events for teens such as the Voyagers dances. He participates in planning meetings, set-up, collecting money, and creating music playlists.

Living History: (Student) his participated with his family in colonial reenactments as members of the Billerica Colonial Minute Men. He started when he was 6, but around 11 he was too busy with other interests to participate much. The last two years he has again been participating in parades and encampments. This year he portrayed Thomas Ditson, a real colonial person from our town who was tarred and feathered for trying to buy a musket from a British soldier. Even though we use molasses instead of tar, it is a sticky proposition. He also has cast pewter buttons and musket balls, helped make brooms and candles, and provided commentary for the tourists.

Yearbook Copy Editor: (Student) wrote and edited copy for the homeschool coop yearbook, *The Voyager*, which was 114 pages. He was the Spring Semester Copy Editor. Unfortunately, the coop only did a yearbook the one year, so he was unable to continue with this activity.

Model United Nations: To participate in a MUN conference, the students first had to take Introduction to the United Nations. They studied the workings of the United Nations, read original UN documents, and learned about different countries' positions on a variety of situations around the world. After completing the semester-long class, (Student) participated in the MUN Preparatory Class. The Model United Nations Conference is an international program run from middle school to college level, which simulates a working day at the UN. Students are assigned countries to represent and the issues come from actual UN proceedings. Unfortunately, although he prepared with students who participated in the high-school level MUN, (Student) could not participate at this level because he was only 13; therefore, he participated in the middle-school MUN at Bentley College. (Student) represented France in the Security Council, which debated the situation in Iraq (this occurred in spring 2003). (Student) joined the UN club, which worked on a variety of projects generated by the group. The club developed a theatre piece in order to educate people about the Convention on the Rights of the Child. They worked directly with the United Nations on this project. However, (Student) came to the conclusion that he did not support the Convention on the Rights of the Child, so he eventually dropped out of the club. He remains very interested in international diplomacy issues, but the club was focused on just the one issue at the time.

Writing: (Student) spends much of his spare time writing novels. He has not published anything yet, but he hopes to someday. He shares his writing on the Internet with other writers. He has participated in National Novel Writing Month. He attempted to start a Writer's Group at our local library, but was not able to attract many members, so it disbanded after about 6 months. He advertised in the local paper, at the library, and on the local cable channel.

Appendix 6

Expanded Transcript

Use the student's transcript as you have prepared it, but include additional details about every course. This will result in a multi-page description of your homeschool.

Official Transcript
~Homeschool Senior High~

Homeschool Senior High
Home Address * City, WA 98000
HIGH SCHOOL DIPLOMA AWARDED JUNE 11, 2006

Student: Gender: **Male**   Birth Date: **01/00/00**

Parents: M/M   **Address**: Home Address, City, WA 98000

Academic Record with Detail

Subject	Class Title	Completion Date	Credits	Grade
English	**English 1: American Literature & Composition** Sonlight Core 100 American Literature (You may choose to list individual books)	06/03	1.0	4.0
	HCC SPCH 100: Basic Oral Communication HONORS Dual Enrollment Highline Community College (You may choose to cut and paste the course description provided by the college.)	12/05	1.0	4.0
Math	**Algebra 2** Saxon Algebra 2 DIVE Into Math Supplemental DVD	06/03	1.0	4.0
	HCC MATH 124: Calculus Dual Enrollment Highline Community College	12/05	1.0	4.0
Science	**Biology with Lab** Apologia Exploring Creation with Biology by Jay Wile Lab experiments from Home Science Tools Apologia Biology Supplemental DVD CLEP Exam score 62	06/03	1.0	4.0
Social Studies	**Civics** Basic American Government by Carson YMCA Youth and Government Program (You may choose to include the approximate number of hours spent on this class.)	06/03	1.0	4.0
Fine Arts	**Music: Piano 3 with Performance** Private lessons 30 minutes each week Piano practice 45 minutes each day Monthly performances at church	06/03	1.0	4.0
Electives	**Economics 1** This is a self-directed course. Studying a variety of books, the student will independently investigate Economics. The student will discuss findings, and write one or more research papers on the topic of his choosing, within that subject. Credit will be awarded based on 150 hours of study and research, and successful completion of a written report. Written work available on request.	06/03	1.0	4.0

	Economics 2 Selected Essays of political Economy by Frederic Bastiat Economic Sophisms by Frederic Bastiat Whatever Happened to Penny Candy? by Richard Maybury Economics in one Lesson by Henry Hazlitt Capitalism for Kids: by Karl Hess Young Entrepreneur's Guide to Starting and Running a Business by Steve Mariotti Economics on Trial by Mark Skousen Myth of the Robber Barons by Burton W. Folson Everything I know About Business I Learned from Monopoly by Alan Axelrod Venture Adventure by Daryl Bernstein Basic Economics by Clarence B. Carson The Making of Modern Economics by Mark Skousen International Encyclopedia of the Social Sciences edited by David L. Sills, The Free Press Legacies of Great Economists by Professor Timothy Taylor of Macalester College, 10 lectures by The Teaching Company, College Level Lecture Series of audiotapes.	06/04	1.0	4.0

	Grade Point Equivalents	Summary
PSAT October 2005: Reading 72, Math 69, Writing 76, Percentile 99 SAT March 2005: Reading 800, Math 740, Writing 750, Total 2290 SAT June 2005: Reading 750, Math 790, Writing 790, Total 2330	A =90-100% =4.0 B=80-89% = 3.0	**Summary** Credits GPA 45 4.0
**Denotes Honors course, documented by passing CLEP exam HCC denotes course taken at Highline Community College	C=70-79% = 2.0 D = 60-69% = 1.0	

CPSIA information can be obtained at www.ICGtesting.com
Printed in the USA
LVOW05s1523141113

361321LV00005B/287/P